MY FATHER'S HOUSE

THE MANSION HOUSE
The children's wing was below the awning in this picture

MY FATHER'S HOUSE

An Oneida Boyhood

By

PIERREPONT NOYES

*Illustrated
with
Photographs*

HOLT, RINEHART AND WINSTON
New York

Contents

Part IV—Rebirth

Part V—Emergence

Illustrations

Foreword

PIERREPONT NOYES has in no sense attempted to write a formalized autobiography in *My Father's House*. Only the first sixteen years of his life are recorded in the pages which follow, and a full half century has elapsed since the events of his final chapter. Had he chosen he might have gone on to write another American success story, a story different, however, from many in that its business success has been based as much on a belief in the essential dignity of labor and value of co-operation as on his own brilliant leadership. He might have developed the themes of industrial and social pioneering, of a humanitarian internationalism at the time of the Peace Conference at Versailles, of a spirit of public service which has created a model community and later directed the successful work of the Saratoga Springs Commission. Some brief outline of these accomplishments follows the text of his book, but the influences which molded them are all implicit in the story of his childhood and of the Oneida Community.

Today the Mansion House, where the members of the Community lived, still stands on the crest of its hill, the warm brick walls, the white columns, the spacious quadrangle, the communal rooms as friendly, as useful, as full of life and meaning as ever. Pierrepont Noyes himself still lives in it, and so do many children of the Oneida Community, and their children and grandchildren, who play across the South Lawn, slide down its gentle slope in winter and romp under its trees in summer just as "Pip" Noyes and his friends of the Children's House did in the days when John Humphrey Noyes was alive and the Community practiced Perfectionism and so narrowly missed achieving it.

Much of the spirit of the original Community survives, a spirit of co-operation and love, a deep satisfaction in work well done and the dignity of work if its end be unselfish, and an appreciation of the fact that men do not live by bread alone. In a unique sense the story of his childhood is the epitome of Pierrepont Noyes's later life, for intrinsic in it are the motivations and ideals which have guided his career as a grown man.

The publishers of *My Father's House* feel for it a particular and personal enthusiasm. They believe that it is an account of one of the noblest attempts which men and women have made in all human history to live together in peace and honesty and a communion of spirit. Such an experiment, seen through the eyes of an active, vigorous, and thoroughly normal boy, makes not only a lively and moving story but an important historical record. The dark days when the Community abandoned most of its spiritual tenets and became little more than a business enterprise uniting a band of men and women who had once lived for perfection is a period of affecting human tragedy. The final account of a boy, thrust suddenly into a hostile world which taunted him with the facts of his birth and sneered at everything which he had been taught to regard as true and noble, might well appear pathetic. But there is no pathos in Pierrepont Noyes; he met the world "outside" the walls of the Mansion House on its own terms and triumphed. *My Father's House* is a complete book, needing no extension or sequel to stand as the narrative of a life lived through to success and integrity.

THE PUBLISHERS

MY FATHER'S HOUSE

Part I

The Oneida Community

I

I WAS born and brought up in a strange world—a world bounded on four sides by walls of isolation; a world wherein the customs, laws, religions, and social formulas accumulated by civilization came to us only as the faint cries of philistine hordes outside our walls. Within that protected area, a prophet and his faithful followers, having separated themselves from the rest of mankind, were trying to live as lived those members of the Primitive Christian Church of whom it is written, "No man called aught his own." That little world was called the Oneida Community, and that prophet was my father.

Every child's life begins with its parents, and my own does so to an unusual degree. I had not only heredity from my father, but the first ten years of my life were spent in a world which he created, a sort of island society which differed at almost every vital point from the accepted institutions of his contemporaries.

It has been no part of my plan to write a history of the Oneida Community; others have done that. This is the story of a child, and I have tried to confine the narrative, as far as possible, to the observations of that child. And yet, since Community life is the background of the story, it has seemed to me that the salient features of that background ought to be sketched before I begin the narrative. Hence this foreword.

3

2

My father, John Humphrey Noyes, was the son of an old and respected New England family. After graduating from Dartmouth, he took up the study of law, but having suddenly experienced conversion while attending one of those enthusiastic revivals which swept the country during the 1830's, he gave up his legal career and there and then dedicated his life to the service of Jesus Christ. He entered Andover Seminary. While there, he became the leader of a band of youthful enthusiasts who swore to "be young converts forever."

Those were the days of perfervid theological doctrinism. Men reckoned "the strait and narrow path" of secondary importance to correct interpretation of every word written in the Holy Scriptures, and naturally Noyes turned to a study of the Bible. He delved into comparative philology. His examinations were word by word and his interpretations literal. Letters and diaries written at Andover reveal a remarkable absorption in his search for truth.

Presently, finding Andover deficient in earnestness or erudition, he transferred his study to the Yale Theological Seminary. There he made his "great discovery." He decided that current religious teachings were all wrong, that Christ did not sanction lives of alternate sinning and repentance, but demanded and promised perfection here on earth.

Being a man of strong convictions and a fighting spirit, he proceeded to preach his new doctrine under the very noses of his Congregationalist professors. He became the leading speaker in the New Haven Free Church. It is related that a friendly member of the faculty called at his room one evening and begged him to lie low the few weeks remaining before graduation; but Noyes was adamant. He barely escaped expulsion from the seminary. Later, his heresy of "perfection" led to the canceling of his license to preach. He then declared publicly:

"I took away their license to sin and they go on sinning; they have taken away my license to preach but I shall go on preaching."

During the next fifteen years he spent his time and much of his fortune traveling about the country preaching "Perfectionism," or editing militant magazines devoted to proving the theological soundness of his new doctrine. By 1845 so many worthy church members in New England, New Jersey and New York had joined his faith that the orthodox clergy regarded him as a serious menace.

At Putney, Vermont, the home of the Noyes family, a group of relatives, neighbors and believers organized in 1839 "The Putney Bible Class." As numbers increased, this Bible class evolved through several intermediate stages— "The Society of Inquiry," "Contract of Partnership," "The Putney Corporation"—to the "Putney Community" in 1846. This final step to organized communism was coincident with acceptance by the group of Mr. Noyes's radical views on marriage and was probably made necessary by the new practices. Which of these steps was cause and which effect is hard to judge. In any case, the virtuous citizens of Putney objected to both and within two years broke up the Community and drove my father out of town.

During September, 1847, he had attended a convention of "Perfectionist" disciples held in a little church at Lairdsville, New York. There, communal living, his recipe for defeating the powers of evil, was warmly debated, and during three consecutive days he struggled with "the spirit of unbelief." He explained very frankly the principles governing the Putney Community; told how he and thirty or forty other believers were trying to live together as the members of the Primitive Church lived between the time of Christ's ascension and His Second Coming. This, according to Noyes's teachings, took place at the destruction of Jerusalem in the year A.D. 70.

Before returning to Vermont, Mr. Noyes announced to the startled New Yorkers that the Putney Community had carried the war against selfishness to its logical end. Quoting Christ's portrayal of conditions in the Kingdom of Heaven where is "neither marriage nor giving in marriage," he stated that the Putney Community had abolished the private ownership of women and had substituted in its place a system which he called "complex marriage." The Oneida Community was conceived at Lairdsville.

3

In the central part of New York State there lies a broad and fertile valley which leads so far up between the wooded hills that its beginnings are lost among the faint blue forms of higher hills which loom on the southern horizon. A century ago this valley was the home of pioneering men. A few Indians still lingered there, having chosen to remain in the home of their forefathers when the federal government moved the rest of the tribe to Wisconsin. These home-loving redskins hunted, fished and trapped, and every fall earned a little money for tobacco or rum by helping the farmers at harvesttime.

The stream that winds its serpentine course down this valley, having added to its upland inheritance the waters of many hillside brooks, runs out into the plain and on to Oneida Lake, a very self-respecting "little river." At intervals along the banks of this river—it is called Oneida Creek

JOHN HUMPHREY NOYES
In the early 1870's

HOUSE OF JOHN HUMPHREY NOYES
AT PUTNEY, VERMONT

THE "OLD MANSION HOUSE" AT ONEIDA

—splashing water wheels furnished power for crude little mills where grains were ground and logs sawed into lumber. One of these mills standing squarely astride its raceway, just where the stream emerged from the valley, was owned in the year 1847 by one Jonathan Burt.

When I knew Mr. Burt in the 1870's he was an elderly man, stout, slow-moving, with a thick neck, heavy jowls and a round gray beard; but in 1847 he was a young man and, I am told, an exceptionally strong, active worker. He was rated high among his neighbors for the kind of common sense so greatly prized in a new country. He was a religious man and, having listened to the preaching of John Humphrey Noyes, had been converted to his strange doctrines.

4

A few months after the Lairdsville convention, Jonathan Burt and Joseph Ackley, a farmer living in a neighboring valley, proceeded to unite their families as the nucleus of a community such as Mr. Noyes advocated. In the meantime the Putney Community had disbanded on account of the militant opposition of certain leading men in that Vermont village, and Mr. Burt invited John Humphrey Noyes to move to Oneida and become the leader of this new group. Thus Burt's log house near the old sawmill became the first home of the Oneida Community. Other families joined the Burts and Ackleys, and the little band of Perfectionists lived together as one family. They were almost without money. During the first winter they eked out a precarious living by operating the mill, to which, in the spring, were added the products of such limited farming operations as Mr. Burt's small landholdings permitted.

When, however, Mr. Noyes, with his wife, a brother,

two married sisters and certain other families who had been partners with him in the previous attempt to found a community in Vermont, arrived at Oneida, they brought some real money. With this, additional land was bought and the Communists began the erection of new buildings to accommodate their ever-increasing membership.

Those first years were years of poverty. Men, women and children worked without stint, and suffered privations cheerfully. They worked and they prayed. They added new members and built more houses, regardless of whether or not the necessary money was in sight. Many a story has come down to my generation of days when they had sizable payments to make and something like three dollars and a half in the till. They "trusted in God" and always "He provided." By 1849 the membership had grown to 87; by 1850 it was 172; by 1851, 205.

5

The group at Oneida had accepted John Humphrey Noyes's theory of the perfect life and had adopted his system of complex marriage with full recognition of what this defiance of public opinion might mean to them personally. Sex relations were freed from monogamic limitations. The widest selections in cohabitation were encouraged and, in fact, insisted upon, but always under strict regulation and governed by spiritual considerations whose sanctions were rooted deep in the Community religion.

Mr. Noyes agreed with orthodox social scientists that the family was the keystone of the world's social system; that men's possession of women—one man's possession of one woman—had been for centuries the strongest support of individualism and a powerful incentive to self-seeking. Engaged, as he was, in a campaign against self-seeking, he eliminated this kind of ownership with the rest.

The Oneida association announced its abandonment of the marriage system in pamphlets and the weekly periodical it published and described its unique method of birth control. Naturally, press and pulpit attacked it as revolutionary and socially subversive, but there is every evidence that the practical application of Mr. Noyes's plan in Community life led to none of that unbridled pleasure seeking assumed by the outside world. Were it otherwise, one can hardly conceive of three hundred men and women living happily together for more than thirty years. It was fashionable during the fifties and sixties and seventies to refer to the Oneida Communists as "free lovers." Mr. Noyes resented this. He had preached against "free-love movements" in Massachusetts and Ohio. He always insisted that in the sex relations of the Oneida Community there was less of that licentiousness suggested by the term "free love" than in worldly marriages—also more of responsibility.

6

This Community, in which "special love" was reckoned a sin and breadth of sexual experience the desideratum, offered opportunity for an experiment in eugenics on a scale never before attempted in the history of the world. John Humphrey Noyes seized that opportunity. Long before the word "eugenics" had been coined, he became interested in the possibilities of selective breeding and outlined a plan of action. Christening this new science "stirpiculture," he wrote pamphlets advocating its practice, and when, in 1867, the Community became sufficiently prosperous to warrant more children, he made the raising of a superior generation the most important business of the group.

Between the years 1868 and 1881 fifty-eight children
were born in the Oneida Community, of whom I was one.
I have no doubt that my father would have disclaimed
any resort to uninspired diplomacy in his handling of Community problems, but I have never been able to free my
mind from a conviction that he used his head in administer-
ing the details of selective breeding and forestalled trouble.

The socially poisonous feature of eugenics is created
by the unequal roles played by males and females. Eugenics,
if organized scientifically and cold-bloodedly, selects only
a few of the best males, while a majority of all the females
must breed to produce numbers. Here is the nub of the
problem: the eliminated males cannot feel contented. John
Humphrey Noyes either purposely or unconsciously avoided
this snare by arranging that all males who desired should have
one child. My memory, running over the roster of Community members, notes that almost every man had one child,
but that, aside from the preferred "stirps," they had *only
one*.

7

As early as 1849 the Community decided to build a
large communal home. All the principles to which Mr. Noyes
and the Communists were committed, as well as the practical ordering of life in accordance with their plans, made
such a unitary home absolutely necessary.

As an instance, the family "meeting," which assembled
every evening through all the years of the society's existence
and was regarded as an essential part of communal life, could
be maintained with difficulty when the members were scattered in different houses. Incidentally, Mr. Noyes quarreled
with the Sunday of the churches. He insisted that the Com-

munity regard every day as holy and the evening meeting, seven days a week, was his substitute for the Sabbath.

Then there were the children. The Perfectionists planned to bring them up as wards of the whole Community rather than the property of parents, and they early discovered that this plan could not be made completely successful unless all were living under one roof.

Perhaps the most urgent need for concentration was implicit in the system of complex marriage. I have said that cohabitation was "governed by spiritual considerations whose sanctions were rooted deep in the Community religion." These sanctions could not be applied or the desirable circulation maintained when the members were housed in small separate units.

The year 1849 was a year of business depression and money was scarce at Oneida, but the Perfectionists were not to be deterred by financial considerations. They cut logs from their wooded farms, sawed them into lumber at the mill, searched out clay beds suitable for brickmaking, and built, with their own hands, what was in later years affectionately referred to as the "Old Mansion House."

8

It was not until 1860 that the large brick Community home, which still stands and in which many descendants of old Community members still live, was begun. The main building is set well back from the highway and surrounded today by spacious lawns and towering trees. It has a classical feeling, with its fine broad gabled roof and white-pillared portico. To the right and left wings extend to square towers and, turning the corners, form a quadrangle, completed by a building set a trifle apart from the others. This building—

called, for some unknown reason, the Tontine—is devoted
to the kitchen and dining rooms.

Architecturally, I presume, most technical rules have
been violated in this structure, but the general effect is pleasing, friendly and hospitable. The rooms formerly devoted to
the children's department are in the south wing, and from
its wide porch the close-clipped sward sweeps down a gentle
terrace to the distant hedge which marked the boundary of
the children's playground. It was here in this south wing and
on these ample lawns that I spent most of my childhood.

9

There was little regimentation of individuals in the
Oneida Community. Committees discussed the work to be
done and the men and women available, and adapted all
tasks as far as possible to the wishes of each. Similarly,
there was no organized scheme of government. The Community's system of "mutual criticism" was relied upon as
a restraining and co-ordinating influence.

Through all the years of Community history, criticism
was the recognized agency for improving character and conduct; the rod which chastened pride and selfishness and
worldliness; the weapon by which law and order were insured. To the righteous, criticism seemed a beneficent shade
under which all virtues thrived; to the spiritual backslider,
it loomed as a threatening shadow.

The rudiments of criticism as practiced in the Community were, I have since been told, imported from Andover
Theological Seminary. There, in 1831, John Humphrey
Noyes and six or eight other enthusiastic young Christians
were accustomed to meet and purge themselves of carnal
weakness by "mutual criticism." The Andover idea, how-

ever, was only a beginning. At Oneida the technique of criticism was developed amazingly and its application extended to curing the ills of the body as well as the soul.

There is still extant, in the Community archives, a voluminous literature dealing with criticism. Sometimes men and women "offered" themselves for criticism. Oftener they were offered, or perhaps were advised to offer themselves. As a rule, the inquisitions were conducted by regularly appointed committees, but occasionally—these were the *causes célèbres*—some member underwent a thorough overhauling of character in the evening meeting with the entire family participating. It is even recorded that men offered themselves for this supreme test of Christian humility and fortitude.

The committees mixed praise with faultfinding. The essence of the system was frankness; its amelioration, friendliness and affection. Yet it was always an ordeal. Without doubt, the human temptation to vent personal dislikes on a victim was not resisted by everyone, but I have heard old members say that the baring of secret faults by impartial criticizers called for more grace—as they used to say—than the occasional spiteful jab of an enemy. The same witnesses have testified that they were always happier and healthier after one of those spiritual baths; also that just because members had the opportunity to criticize each other openly, Community life was singularly free from backbiting and scandalmongering.

10

In 1848 the ambitions of the Communists were simple. At first, like most of the sixty-two groups that essayed communism in the United States during the nineteenth century, they hoped to support themselves by agriculture and horticulture, and, like most of the sixty-two, they found at the end of three or four years that their capital was seeping away. The $107,706.45 brought in by members had dwindled to $67,272.22. It was then that New England thrift convinced our forebears at Oneida of the necessity for some kind of industrial enterprise. In the record of that period I find my father urging that "we must make business a part of our religion."

They first experimented with the canning of their crops for sale to grocers. Thereafter, for more than seventy years, "Community fruits and vegetables" enjoyed a high reputation throughout the United States.

The financial backbone of the Community, however, was the manufacture of steel traps. Sewall Newhouse, a trapper and trader with the Indians, who was living in the adjoining village, Oneida Castle, when the Community moved to Oneida, manufactured traps and assembled rifles in his blacksmith shop. These he sold to the Oneida Indians. After he joined the Community, he was allowed to continue trapmaking in a small way, and when, in 1852, the responsible heads decided that the Community's labor must be turned to more profitable ends, the making of "Newhouse traps" emerged as an industry. The story is told of a trip to Chicago, made by Mr. Olds, with a trunkful of traps. He called on a hardware dealer and with some misgivings exhibited his merchandise. The buyer said, "I'll take all you've got." That started the trap business. Whenever a large order was received, the entire family worked long hours making the traps. My father ran a forge; women, as well as men, labored until the order was completed.

By 1860 the Newhouse trap had become the standard of the United States and Canada. Professional trappers would accept no other brand, and for nearly seventy years all the steel traps used by the Hudson's Bay Company were made at Oneida. Later, Community traps caught sable and ermine in Russia, rabbits in Australia, and nutria along the rivers Parana and Uruguay. Thus an industrious community became, by force of circumstances, an industrial community.

In 1865 another industry was established. Certain of the early Community joiners had been peddlers back in New England and when money was lacking at Oneida they took to the highroads with articles to sell. Their assortment included skeins of sewing silk. The men traveled in pairs, usually a young man with an older one, and often they were away from home for several weeks. When they returned, these men were subjected to a spiritual bath before being allowed to associate with the Family—a cleansing designed to remove any possible contamination resulting from their worldly contacts. They were given a criticism.

When skein silk proved the most salable merchandise in the peddlers' packs, the Community decided to experiment with manufacturing silk. Three young people, Charles Cragin, Elizabeth Hutchins and Harriet Allen, obtained employment in a Connecticut silk factory from which they returned with sufficient knowledge of processes to start silk manufacturing at Oneida.

These were the Community's industries at the time of my birth. Later, in 1877, the Wallingford branch was provided with an industry of its own, the making of tableware: spoons, forks and knives. It is related that when the Community was preparing to enter this field the leading manufacturer of silver-plated tableware, whose plant was located in a neighboring city, showed his fear of Communistic competition and the shrewdness that later built his institution into one of the country's great commercial enterprises, by promptly offering to buy the entire output of the Community factory.

A contract was closed with him which insured profitable returns to the Wallingford family. It remained for me to discover in later years that this masterful Captain of Industry immediately sold our contract to a large Western wholesaler and thus forestalled dangerous competition without expense to himself.

The Communists' first love—the farms, orchards and gardens—continued for many years to be their best love. Long after the increasing work in the shops forced them to hire Outsiders, the farms were cultivated exclusively by members of the Community. Until Civil War times the Community hired little outside help, did most of its own work of every kind, and I have heard old members say regretfully, "Those were our happiest years."

II

Most of the incentives that call men to the struggle for individual wealth were eliminated in Community life. There food, housing and warmth were provided equally for all, and the simplicity of "dress" made competition in that field nonexistent. Luxuries were no problem, since vanities and all forms of dissipation were abhorrent to men and women striving for salvation.

This left only three of the major human desires which urge men on to the pursuit of money. The first, to provide for children, lost its potency because all children were cared for by a children's department, and no parents had any power to obtain preferences for their own children.

The second, ambition for power, was largely denaturized by a system which rotated jobs so far as individual ability made this possible. Of course, not all work was equally agreeable, but the Community succeeded in making all classes of work equally honorable. The man who helped with the dishwashing, if he performed his work well, was praised and had fully as good a social standing as had the superintendent of a factory. The Community discovered that men do not really enjoy work beyond their abilities. In the world the multitude who have had no chance to experiment with responsibility call loudly for such a chance, but in the Oneida Community a few embarrassing failures furnished object lessons for the overambitious. I have heard men who in Community days served always in minor positions speak very appreciatively of those in high places.

And lastly, there is money as a means to attract women. In the Oneida Community, where mating was based on personal affection and its freedoms on "spiritual states," no one looked toward money as an advantage. The question of "spiritual states" was a very real one. It hinged partly on the approval of John Humphrey Noyes and partly on the consciences of the mates desired.

So, unless a member of the Oneida Community abandoned his pursuit of Perfection and Salvation or faith in Father Noyes, the economic problems, at which students of social systems balk, were nonexistent in the Oneida Community.

12

From all the foregoing the reader may infer that life in the Community was of an experimental nature and surrounded with an atmosphere of theory rather than of vital human living and feeling. This would be far from the truth. When I was born the Community had been firmly established at Oneida for twenty-two years and my elders had long since accepted its pattern of life as normal and entirely right. My mother-in-law once said to me, "It was never, in our minds, an experiment; we believed we were living under a system which the whole world would sooner or later adopt."

If my childhood was spent in surroundings totally unlike any other existing then or now, there was nothing tentative about that environment, either spiritual or physical. The framework of our religion seemed final, human relations fixed, and both buildings and businesses showed that the Community fathers planned with faith in their permanence.

Part II–The Children's House

Chapter I

An East Room Child

I WAS born at high noon, August 18, 1870. A band was
playing at the time and just outside my nursery window
the usually quiet old Quadrangle, with its spreading shade
trees and moss-grown, ivy-covered "reservoir," was alive
with hurrying strangers. An "Excursion" had arrived, one of
those Ontario & Western Railway excursions which periodi-
cally, during the seventies, brought a thousand or more visitors to eat the Community's far-famed vegetable dinner, to
wander about the grounds, and, I suppose, to see what manner of people lived in this Community and how they lived.
At that particular moment these excursionists were being
entertained with a concert in the great hall of the Mansion
House.

All this I learned from my mother. At about the same
time someone added a dramatic touch to my picture of that
day in August by announcing impressively: "Pierrepont, you
were born on the day of the Battle of Gravelotte." This completed my horoscope. Others may study the stars and the
signs of the zodiac for information regarding their character
and possibilities, but my "natal influences" are associated, for
good or ill, with a noonday sun, hurrying crowds, a band
playing, and the Battle of Gravelotte.

2

Somewhere in the misty dawn of life I made the discovery that the world into which I had been born was called "Oneidacommunity." I learn from the report of relatives that, like other Community children, I remained in the care of my mother until I was able to walk: probably fourteen or fifteen months. Then, at the age when all Community children were brought together, I was transferred to a department called the Drawing Room. I remember nothing about my life in the Drawing Room, but assume that I was cared for meticulously, as I afterward saw the Drawing Room children cared for. I have been told that in the early 1870's the stirpicultural experiment was a general family enthusiasm and the Drawing Room was frequented by visitors.

It may be imagination, but I seem to remember a time when the Mansion House with its surrounding park was the entire world and "our folks" the population thereof. Later, but still in that twilight zone, I made another discovery. We children were watching the cows being driven along the road to their milking. Behind them I saw a man and a dog and someone told me the man was a "hired man." I remember puzzling for a long time over nice, old, bewhiskered Mr. Taylor. What was a "hired man"?

The answer to that question enlarged my horizon. We were still the center of the world just as, for the ancients, this earth was the center of the universe, but I now recognized that there were, somewhere "beyond the hedge," many strange people sometimes called "hired men" and again "outsiders."

So much for the period of infancy wherein the distinction between fact and fancy, between one's own recollections and the reports of others, is a doubtful one. My first valid memories begin at the age of four.

3

We were in the East Room. There were six of us sitting in high chairs about a large, round, maroon-colored table eating oatmeal and applesauce. The oatmeal half filled homemade tin porringers and the applesauce took the place of sugar and cream. I remember especially the pink color and delicious flavor of that applesauce. It must have been made from the fruit of an Early Joe tree which used to stand on the north lawn above the Dunn Cottage, for whenever I have been served with Early Joe applesauce the flavor has taken me back to the East Room.

The East Room, by the way, stood for something more than a room. It was a badge of class, a sort of sophomoric class, located between the babies of the Drawing Room and the older children of the South Room. My memories of life in the East Room are extremely vague. From the reports of older people I judge that it was much like life in the modern day nurseries to which children of three or four years are sent, excepting that the women who tended us in the East Room were also responsible for our sleeping arrangements. We had many playthings—blocks, marble rollers, rocking horses, and, I am told, were encouraged to pore over picture books, mostly homemade linen scrapbooks.

From what I have heard I am led to suspect that the desire of our elders to discover moral superiority in us "stirpicultural" children was disappointed, that those who lived closely with us acknowledged, at least to themselves, that at the age of four we were much like other children of the same age. We were selfish little animals. The women who cared for us spent much of their time settling differences of opinion as to who should have a certain toy.

I remember clearly just one feature of the East Room. It was a prancing horse with flowing mane and tail and its body all covered with hair. Shockey—that was the horse's name—pranced on delightfully elastic springs. To sit in a real saddle on its back with our feet in bright nickeled stirrups, and pitch back and forth with the motion of the pony, was the most popular amusement in the room. I think that the first time I ever encountered the word "quarrel" was in connection with that pony. Probably I had been unduly insistent on my turn at riding. The East Room impresses me as another of those remarkable anticipations of modern systems for child training which I find throughout the recollections of my earlier years.

I have a vague recollection of visiting the Drawing Room where many infants were creeping around the floor or playing on a platform, raised and railed-in so that they might safely look out the windows. More distinctly I remember our feeling of superiority to them. Were they not confined and watched and taken outdoors in carriages, while we of the East Room were allowed, within certain limitations, to play by ourselves in the sandbed and even wander over the lawns?

On the other hand, the South Room children, the older children, were granted a freedom which to us seemed infinite; even more, they had attained to such dignity of personality as to command our respect and envy. There were twenty or thirty of those privileged seniors, boys and girls between the ages of six and twelve, and they constituted the solid citizenship of the Children's House.

There again is a name which was more than the designation for a place. The Children's House was an institution. At the time it never occurred to me to question the applica-

bility of the word "house," although the children's department occupied only a small section of the Community buildings. It was years later that I learned the origin of this col-
loquialism. It seems that, in the earlier days, the children's
quarters were in a wooden house which stood at the edge of
the south terrace and, when the great brick mansion was
built in the 1860's and the children were installed in its
southern wing, the earlier name persisted.

4

After that breakfast of oatmeal and applesauce, I find a
hiatus in my memory—a period of obscurity, unillumined by
any clear recollections or well-defined pictures—a hiatus ex-
tending to my Wallingford visit, in 1875. I do remember one
rather unusual problem which, in that earlier time, engaged
my mind and the amusing if not very elegant solution at
which I arrived. We were forbidden to speak to "hired men"
or "outsiders." These two designations seemed applied to
strange people indiscriminately, and yet I felt sure there existed a difference. In the end I decided that "hired men" spit
brown and "outsiders" spit white. The data upon which I
based this bizarre conclusion was evidently the fact that the
Community's hired men—carpenters, teamsters, farmhands
—chewed tobacco, while the higher class of outsiders, visitors, did not.

Wallingford, to us Oneida children, seemed a faraway
land of adventure; a place where children lived much nearer
to horses and cows and much more intimately with grown
folks; also, where grew those nice-smelling yellow quinces
which returning members always brought in their trunks.
Specifically, our Wallingford was a branch of the Oneida
Community, which occupied a little plateau on the eastern

slope of Mount Tom just across the Quinnipiac River from the Connecticut village of Wallingford.

The Wallingford branch of the Community was always associated in my mind with the Allen family. Mr. Henry Allen, a leading citizen of Wallingford, joined the Community in 1852, bringing with him three sons and a daughter and contributing his large farm. Soon thereafter buildings were added, and the Quinnipiac River was dammed to create water power for a large mill in which the Community's very considerable printing business was conducted. For a time Mr. Allen made his principal residence at his old home, but in the end he moved to Oneida where both he and his children were, throughout the life of the Community, prominent and loyal members.

My brother, John Humphrey, one year my senior, had been living at Wallingford for some time before my visit. I am told that I accosted him with a quotation from the thirteenth chapter of First Corinthians which the children at Oneida had been learning by rote, "I am become as sounding brass or a tinkling cymbal." I cannot believe that he was greatly interested by either the brass or the cymbals. I was just a new boy to him and soon he was showing me all the wonders of the place, the pet lamb, the "mustang pony" and the yoke of huge oxen named Buck and Berry which Mr. Bristol used for his plowing.

I had not been there long before he took me back of the woodshed and proceeded to demonstrate his skill in cutting up potatoes. Whether he was cutting them for planting or for rat-bait, or merely seized on potatoes as excuse for exhibiting his dexterity with a new knife, I do not remember. What I do recall is the ugly gash inflicted on his finger when the knife cut through the potato in his hand. To this day Humphrey has a little finger made stiff by that cut.

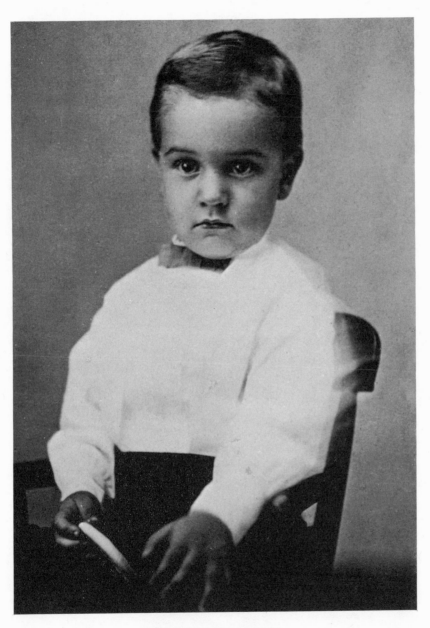

PIERREPONT NOYES
Aged four

THE WALLINGFORD BRANCH FROM THE VILLAGE
OF WALLINGFORD

That seemed bad enough, but worse was to follow. After his finger had been dressed, I sought to comfort him by sharing one of those little, hard "motto" candies which we children set much store by and, in trying to cut it, sliced off, or nearly off, a section of the fleshy portion of my thumb. Thereupon a "meeting" was called and we were introduced to our first "criticism."

My father summed up our moral turpitude by the statement that we were evidently "under a bad principality." "Principalities and powers" were familiar and awesome portents in my childhood and always depressed my spirits as much as normally buoyant spirits could be depressed. In some of my father's early writings I find a discussion of evil principalities and powers based on a quotation from Ephesians 6:11, but when a child I supposed that these were in some way connected with the Primitive Church.

My memory of the family sitting room at Wallingford is colored with the gloom of that criticism. It was a large room with a great fireplace and marble mantel at one end; the first fireplace I had ever seen. I remember it as a dark room. This, however, may have been a measure of my spiritual depression at the time. We two little culprits sat side by side on a great haircloth sofa with our hands bandaged and our feet sticking straight out in front of us. My father, as I recollect it, kept his eyes closed most of the time and wrinkled his forehead with a flexion of the skin which fascinated me. I remember also that Mr. Herrick and my aunt Harriet Skinner were there and that they did most of the criticizing.

Mr. Herrick was a strange combination of hearty camaraderie, quick sympathy and warm human affection, with a fanatic religiosity. In general, he was our companion, almost our playfellow, but always his affectionate smile could change

on the instant to tight-lipped severity, and his voice ring
with a challenge to the powers of evil. This meant anything
condemned by John Humphrey Noyes or his theology. Mr.
Herrick was a typical Community joiner. He left a wife and
children and a high church pulpit in New York City to come
to the Community, and thereafter his wife taught his children that their father was insane.

Aunt Harriet was my father's sister and his stanch sup-
porter through all his life; she was beautifully homely, at
least in my eyes, with many freckles, sandy hair and almost
masculine features. Aunt Harriet possessed many of the same
qualities as Mr. Herrick. She was fond of both Humphrey
and me, but held the Community's war against sin and
worldliness above all other considerations. Often, as a child,
I sensed a struggle between her love for "John's children"
and her loyalty to his spiritual severities. I can still see her
strong profile as I saw it that day in the Wallingford parlor,
and can hear her say with judgment-day sternness, "You
boys will have to learn—"

The only other person I recall, in the circle which surrounded us during this criticism was "Miss" Fanny Leonard
(we called all adult females Miss). She was a middle-aged
woman with a sweet, kindly face and a large goiter which
somewhat distracted my attention from the proceedings, in
spite of their solemnity.

5

At the end, if I remember rightly, we were convicted of
"pleasure seeking" and were told to "confess Christ a good
spirit." That formula—"confess Christ"—with or without
specific additions was an essential part of the Community
liturgy. Of all the holidays and feast days and fast days cele-

brated at Oneida, the 20th of February had first place. It was on that date in 1834 that John Humphrey Noyes "confessed Christ his Savior from all sin."

The group of believers who gathered around him at Oneida in 1848 adopted his "confession" as a ritual. The words, which meant little to me when a child save as the formula for getting into good relations with a dimly sensed heavenly hierarchy, were to them an acknowledgment that Christ had the power to free their lives from sin. We children said, " 'fess Christ" or " 'fess Christ a good spirit," without clear understanding but with firm confidence that we were in some way acquiring merit, just as orthodox Protestant children probably feel when they kneel down to pray, or Catholic children when they say their beads.

6

Another memory of Wallingford surrounds a word and a sled. The incident was trivial but the vividness and persistence of the memory has always interested me because then, I believe, for the first time my mind was exercised by one of the moral issues of life. I had learned at Wallingford that children could not climb Mount Tom, nor go to the pond, nor do other unusual and interesting things without getting "liberty." The process of getting liberty was hazy in my mind. I heard much of it from the older children, but I remember a puzzlement from the start as to the personal application of liberty. Why was it that Theodora seldom asked for liberty and was never refused; while Ormond seemed always in trouble with liberty?

On this particular day I was trudging down the hill toward the pond with the older children. It was a winter's day when all the world was white and sprays of snow whisked in our faces as we plowed through the drifts, bent on finding a place to slide. Suddenly one of the boys turned around and yelled to those behind, "We forgot to get liberty."

Now, among our sleds was one that I admired greatly, a sled with the name "Liberty" painted on its purple back. As I stood there listening to the discussion as to who should go back for liberty and uncertain whether they referred to release from adult prohibitions or to the sled, there came to me a new, though somewhat nebulous, perception that the same act might be made right or wrong by its relation to other people. The boy came back without the sled but with permission to go on to the hill.

7

I would not have anyone think, from the incidents related, that my stay at Wallingford was somber or unhappy. On the contrary, it was, in general, a season of fun and adventure. Humphrey and I helped feed the chickens and water the horses; at least we thought we helped. We visited the great dam, under proper guardianship, and when the ice on the pond grew thick we slid around among the skaters. Often we rode about the farm with Mr. Bradley on a flat sled drawn by horses.

Mr. Bradley! I can see him now: a little man with a chunky body, a round head made more globular by the curved cut of his iron-gray beard, and twinkling eyes which closed when he laughed. I have heard that, before my day, when he was head of the Children's House, he greatly overdid whippings. Mr. Bradley journeyed from New England to join the Community in 1849 when the Erie Canal was the popular method of transportation up the Mohawk Valley, and he evidently brought with him an early New England conviction that punishments, often and painful, were profitable for the spiritual development of a rising generation.

I have also heard that his discipline became so thoroughly Squeersian as to bring down upon his head my father's spiritual thunders. He was criticized, deposed, and relegated to the farm. He must have taken his criticism to heart since, when I was at Wallingford, he seemed a jolly little man, willing to go out of his way to interest boys.

Aunt Charlotte Maria—beautiful Aunt Charlotte who, on one of my first homesick days at Wallingford, took me in her arms and comforted me—used to help me set type in the printing office. Those were magnificent letters I concocted for my mother at Oneida. They were adorned with great woodcuts, horses and groups of men, and one, which I still have, is mostly taken up by the picture of an enormous eagle. That particular letter says, "Humphrey and I have lots of fun. We skate on Noyes Pond. We each have a skate." I remember Noyes Pond, a frozen ditch beside the road which Mr. Herrick named for us; and I remember the skating, Humphrey with one skate and I with the other. We felt quite grown up.

Another memory of Wallingford, an incident which had its painful side, has stayed with me through the years. One day Humphrey and I, in our roamings, visited the old blacksmith shop halfway down the road to the Mill. Boylike, we explored the attic where untidy heaps of miscellany lured us. Poking into a pan of meal, my finger was caught by a steel trap set there for rats. I assume I yelled lustily, for I can still remember how it hurt, but the tragicomic afterscene is what I particularly recall: when we led Mr. Herrick to the attic to show him how it all happened, I again got my finger in the trap. It was typical of Mr. Herrick that, after a word of reproof for my carelessness and another word of sympathy, he laughed long and loud. He laughed and said nothing about a criticism.

8

My return to Oneida involved a sleeping car. I had never before seen a sleeping car and was full of curiosity, hence wakeful. I must have been a "trial"—as they used to say in the Community—to Mr. George Hamilton under whose care I made the journey. I was awed by this magnificent big man. He was over six feet tall, with an impressive beard—every man wore a beard in those days—and an earnest, pleasing voice. When he spoke to me I had a feeling that the heavens spoke through him. Perhaps it was because he was so tall and I had to look far up to see him—as I did to see the sky where God was.

Our carriage turned up the shady drive. I could hardly contain myself; between the trees I saw children playing on the lawn. Then a glimpse of the Mansion House, the dear old North Tower which, until my New York visit, I believed the tallest structure in the world. A moment later our carriage stopped at the front stoop. There stood my mother, waiting and eager, but suppressing her eagerness and struggling to keep her demonstrations of affection within approved bounds. It was a great home-coming! I was overjoyed to see my mother, but suspect that I did not give her full satisfaction. All too soon I disappeared with a crowd of playmates as anxious to hear my tales of Wallingford as I was to tell them.

9

This chronicle of early childhood, of what I may call "pre-South Room" memories, would be incomplete without the addition of an unpleasant incident which has stuck fast in my mind. It is an unfortunate trick of memory that tragic happenings come back in pictured detail while only the general aura of happy times is preserved.

In those early days we went to school to Aunt Susan Dunn. Aunt Susan's school was really a forerunner of the kindergartens which have, since that time, spread over this country. On the walls were great charts where, in alternate squares, animals and simple objects were seen and described; a cat, then C-A-T; a dog, D-O-G. We played with blocks for all the world like the modern kindergarten blocks—square blocks and round blocks and groups of conic sections which fitted together to form irregular figures. We folded paper and cut out pictures, learning to follow with scissors all the intricacies of trees and animals and people.

In a drawer of her stand, Aunt Susan kept a supply of motto candies which she doled out to us sparingly on suitable occasions; usually as rewards. One day she called us all around her and solemnly informed us that some child had taken a motto without permission. She began at one end of the line, asking each child, "Did you take it?"

"No."

"Did you?"

"No."

It came my turn.

"Did you take it, Pierrepont?"

"No."

Aunt Susan lunged at me.

"Yes, you did!"

At the time I was sure she leaped from her chair. Probably it was only the sudden thrusting out of her hand and the explosive savageness of her tone which gave me that impression of attack. In any case, my childish mind registered terror . . . a terror that has preserved the incident in all its vividness.

I have no recollection of the punishment which unquestionably followed, nor do I remember stealing the candy; probably I did. The entire canvas is taken up by the bulky figure of Aunt Susan towering over me, her great, accusing eyes boring me through and through and her words exposing my guilt to all my companions.

Chapter II

I Graduate to the South Room

I

BEFORE beginning the story of my life in the South Room I could wish to fill a canvas with color—nothing but color—which should represent the totality of my Children's House memories. When, however, I essay this task, I find the coloring inseparable from form, from the environment and activities of my childhood. Perhaps I must content myself with a brief general description of that environment and those activities with the hope that collectively they will suggest the warm colors which enliven all my early recollections.

There were about thirty of us turned loose each morning south of the house. Every day then was an aeon and avidly through its long hours we romped and played and explored the physical world about us, enlarging our infantile horizons under conditions only slightly modified by the interference of "grown folks."

When I turn to the specific elements of that emotionally integrated picture, I find myself torn between memories of summer and of winter. At one moment I see the broad expanse of the children's playground below the South Terrace with its grass and bordering trees painted in vivid green and sunlit yellow; I see it surrounded by much equipment for sport, swings and sandbeds and croquet grounds and teeters, green and red, and the Crooked Stump where we climbed and played that we were sailors on a ship. If I look over the

35

evergreen hedge, I see the Cragin Meadow sloping away to the creek, and beyond, the old Mill, behind which a clump of trees marks the entrance to "Parson's Gulf" with its endless possibilities for exciting adventure. Toward the west I can see, through the latticelike barrier of a railway trestle, the Island Woods where squirrels and butternuts and birds' nests abound and where begins that limpid backwater we called Above the Dam.

These pictures, this composite, is almost as vivid today as it was on those mornings years ago when my bedfellow waked me, or the sun pried open my eyes, and I rejoiced at the beginning of another day.

On the other hand, the South Terrace itself belongs, in my memory, mainly to winter scenes. I find difficulty in separating it from sliding downhill and snow men and snow forts. Those also were aeons, those days when, clad in heavy jackets and prickly mohair caps and leather boots which, after a wetting, often grew stiff and wrinkly, we vied with each other for the farthest slide, or rolled immense snowballs, or played fox and geese in the field below.

This picture also has its distance. Beyond the trestle lay the old bed of the creek and skating. Over by the woods and above the dam we later trapped muskrats, and, in certain prized valleys, found huge drifts where we could dig caves high enough for boys to stand upright.

Put together these two pictures, a white world and a green and yellow world, then add a lot of healthy children of about the same age conspiring together, with only such control as served to maintain well-recognized rules, and you may glimpse the color of my childhood and boyhood as it comes back to me after fifty years.

I have described our out-of-doors as though that were all of our physical environment worth mentioning. As a matter of fact it was, or at least it is now as a memory, our most important and interesting field of action. Indoors, we were segregated in the south wing of the Mansion House. Seven large rooms were set apart for the children's use. The East Room, South Room and West Room were indoor playgrounds and were furnished accordingly. A substantial wainscoting protected the most vulnerable portion of the walls, the floors were bare, and the wooden chairs and settees were uncushioned. I remember a few pictures hung high on the walls of the South Room. Only the Girls' Room showed any attempt at decorative furnishing and for this very reason it always remained exclusively a girls' room.

The Nursery Kitchen, although designed originally as an adjunct to the near-by nursery, attracted both old and young. It was a cozy room. The special feature was a small cookstove in which a coal fire was kept burning day and night, year in and year out, and on which there always purred a kettle of boiling water. In addition there was a sink, a soft-water pump which we children loved to exercise, an immaculate ironing table, and against one wall a frame for drying clothes.

But the Nursery Kitchen was much more than a serving room. That it was a gathering place for grown folks as well as children was recognized long before my day by the addition to its furnishings of a large comfortable sofa and two well-padded Boston rockers. The room had a quality peculiarly its own—an odd combination of publicity and privacy. People were continually passing through it on their way from the children's department to other sections of the house, and yet small groups or interested couples sought the Nursery Kitchen for more private conversation than could be enjoyed in the larger sitting rooms. Sociable or lonesome men and women often sat in the rockers for the sake of brief, friendly exchanges with any who passed that way. Elderly people would happen in after meeting, concoct a hot peppermint sling or brew a cup of strawberry leaf tea and chat while they enjoyed the cheery warmth of the fire.

We children found much to interest us in the Nursery Kitchen and in winter looked upon it as a place of refuge. Wet clothes or mittens were dried there. We boys thawed out our skates on the back of the stove, and after those evenings when we had "iced the slide," we gathered there to reduce the numbness of hands and feet in the genial warmth of an open oven door. The Nursery Kitchen was a simple, homely room but, like a plain person with a kindly heart, it attracted everyone.

2

When we were very young we knew little about the interior of our home beyond the children's wing, but as we grew older other parts and especially the public rooms became available for adventure. Whenever we were given leave to wander beyond the children's quarters, we made directly for the room nearest the front door, the Reception Room. It was a large room. The furniture was Victorian mahogany brought to the Community by well-to-do joiners, and on the walls were hung historical engravings. The effect was rather austerely impressive.

We forgot this, however, when smiling and friendly Aunt Julia, who "waited on company," let us look into the stereopticons. There were two of these, black walnut boxes with lenses and eyeholes through which could be seen enlarged pictures carried on a revolving frame inside. We would sit for an hour or until the entrance of some visitor sent us away, turning knobs which brought before our eyes, in succession, scenes from far-off lands, well-censored comics, and best of all, the adventures of some unfortunate visitors in the Hadean world. With these were imps with forked tails, and devils on velocipedes, all in luminous color. They gave us the shivers, but we were never tired of looking at them.

Farther along the front hall we peeped into the Back Parlor, but that was gloomy and uninteresting with its heavy, marble-topped furniture. The Library, opposite, lured us. We tiptoed into that silent room where men and women, seated in comfortable armchairs, were reading, while others bent over a long table scanning the files of newspapers. We were awed by the immense number of books to be seen in the alcoves and glass-doored cupboards that reached to the ceiling. Miss Beulah, the librarian, tolerated us if we were very quiet and did not "meddle." She would even bring from one of the cupboards a book with interesting pictures and, seating herself beside us, whisper stories about them.

There was one other room we visited, if no officious adult took it upon herself or himself to send us back to the Children's House: the Upper Sitting Room. It was only one of several sitting rooms in the Mansion, but to us it seemed the nicest. The Oneida Community discouraged personal isolation or exclusiveness. Members were urged to "keep in the circulation," and sitting rooms were scattered through the building in order to make association easy and attractive. For the same reason the two hundred or more bedrooms were small; comfortable as sleeping quarters, but frankly not intended for living rooms.

The Upper Sitting Room was a sunny, spacious room, lighted by four high windows which looked out on the eastern lawns. Two tiers of bedrooms opened out of this sitting room. The upper tier was reached by a balcony on the front of whose wide-paneled balustrade there stared at us a collec-

tion of small engravings, each showing a classic head. All the
Muses were there, and Homer with his blind eyes and curly
beard, and Socrates, and Pythagoras, and Vergil, and Pindar,
and Plato, and others of ancient renown. These, I understand, were given to the Community by a former Italian
priest. I never tired of studying those pictures and more than
once was reprimanded for sneaking up to the "Corridor," as
the balcony was called, and leaning far over its balustrade
to get a better view of Homer. In later years I was surprised
to find some of those pictures looking down at me from the
walls of the Vatican. The bareness of the southern wall which
rose unbroken to the ceiling was relieved by a huge painting,
darkened by age, which pictured, we were told, the Israelites
gathering manna in the wilderness. Its Biblical obscurity fascinated us and I can remember groups of children gazing upward at it, engaged in a competition to recognize Moses in
some of the fragmentary forms and features that emerged
from the general duskiness.

The Upper Sitting Room was not only light and cheerful, but was usually enlivened by the presence of young
people. I remember that after the evening meeting this room
was filled with grown folks, young and old, and noisy with
conversation.

The Lower Sitting Room, just underneath and of the
same size except that it was only one story in height, had no
such attraction for children. The elderly people who usually
visited together there spoke to us patronizingly, but evidently
expected that we would "be seen and not heard."

The interior of the house interested a boy only on rainy
days or in the evening. My vivid and significant memories, as
I have said, surround our life outdoors.

A CORNER OF THE UPPER SITTING ROOM

THE SHOW CASE

CORINNA KINSLEY
Now Mrs. Pierrepont Noyes

DICK

3

It was some time before my sixth birthday that I was graduated into the South Room. Sixteen others, nine boys and seven girls, were graduated at the same time and our common emergence laid the foundation for a class spirit which has remained strong upon us all to this day. I have a vivid recollection of the excitement attending our "moving up": the discovery of our names over hooks assigned for outdoor wraps in the South Room closet; the locating, each child, his locker in the sinkroom cupboard where, thenceforward, he was to keep rubbers and leather boots; more than all, our freedom to wander over the home domain with less oversight.

One incident that comes back to me suggests a megalomania to be accounted for—and perhaps excused—by our sudden elevation in the social scale. Several of the younger boys, left behind in the East Room, were playing in the sandbed near the South Tower: Ethelbert, Karl, Grosvenor, I remember. Dick and I, self-hypnotized by our new dignity or being just ordinary liars—I am not sure which—proceeded to establish a temporary dictatorship over them. We insisted that we had the authority to admit them to the South Room or keep them out as we pleased. If I remember rightly, Karl revolted, and refused to obey our orders, whereupon Dick pronounced an edict of excommunication against the rebel and assured the others that they alone would be graduated.

As the reader will have inferred, the children of the Community were brought up, not by their parents, but by a "department." Mr. William Kelly—we called him Papa Kelly—was the head of that department. Miss Chloe and Miss Libby, the "mothers of the Children's House," put on our mittens and rubbers and made sure that when we came indoors our clothes were dry. They fed us wormwood tea and sulphur-and-molasses every spring, administered "drops" when an epidemic of sore eyes threatened, and saw to it that at least three times a day we were clean and properly fed.

Papa Kelly was an earnest man, lean and spiritually athletic. He had a thin, sandy beard, and an equally thin voice which rasped and clicked whenever he approached serious matters. He presided at five-o'clock Children's Meeting. Sometimes he quoted from one of John Humphrey Noyes's "home talks." Always he read passages from the Bible and expounded texts, mostly dealing with "love your neighbor," "disobedience," or "God's punishment of the wicked."

In the *Oneida Circular*, 1874, I read that at the age of three I asked my mother:

"Is God really good?"

"Of course, child."

"Is He ever funny?"

"Yes, He does funny things sometimes."

"Well, does He ever laugh?"

This story brings back to me the naïve mentality of an age when I was incapable of conceiving any but an anthropomorphic God. Even at the age of five, He was still a man, a good man, an all-powerful man; in addition, God seemed stricter than Papa Kelly. I recall how intimately that word "strict" was associated in my mind with Papa Kelly.

At times he meted out punishment for the spiritual good of some erring youngster and as a warning to others. I respected him highly. Dick maintains that he resents his whippings to this day, but, personally, I cannot remember any unjust punishments. As a rule, when whipped, I knew my guilt and felt it a fair and just comeuppance. Further, I believed Papa Kelly to be a custodian of that "salvation" which was the special and wonderful asset of the Community.

At an early age we were impressed with the primal necessity
of being "saved" and I recognized in him a plenary repre-
sentative of my father who, I knew, dealt directly with the
heavenly agencies of salvation.

When Children's Meeting was over, we filed into the
sinkroom where we washed our hands and faces under the
rigid inspection of one of the mothers of the Children's
House. In the next room Miss Jane Abbott brushed our hair.
She had a habit of grasping our chins and tapping our heads
smartly with the brush as she asked, "Right or left?" Then
she parted our hair on the side where we had announced a
"cowlick." I have a vivid recollection of a wart on Miss Jane's
nose which her viselike grip always brought into the direct
line of my vision. After her ministrations we marched, two
and two, across the Quadrangle to the dining room.

There were two dining rooms, airy and well lighted and
large enough to accommodate a dozen oblong tables each
seating six people, and two or three "round tables." The
round tables had stationary rims wide enough to hold a plate,
cup and saucer, while the circular center with the service of
food and condiments revolved. This central portion could be
easily turned to bring anything desired opposite a diner's
plate. The round table was hailed as a valuable invention, but
I have heard members admit that its mechanics offered temptation to bad manners. There was a story that old Mr. Newhouse would let others turn the table until a desirable dish
was opposite his plate; then with his thumb he would stop it
and help himself to the food he wanted. We children were
grouped together at the long tables and it was a proud day
for me when a friend or parent invited me to sit with them
at one of the round tables. Perhaps when I grew older I could
sit there every day.

In the early days of the Community, the menus were

simple—meager, in fact, according to the stories told us. But when I was a child the food was both abundant and excellent, although still simple. We had a wide range of vegetables, nicely cooked, delicious homemade wheat and graham bread, plenty of milk, and, in place of meat which was rarely allowed, eggs, fish, cheese or creamy meat gravies. Although living in the pie belt, pie was regarded as a menace to children; so our dessert covered a wide range of puddings—rice, tapioca, sago, custards. Our diet, and our manners as well, were carefully watched by mothers of the Children's House.

At what age we were allowed to carry our used dishes out to the dishwashing room, I do not remember. We were ambitious to do as the grown folks did, but I suppose we were obliged to wait at least until we were tall enough to lift the dishes to the high tables surrounding those great copper vats in which they were washed.

4

My memory is not clear as to our early sleeping arrangements; there must have been some regular progression governed by age. I remember sleeping with Dick and I remember that he snored annoyingly. At a later time I slept in Mr. Towner's room up in the mansard. Paul, then only one stage removed from babyhood, slept near me in a trundle bed, one of those low, square, boxlike cribs which in the daytime disappeared under larger beds. Often when the grown folks were gathered in evening meeting, Paul would start crying and his crying there in the darkness was, for me, a tragedy. When I could stand it no longer, I used to peep in at the door of the gallery which ran around three sides of the great meeting hall and try to attract the attention of someone. I say peep because the Big Meeting seemed to the children a solemn affair, and those peepings were undertaken with many misgivings and only as a last resort.

It was through the crack of the gallery door that I got my first glimpse of the Community assembled. I was greatly impressed. I remember that the hall below seemed filled with people; men were sitting bolt upright with solemn faces and arms folded; women were sewing or knitting at little tables where the cheerful yellow light from kerosene lamps with green paper shades competed with the general illumination. I had a momentary view of my father sitting near the stage— not on it—with his eyes closed. Uncle Frank was explaining to him in a loud voice—for he was then quite deaf—some question a member had asked. At another time I heard my father talking and could get no one in the gallery to pay any attention to me until he stopped.

Those were harrowing experiences, pattering barefooted down the long hallway, clad only in a nightgown, to a door I hardly dared open. The worst of it was that after some good Samaritan had come to my rescue and frightened or cajoled Paul into silence and had returned to the meeting, his crying often began again.

I remember sleeping in the drawing room with five other boys. We were forbidden to get out of bed, but managed to gratify our passion for sociability, without too greatly searing our consciences, by fastening a rope to a baby basket —a wicker affair which rolled on wooden wheels—and ferrying each other from bed to bed in this.

Still later—it must have been later because the ban on roaming had evidently become a dead letter—we had that adventure and committed that classic blunder which has become a tradition of Children's House days.

It happened thus: In the Nursery Kitchen closet was kept a fascinating assortment of supplies. I can still smell the odor of that closet—sage and catnip and strawberry leaves for making tea, peppermint for tummy-aches, and what was of greatest interest to boys, two wooden firkins, one filled with oyster crackers and the other with sugar. One night, when all grown folks were in Big Meeting, we decided on an expedition to the Nursery Kitchen for sugar. Unfortunately, the shelf was high and the firkin heavy, and by some mischance it slipped from our hands. There was a crash and a scattering of sugar over the floor.

We were panic-stricken. Hastily sweeping the sugar into a pile, we retreated to our beds where a council of war evolved a very stupid plan of action. Clifton, then a baby or nearly so, was sleeping in an adjoining room with Mrs. Waite. When that worthy woman came down from the meeting we sent one of the boys to inform her that we thought Clifton had been stealing sugar and had spilled some on the floor. It goes without saying that we were convicted of the crime.

5

Beyond the children's wing in the great rambling Community buildings there lived two hundred and fifty men and women, all of whom I knew, at least by name. Some I liked, some I feared, some I cordially disliked; all I respected. My impression was that they were a people set apart from the world by lofty ideals of human conduct and were possessors of the only true theology. Not that I could have told what their ideals were or defined the word "theology." In fact, I think my early conception of theology ranked it among the religious errors of Outsiders.

What I sensed in the people about me was their jealous guardianship of a certain spiritual integrity which seemed in some way intimately connected with the "second coming of

Christ" and the Perfectionism of the Primitive Church. There was to me, as a child, something final and complete about the character of the grown folks of the Community. I was especially persuaded of their genuineness and solidarity. Old and young, the naturally saintly as well as those whose youth or appearance might have led one to suspect an all-too-human temperament, presented a united front—to the children, at least: a front of spiritual consecration.

I remember once being greatly impressed by the righteous indignation of a young man, George Burnham by name, when confronted with wrongdoing. It was this way: Dick and I, gratifying a congenital necessity for adventure, had stationed ourselves by the highway where the terrain, we thought, concealed us from the folks, and were brazenly "sassing" strangers who passed by. Our "sass" was undoubtedly confined to calling out, "Hullo, outsider-man!" or something of the sort.

We were so pleased with our experiment in wickedness that we failed to note George Burnham's approach until he was upon us. Seizing each by the arm, he accused us of disrespect and breaking bounds and asked sternly if we did not know where disobedient little boys went to. In the end he took us to Papa Kelly for whatever immediate punishment seemed fitting. I knew George Burnham in later years as a very sophisticated man, but on that occasion his reproof was blunt and his tone expressed impatience with sin.

So it was in all my dealings with the older generation of the Community. Never, in their contacts with the children, was there any suggestion of uncertain standards of conduct or any compromise with wrongdoing.

The sincerity of the preachment and practice of Perfectionism in the Oneida Community was partially confirmed also by its effect on the children. As far back as I can remember, the Bible had its place as one of the astounding realities of the world I had been born into. Those stories of the Creation, of Abraham, of Noah and of Jonah were most important history. God seemed rather terrible, but a friend of the Community; while Christ I loved and His words wove themselves progressively into my expanding vision of life and human relationships.

We "did a good turn" to our fellows and elders with the same belief in its necessity and its efficacy for our own good that the Boy Scouts, for instance, do their "good turns." We read the Bible, partly no doubt to ape our elders, as other children do when they play school or dress up; but we did it also to "please God" and with a feeling that we were putting our feet on the same path those elders were treading, a path we fully believed led to heaven. As a child I felt surrounded by "good people," who loved Jesus Christ and wanted me to love Him, and my naïve conception of them as earnest and honest and in possession of truths not vouchsafed to the rest of the world was the background of life in the Children's House.

Chapter III

A Child's World

I

MY cousin Dick is, perhaps, the most vivid memory of
my childhood. We were by choice inseparable; so much
so that often we were "separated" for falling into the spiritual error of "partiality." That verbal noun had a definite and
serious, not to say sinister, significance in the Children's
House. The penalty, upon conviction of partiality, was a
sentence of separation for several days. The sentence usually
ran like this: "Richard and Pierrepont must not speak to each
other for three days."

I did not realize at the time that Papa Kelly's struggle
with partiality was but the echo of a warfare against exclusive (called selfish) affection, waged unremittingly in the
regions beyond the children's wing. It was not alone that the
Community religion rated "special love" between the sexes as
a sin, but any friendship that excluded others came in for
censure, and those Perfectionists believed in uprooting tares
as soon as they showed themselves.

Dick and I found a way to avoid the more serious in-
conveniences of separation. Papa Kelly undoubtedly expected
that we would remain apart, but his words said only that we
"must not speak to each other." It happened that a younger
boy, Berton, had a persistent ambition to join our expeditions. So, having arranged everything in advance, Dick and
I rendezvoused down back of the playhouse and took Bert

49

with us to the "locusts" or over by the beehives or wherever
we were building a tent. (For some reason we called our
crude cabins or cubbies or tree platforms "tents.")

At such times our conversation usually ran like this:
"Bert, tell Dick that looks like a good tree for a tent." Answered by: "Bert, tell Pip (I was called Pip until I was well
in my teens) it's too hard to climb." Berton, all the while,
maintained a prearranged silence. This avoidance of direct
disobedience was, it must be admitted, highly technical, but
it satisfied our somewhat rudimentary moral senses.

At one time we had a passion for creating little secret
societies. This must have been shortly after acquiring the new
freedom of the South Room, since some of the rituals of
those "sides" (our word for cliques) suggest simple minds.

One in particular I remember. Either Dick or I picked
up somewhere a bit of poetical wisdom. "Evening red and
morning gray, starts the traveler on his way. Evening gray
and morning red, keeps the traveler late in bed." This evidently appealed to us as something more than a scientific formula, and we proceeded to organize a cult with "Evening
Red," etc., as its abracadabra.

In the great woodpile near the Playhouse a secret chamber was excavated with much labor. There we foregathered
to nurse our mysticism and initiate other boys. Dick had a
genius for dramatizing novel ideas, first for himself, then for
others, and his explanation of the mystical significance and
practical value of "Evening Red" greatly impressed five-
year-old initiates. Bert or Holton, crouching in the dim light
which filtered between the slabs of boiler room wood, listened
to his elaborate dissertation on the prophetic possibilities of
this cabalistic jingle, with faces as solemn as little owls.

At another time we met down cellar in a small rough-
boarded room where were stored pipe fittings, and whittled

out little wooden fairies. Someone—I think it was Miss Chloe
—had been reading to us from *Grimm's Fairy Tales*. I am a
little surprised that my father, who frowned on dolls, allowed
the children fairies, but Grimm's was certainly in the South
Room library. I cannot think that we really expected our
little images to turn into fairies, but an aura of fairyland certainly surrounded our labors. Perhaps at that age a child's
mysticism does not include definite expectations. Nevertheless, down in the boilerman's room, we were getting as near
as we could to fairyland.

Another enterprise that engaged our enthusiasm was a
"Magic Lantern Show." Readers of my age will remember
that the magic lantern was the father—or grandfather—of
the movie. Some enterprising member of the Community
bought or manufactured an outfit and gave a showing in the
Hall. We children were fascinated by it. One of the boys
noticed a knothole in a large woodbox in the cellar under the
Nursery Kitchen stairs, and being a genius, saw its possibilities. We borrowed a "bull's-eye lantern" from one of the
older boys, and by sliding strips of glass covered with sil-
houetted figures across the opposite side of the hole, we repro-
duced crude pictures on a sheet stretched across the box. I
remember a formal exhibition in the cellar, attended by complacent adults, mostly, I suppose, parents.

Dick and I were not really exclusive. We played games
with the others—escape; I spy; King, King castle; prisoner's
base; and the ball game called "one old cat." Those were
for the interims of school and after supper; it was during the
long afternoons and on days when there was no school that
we went about the serious business of life.

We planned our expeditions in advance. They seemed
like expeditions, although at that age they could hardly have
extended farther than the "locusts" or over by the "bee-

hives." We went alone, except that occasionally, especially when our plan involved much work, we admitted one or two trusted subordinates. We had a passion for finding "secret places," or arranging lairs, among the barrels of the woodshed attic, in the dark places of the mazelike cellar of the Mansion House, and more often in trees.

Another of our activities was bird's-nesting. This sounds unethical and is now unlawful, but in the 1870's little was thought of it. In fact, collecting birds' eggs seemed to our elders, I am sure, a rather commendable variation of a boy's activities, like collecting stamps or coins. There was a tacit understanding that we ought not to take *all* the eggs in a nest, but if it was a rare find, an owl, a hawk or a vireo, we did take them all as trading stock with the other boys. Dick and I kept a mental inventory of the hopeful trees on the lawn and in the immediate neighborhood and each season felt that we had not done our duty until every one of them had been climbed. As we grew older we searched the woods for miles around.

2

In the early days, before we were allowed to roam, one of our greatest joys was the New Yard. This special playground lay at some distance east of the home grounds and was surrounded by a high board fence. Whenever Papa Kelly granted permission to play there, he was likely to add: "Remember, you must not go outside the fence."

The lure of the New Yard came partly from the novelty of some of its equipment (a Maypole and a latticed arbor wonderfully adapted for children's climbing) and partly because of its distance from the home grounds and adult oversight; but even more, we were fascinated by the *terra incognita*, the tantalizing regions for possible adventure, to be seen on every hand beyond the fence.

Our journey to the New Yard, too; that was exhilarating. First came a crossing of the main highway, which in itself gave us a pleasant sense of freedom. Beyond, the path lay between rows of grapevines, the especial care and pride of one Henry Thacker. I remember how hungrily we looked at the bunches of luscious purple grapes and how suspiciously Mr. Thacker looked at us. His nearsighted eyes peered down the line of a large Roman nose and followed us until we were well past the grapes.

The dour expression on his face, which in my early childhood led me to classify him with the ogres, may have been an index of his premonition. He may have anticipated a later day when he would be chasing us with threatening hullabaloos among his vines. I might add that Mr. Thacker lived long enough for one of his grape stealers to recognize that he was a kindly soul—except where grapes were concerned.

At the far side of the vineyard we came to a tall barberry hedge. This I early associated with a certain hedge—it seems to me it was called hedge thicket or thicket hedge— which played a prominent part in one of my favorite fairy stories. It may have been *Rumpelstiltskin*—I have forgotten. All I remember is that on the other side of that hedge the boy in the story met a little brown dwarf who asked him three questions.

As a five-year-old, when passing through the narrow opening in the barberry hedge, I cherished a secret hope that I would find a little brown dwarf in the regions beyond. That was the mysticism of a five-year-old. By the time I was six, dwarfs and fairies were more doubtful, but still the territory east of the New Yard, between it and the creek, and over the hill beyond, retained a part of its mystery: a more rational mystery but equally alluring, the mystery of unexplored lands. More and more, when tired of the sandbed and Maypole and arbor, Dick and I would hang over the fence looking longingly at the forbidden territory outside and discussing its possibilities.

Through what period of time we were satisfied to look and long, and just when we began making little outside explorations, I cannot tell. We must have ventured often and ranged widely, for to this day I have a possessive feeling toward the terrain east of the vineyard. I can still find the big buttonball tree which we tried to climb, and the slippery stones at the creek fords, and the ditch we dammed, and the wooded gully across the creek in which our imaginations located thrilling adventures taken from *Nick Whiffles* or *Frank on the Prairie*. To all these there still clings a trace of that coloring painted only at the dawn of life.

3

On one occasion our venturesomeness was near to bringing me the wages of sin. We had crawled down the steep creek bank where an eddy circled darkly under the roots of an overhanging tree. Probably we were searching for muskrat holes about which we had read in the *Trappers' Guide*, a book printed by the Community.

Suddenly I lost my hold on the roots. There was no splash; I simply slid into the water and down, down, it seemed, toward the bottom of a deep hole. I can still remember the terror of that moment; I could not swim and there was nothing to get hold of on the bank. It is odd, but I remember seeing, among the patches of foam floating on the surface, hundreds of seeds from the maple trees upstream, little green nubs with curved membranous wings. For years thereafter those winged maple seeds were associated with terror and death.

Evidently Dick kept his head. In some way he managed to grasp my arm and hold on until, with his aid, I crawled back onto the bank. It was near evening, or a cloudy day, or both. All the face of nature seemed dark and ominous. Behind us lay the black monster whose jaws I had so narrowly escaped and, to our frightened imaginations, unseen agencies of danger lurked all about.

And then, to the eerie terrors of that newly discovered reality—death—were added the hobgoblins of disobedience and sin, while the grim specter of Papa Kelly loomed in the background. On the bank of Oneida Creek, as the sun was setting, there stood two little boys wet and cold and beyond their depths in misery.

4

"Snow! Snow! See the snow! It's covered up everything! It's deep!"

We boys, six of us sleeping in the same room, scrabbled into our clothes. The before-breakfast gathering in the South Room was a pandemonium of joyous exclamations and expectations. "Oh! ooh! see the hill and the sliding!" "We can roll in the snowdrifts and build forts." "Yes, and make fox-and-geese tracks all over the lawn."

Miss Libby, struggling to get us washed and our hair brushed, had to give it up; and later she had to give up trying to persuade the herd of excited youngsters to "eat slowly and chew your food fine." After breakfast came a pell-mell race back to the South Room and another race to see who could first don snow pants, cap and boots. I remember Miss Libby, hurrying from room to room, scolding, helpless, unable to make sure that every child was properly dressed for the snow. Marvelous memories.

We must have been an odd spectacle as we emerged on the terrace. Our snow pants were held down by straps under the instep, and belted over heavy jackets. Around our necks knitted "tippets" were securely tied, and our costumes completed by the prickly mohair caps I mentioned before. These caps had a skirtlike fold, pierced with eyeholes and mouth holes, which were pulled down in very cold weather, completely encasing our heads. We looked like a band of Oriental masked demons or little Ku-Kluxers.

How we romped in the snow! If, at first, it proved too deep for easy sliding, we rolled over and over in the drifts and down the hill—rolled each other over. We ran around the field with our sleds, playing horse-and-cutter or that the whole procession was a train of cars. Then, when the older boys had trampled the snow on the hill, we tried sliding again.

We were forbidden to slide on the fast track. When we tired of the slow speed in the softer snow, we sought excitement by hitching together a string of sleds which usually ended in a grand smash at the bottom of the hill. I can still see the picture—Dorr and Ruddy and Holton and George and very likely several girls, Althea and Elinor, disentangling themselves and their sleds from the wreck and arguing loudly as to whose fault it was. Perhaps Dick and Felix and half a dozen other boys, engaged in building snow forts over by the garden, were attracted by the fun and ran over to join us.

Still farther along in the deeper snow three-year-olds and four-year-olds—Paul and Karl and Stephen and Grosvenor, and the little girl Corinna who afterward became my wife, were tucked onto little snub-nosed sleds by Miss Libby or Miss Chloe and pushed over the brow of the hill. Their unsteered sleds always ran off at unexpected angles. Often they slued sideways and tipped over, and the tots came up little snowmen and women all white from head to foot.

The "four big boys"—Ransom, Amos, Eugene, Deming —were allowed to slide on the fast track and even experiment with plunging down the "platform." This was a steep wooden ramp which a still older class, Harry Kelly and Ormond's class, not satisfied with the height of the hill, had built to increase speed and double the length of slide.

At such times, when the white playground was alive with speeding, plodding or wriggling children, Papa Kelly seemed everywhere. Oftener than not, he would appear from nowhere in particular to balk the plan of a small boy who had edged over toward the fast track. However, in spite of his watchfulness, we, one by one, learned to steer. I was very proud the first time Papa Kelly stood by without objecting while I slid down the icy path, and I remember his chuckle of tolerance, almost approval, as I again climbed the hill.

5

I had not been long accepted as a competent steerer when overconfidence got me into trouble. Aunt Sarah Johnson, middle-aged and stout, was through all my childhood a sort of foster mother to me. I never knew why. She was childless and her partiality for me may have been a manifestation of thwarted maternal love. There were many similar cases. I remember boys and girls "aunty-ing" or "uncle-ing" women or men who were neither their aunts nor their uncles, but who, we children thought, petted them more than their own parents did. Which suggests that the Community recognized the urge of parental love and encouraged childless persons to associate freely with children of whom they were fond. I liked Aunt Sarah, but secretly objected to her calling me "Ponty."

One morning, inflated with the pride of accomplishment, I teased Aunt Sarah (Papa Kelly always severely criticized "teasing") to let me take her for a ride down the hill.

I remember sliding alone several times to prove I could steer. She was a timid woman, and even now I am surprised that she yielded to my persuasion; but she did.

From under the "platform" I brought "Old Peakie," an extra large sled. On this Aunt Sarah adjusted herself. She occupied most of the sled while I, with one knee on the limited space remaining and the other foot trailing as a rudder, managed to push off. Now there was—and still is—at a little distance from the sliding track a huge elm tree. My start was wobbly and some demon of ill luck directed me toward that tree. Then the fatal attraction for approaching obstacles which at times seizes fearful souls did the rest. I saw the tree rushing toward us and struggled, but my little leg was too weak to deflect a sled weighted with at least two hundred pounds avoirdupois. We ran squarely into the "big elm."

I was not injured, only shaken up. But, oh, Aunt Sarah! Over her eye I saw a savage gash, and blood was running down her face. She did not scold me; she seemed mostly concerned as to whether I was hurt. In her comfortings there was even a hint of anxiety lest I had brought upon myself departmental displeasure and possible punishment. As a matter of fact, I feel sure that she herself received a criticism for recklessness or "uninspired dealings with the children."

For me it was a catastrophe too appalling for the emotional capacity of a six-year-old to encompass all at once. I do not recall that I was either punished or criticized; in fact, I have a faint recollection of being comforted by women who feared I was injured. I do remember, however, a sickish feeling in the region where we had been taught our hearts were located, a feeling which expanded as I recovered from the first shock and which, for the time being, led a very objective boy to serious subjective thinking. I felt responsible for Aunt Sarah's bleeding face.

I am not sure that I retained for any length of time a look-before-you-leap complex sufficiently strong to deter me from future recklessness. I am almost sure I did not. But I do believe that on that day was born a recognition of responsibility for injury to others as result of my own acts. Surely none but a boy of very callous nature could run his aunt Sarah into an elm tree without taking on a certain amount of what Papa Kelly called "sense of responsibility."

6

Often after a rain had turned the snow to deep slush Dick and I, with wet mittens hanging from our sleeves, worked at making little rivulets; worked until our hands were badly chapped and we had to stay indoors for a whole day as penalty. Then there was (or were) chilblains, a winter scourge prevalent in Children's House days. I remember freezing a cheek and hearing Miss Libby or Dr. Cragin or someone else say, "He is likely to have chronic catarrh." This registered in my mind as one word and seemed to promise a distinguished disease. For a long time thereafter I supported a superiority complex on the belief that I had "chroniguitar."

In general, however, the social distinction we founded on interesting diseases was denied me. I failed to come down with measles or whooping cough during those epidemics, and when poison ivy was the popular scourge I could not get it, try as I would; even when I rubbed my legs with ivy leaves, the poison would not take. Similarly, my ankles would not sprain.

Once, after nearly all the other boys had, at one time

or another, enjoyed a sprained ankle, I took advantage of
a twisting of my foot to claim that status. My ankle
was bandaged and I was ensconced in a chair on the South
Stoop. My meals—and those were meals we all coveted—
were brought on a tray. I hope, for the sake of my own self-
respect, that the joint hurt me enough to warrant the belief
it was sprained. In any case, the privilege and distinction
were short-lived. On the second day, the approach of a
tray with that unusual food excited my gustatory sense
unduly and I ran to meet it. That ended the pleasures and
social advantages of a sprained ankle.

I did get "sore eyes" (probably pinkeye) when the
rest did, and finally accomplished the mumps. In fact, my
siege with the mumps served for several years as a satisfactory offset to the bragging of other children about the
diseases they had had. Unfortunately I had gone in swimming before the mumps was diagnosed, and took cold in a
gland. The fever and final lancing of my jaw were hard
experiences, but, after it was all over, I felt amply repaid by
the hero aura which surrounded me.

7

Some memories with an unusually high percentage of
emotional content pierce the haze of distance and bring
back pictures definite and clear-cut. Such a one is my memory of a certain quarrel—we never spoke of fighting, always
"quarreling."

The Community religion was one hundred per cent
pacifistic. Christ's admonition, "If thy enemy strike thee
on thy right cheek, turn to him the other also," pervaded
the Children's House. It came to us mediately from "upstairs" where the moral and ethical laws for our little world

were made, but its "thee's" and "thy's" stamped it as being unquestionably of heavenly origin. Any uncertainty as to whether the injunction applied to a cheek only was dissipated by Papa Kelly's simpler formula, "Do good for evil." This we fully understood.

There was an even loftier spiritual plane to be reached by "heaping coals of fire" on your enemy's head. "Good for evil" seemed just an ordinary everyday rule of conduct, but heaping coals of fire—well, I remember the sparkle in Papa Kelly's eye and the crackle in his voice when he talked of it; also the somewhat romantic feeling about myself which followed his praise in those metaphorical terms. Although the ethics of the "coals of fire" parable seemed to me obscure, I remember no negative reaction to the idea of burning coals on another child's head. In some way it represented self-abasement—self-abasement for the heaper.

Our elders succeeded surprisingly in planting this fundamental principle in our childish minds. Quarrels were exceptions. Little quarrels we knew were sins and big quarrels tragedies. It was one of the latter I am about to relate.

We were playing in the sandbed, making what we called "marble rollers"; heaps of wet sand honeycombed with tunnels from which marbles ran out at unexpected places determined by the shifting of internal switches. Building these structures called for much careful workmanship. On this particular occasion the sandbed was crowded with children, all working emulously to create the most intricate tunnels. It happened that my foot or some stick I was using accidentally damaged Dick's marble roller. Impulsively, he struck me; what was worse, with another blow he demolished my roller. Thereupon "good for evil" and "turn the other cheek" were forgotten. I struck and Dick struck and we rolled over and over in the sand, with one idea only—to hurt each other. There was great excitement in the sandbed. Other children, their inhibitions untouched by anger, called to us excitedly to stop. "You mustn't!" "I'll tell the folks." And one child ran over to the flower garden calling to Miss Chloe who was working there, "Dick and Pip are quarreling!"

As a result of all this I suppose we were spanked, but my memory tells only of sitting for a long time in a dark corner of the great South Room closet, while I meditated on my wickedness and recovered a "good spirit." Dick was not in the closet, but I assumed (probably hoped) he was having to "sit down" also. I say hoped because I remember some doubt as to whether he was as guilty as I. A child's mind is extremely literal and all the formulas I have referred to aimed their shafts at the boy smitten, without ever a word of admonition or reproof for the smiter. "Do good for evil" seemed to let the provoker of quarrels off scot free. As a matter of fact, I think that even Papa Kelly was unconsciously affected by the wording of his own injunctions, for he always seemed especially outraged by the receiver of blows who failed to "turn the other cheek."

A bit of puzzling psychology comes back with this memory. The first impulse of the other children was to threaten us with "telling." "I'll tell! . . . I'll tell! . . . I'll tell the folks!" rang in our ears. This was by no means poor sportsmanship on their part; we were taught that "telling" represented the highest virtue. We must tell when we saw any child doing wrong. Christ knew all about it anyway, and for the sake of the sinner, as well as ourselves, the quicker he got *en rapport* with the agencies of correction the better.

The puzzling thing about this is that while I am sure we really believed in the righteousness of "telling," I remem-

ber on more than one occasion children surrounding a boy,
pointing their finger at him and reciting jeeringly, "Tattletale, tattletale, hang him on the bull's tail; when the bull
begins to run, shoot him with a leather gun."

I cannot make these two memories fit.

8

The etiquette—if I may use that word—of the Children's House was as definite and fixed as its moral code. We
said "Yes, sir" and "No, sir" to our elders or were reported
to Papa Kelly as "saucy." We addressed all grown folks as
"Mr." or "Miss" excepting our parents and those who by
reason of relationship or custom we could call "Uncle" or
"Aunt." Even in conversation among ourselves we were expected to use these "respectful" titles.

The human aversion for obeying rules was sometimes
in evidence among the usually well-disciplined Community
children. My brother Holton often dropped the "Mr." or
mumbled it unintelligibly in speaking of men he disliked,
while both he and Karl, when telling their inimitable stories
in the sanctity of an all-child audience, dramatized their
victims as "Old Perry" or "Old Randolph." Those were
daring adventures in lawlessness.

I also remember Dorr's sullen silence when criticized for
saying "Yes" to Miss Libby. Dorr was a thoughtful boy and
very temperamental. He seemed possessed of an inner compulsion to ask "the why" of interdictions which the rest of
us accepted on the sole authority of adults. As a rule he
asked the questions only of himself or grumbled confiden-
tially to a companion, but at times he, quite unnecessarily,
got himself into bad odor with Papa Kelly by insisting on
a childish rationalization of some case of disobedience. I

retain a mental picture of the exasperated Papa Kelly leaning far forward in his chair, his head shaking and a finger
pointing menacingly at Dorr as he ordered: "Stop excusing
yourself, Dorr! Stop excusing yourself!"

I do not recall being taught any of the ordinary formalities, bowing, or taking off hats, or rising when a woman
entered the room. Perhaps we were so segregated that there
was little occasion for such. I do believe, however, that the
essence of good manners was drilled into us under the head
of unselfishness. "Do unto others as you would that they
do unto you" was more than a golden rule to be read on Sunday and forgotten the rest of the week. It was kept continually before us as a standard of conduct. I will not assert
that we always lived up to this ideal, but the conviction
that we had a responsibility for the happiness of others
became as real a part of our moral code as "obedience" or
"telling the truth."

If the gospel of unselfishness influenced our manners,
as I have suggested, that was quite incidental. Beginning
with our earliest years we children were impressed with the
fact that unselfishness was one of the basic constituents of
goodness, and Papa Kelly never allowed us to forget this. A
selfish child was always a "bad child."

There was another much-criticized error which, of
course, violated the code of morals rather than manners;
it was called in the Community "stickiness," more especially
being "sticky" to one's parents. I think that this sin was
more prevalent among the girls than the boys. My wife
remembers an occasion when the sight of her mother led
to a violent and, from Papa Kelly's point of view, disagreeable exhibition of "stickiness to her mother."

Chapter IV

My Mother

I

WHEN I was six years old my mother was allowed to arrange a birthday party for me. I remember two little chairs and a low table set out under the tulip tree in the Quadrangle. There were only two at the party, Dick and I, but it was a real party and we had cake.

I think my mother got even more pleasure than I did out of that party. The Community system was harder on mothers than on their children. Whenever I was permitted to visit my mother in her mansard room—once a week or twice (I have forgotten which)—she always seemed trying to make up for lost opportunity, lavishing affection on me until, much as I loved her, I half grudged the time taken from play with those toys which she had—I think somewhat surreptitiously—collected for my visits.

Hers was a pleasant room, lighted by two windows set deep in an embrasure made necessary by the slant of the mansard roof. In the broad window seat I played that I was on a stage or, with the sky and clouds outside as my sea, imagined I was steering a boat as I had seen Mr. Inslee steer the boat he kept above the dam. My stage or boat was reached by climbing a coil—when it was not too hot. The Mansion House was steam-heated at a time when central heating was rare, and every room had a homemade coil consisting of many horizonal lengths of iron pipe connected at their ends by curved "unions."

At one side of my mother's room was a wardrobe with ample drawers below. In addition, there was a desk and desk chair where she did her writing, a comfortable rocker, and a bed. Hanging on the wall was a whatnot. I especially remember this because on its three shelves, of diminishing size, were many articles that I used to tease my mother to let me take—figurines, little boxes, sparkling cards, daguerreotypes in marvelous frames, and a miscellaneous collection of little mementos. Hanging also on the walls were several pictures and a mirror in an old-fashioned wooden frame.

The afternoons with my mother meant a great deal to me, and it is no disparagement of my filial affection to add that freedom from departmental oversight as well as the petting and peppermints to be expected on such occasions enhanced their attractiveness. Certain it is that I often wept bitterly when the time came to return to the Children's House. I remember my mother's terror lest my crying be heard. She knew that Father Noyes frowned on any excess of parental affection as he did on all forms of "special love," and she feared that such demonstrations might deprive her of some of my regular visits.

As a matter of fact, she had concrete evidence of this danger. Once, as a punishment for some childish sin, Papa Kelly forbade my weekly visit to the mansard. I promptly went berserk. Forgetting my Children's House training and my fear of its head, I raged; I howled, I kicked, I lay down on the sinkroom floor and exhausted my infantile vocabulary in vehement protestations and accusations. Whereupon Papa Kelly seized me and shook me and commanded in a voice charged with indignation and authority—just such a voice as I imagined Jesus Christ used when casting out devils,

MY MOTHER, HARRIET WORDEN

DR. THEODORE NOYES
(From a painting by Kenneth Hayes Miller)

"Be still, Pip, be still!" Then, firmly, "You have evidently got sticky to your mother. You may stay away from her another week." The turbulence was mine, but the greater tragedy was my mother's.

A child avid for play forgets easily; but whenever, as I played on the floor, she bent over me, her dark eyes appealing, and asked, "Darling, do you love me?" I always melted. My marbles and blocks were forgotten. I would reach up and put my arms about her neck. I remember how tightly she held me and how long, as though she would never let me go.

On the other hand, I recognized in a vague way that in my mother's heart were spiritual consecrations which often struggled with her love of me. At times I was mystified by her hardness. I distinctly recall an occasion when her sudden transformation from the embodiment of tenderness to the severity of a Roman matron ended a stormy rebellion but left the rebel, for the moment, heartbroken. She had followed me to the head of the mansard stairs, begging me to stop crying. I must have burst out afresh. Suddenly she leaned over me: "Pierrepont!" That was a warning; she rarely called me Pierrepont. "Stop crying instantly! It's a bad spirit in your heart. If you don't stop I shall not let you come to my room."

With one hand on the banister rail I looked up into her face. My mother had a broad, high forehead and a Roman nose and her mouth and chin completed a profile which could look dangerously determined. I went slowly down the stairs. All the world seemed heartless and cruel. My mother was just like Papa Kelly . . . wanted me to be good whether I was happy or not.

2

That was her other side. In general, my mother ex-
emplified for me love and beauty; I thought her beautiful
beyond all others. Later I knew her as a strong, eager woman,
passionate in her religious faith, passionate in her craving
for education, and above all, passionate in her insistence
that life be big and worthwhile. For this last she relied
primarily on religion, on a John-Humphrey-Noyes interpretation of Christ and the Primitive Church and his intimate
relation with them. She never faltered in that faith. To her
dying day, eleven years after the "breakup," she believed im-
plicitly in my father's true inspiration.

After religion, her enthusiasm was for improvement. I
am sure that in those days she called it improvement rather
than education. It seems to me that, even in childhood, I ap-
prehended a spiritual implication in the distinction between
those words "improvement" and "education." The Community was suspicious of education for itself alone. Papa
Kelly often talked earnestly to the children about improvement, but I do not remember his ever using the word "education." It is true that secular studies were approved and
encouraged, but only if made secondary to spiritual advancement. As a matter of record, I have heard that, under the
other name, education was an enthusiasm among the Community members; that men and women sixty, seventy and
even eighty years old, whose early education had been
neglected, studied the three R's and more advanced subjects
earnestly and persistently. In 1864 Theodore Noyes and
several other young men were sent to New Haven where
they studied medicine, science or mechanics in the Yale
Scientific School.

The Community records mention one study class whose

title sounds, to say the least, unusual—a "class for the detection of counterfeit money." It seems that after the Civil War an epidemic of counterfeit money spread over the country and our Cashier's Office suffered very considerable losses from this source. It evidently seemed to our elders a practical and desirable subject for study.

I remember that my mother studied French (*Legendre*, I am sure was the name of the book) with Mr. Hinds, and the Greek version of the New Testament with my aunt Harriet Skinner; also Latin and some kind of mathematics in classes. I recall a large black book in her room between whose leaves were sheets of paper barred with parallel lines on which were penciled endless hieroglyphics. This, she told me, was "thorough bass."

It seems that a musical genius—Felix Schelling by name—joined up in the early sixties and introduced the science of musical composition to a community which had always had an enthusiasm for music . . . just music. My mind was foggy as to exactly what "thorough bass" meant, but I had great respect for it on account of the reverent way my mother spoke of it.

She must have been a capable woman, intellectually capable, since for seven years she was editress of the *Oneida Circular*, that weekly paper which the Community sent out into the world, telling of its religious beliefs, its social system, and its hopes for world communism. Once in a great while I was allowed to visit her editorial sanctum, up the long flight of stairs leading to the second floor of the old Arcade. I remember sitting on the floor—I must be very quiet—playing with strips of gummed paper or abandoned fonts of type.

The real joy of those visits came, however, when Frank Tuttle (he with the flowing beard, notable even in that age of beards) or Eddie Blood took me down to the pressroom. There I stood fascinated before the great revolving cylinders and the ponderous slabs of type matter, jerking noisily back and forth between a maze of inky rolls.

3

I owe immensely more to my mother, in the warp and woof of character, than I do to my father. He never seemed a father to me in the ordinary sense. I revered him, but he was much too far away, too near to heaven and God. He lived somewhere upstairs and, whenever I saw him, was usually surrounded by men like Mr. Hamilton and Mr. Pitt, who were associated in my mind with the Apostles.

In his place I had an "Uncle Abram," whom I loved as a father. My relation to him was an unusual one. He was not really my uncle, but the father of my half brother Ormond—seven years older than I. It saddens me when I think that Ormond—now dead—felt that his father loved me more than he did him. This foster father showed his affection in many ways; had me with him as much as the regulations permitted; mended my skates and sled; took me down to the Mill where I played in the shavings and made little things with sticks while he worked. When he and Birdsey Bristol went hunting, minus a dog—I was older then— they frequently allowed me to go along and I remember Uncle Abram's pride in the vigor with which I ran up and down the sides of the ravines to flush partridges for them.

Uncle Abram was a homely man, homely and awkward and simple. I remember once returning with him from a visit to "Joppa." Joppa was the name of a rough but commodious camp the Community built on the shore of Oneida

Lake in the days before that primeval forest and wonderful sandy beach had been invaded by peanuts and popcorn and merry-go-rounds and named paradoxically "Sylvan Beach." We had been pulled across Fish Creek on a rickety ferry by one of the Spencers, who owned "Forest Home," a fisherman's retreat and the only other house at that end of the lake. Another Spencer had driven us through the sand to a lonely station of the Ontario & Western Railroad. There we sat on the ground while we waited for a homebound train.

A score of other people, Outsiders, were sitting on the ground about us and, when the long wait had grown tedious, someone entertained the company with stories. Then Uncle Abram—I can see him now—rose to his knees and, with his hands folded awkwardly in front, sang several old songs: "Rock of Ages," "Men of Harlech," and something sentimental like "The Last Rose of Summer" or "Kathleen Mavourneen." I was terribly embarrassed, but the listeners applauded and kept calling for more.

He really had a fine voice. When in 1879 the Community staged the opera *Pinafore*, Uncle Abram sang the lead, Ralph Rackstraw. He was given the part not for his histrionic ability, but because he was the only tenor who could take the high notes. I was then old enough to sit in the gallery during rehearsals and I enjoyed his singing more than all others. As always, he was awkward, holding his hands clasped against his abdomen, more like the carpenter, he was, than a romantic lover.

At those rehearsals of *Pinafore*, I entirely missed the Gilbert and Sullivan satire. When Uncle Abram sang, "Farewell, my own! Light of my life, farewell!—For crime unknown I go to a dungeon cell," I wept; and when Dr. Noyes, with his portly figure and beautiful spade beard, sang, "I polished up that handle so carefullee—That now I am the Ruler of the Queen's Navee," I took it as a serious explanation of grandeur.

4

I loved my mother and find it difficult to explain the fact that I suffered so little over separation from her. Perhaps the aspirations of those men and women who formed the background for life in the Children's House had something to do with this. They struggled to concentrate their primary affectional impulses upon heavenly beings and Papa Kelly explained this as best he could to the children. My conception of the grown folks' ideal was undoubtedly vague, but their antagonism to excessive human affection was neither vague nor meaningless. It came to us in the form of oppositions and prohibitions which affected our daily lives and whose intent even children could understand. A child has little capacity for loving that which it can neither see nor touch. Hence the pressure to elevate the love emotion reacted with us as a suppression and, at least in my own case, oriented my interest toward material things. Whether or not this orientation prevented my greatly missing the parental love and tenderness that commonly surround children, I am not sure; certainly our daily routine with its many interesting activities left few unsatisfied longings.

I recall an incident which suggests that this attempt of our elders to keep down the temperature of human love penetrated my consciousness at an early age. Sitting on the floor in that mansard room, I once heard Uncle Abram say to my mother, "Harriet, that is idolatry." I knew they had been talking about me, and this sentence, uttered with the Christ-and-the-Primitive-Church accents I associated with Papa

Kelly's Bible talks, caught my attention. I liked the word "idolatry," with, of course, not the faintest conception of what it meant; but I sensed criticism in Uncle Abram's tone. What has persisted in my memory—and this rather astonishes me—is the fact that I connected his words with my mother's less affectionate attitude toward me during the remainder of that visit. "Idolatry" evidently referred to the way my mother sometimes petted me and Uncle Abram was criticizing her.

Chapter V

I Begin to Look Around

I

A CALF has no idea that it will ever become a cow. Equally, a very young child does not connect its own future or that of its companions with the ruling and providing race of beings called "grown folks." They are just a part of its permanent environment. At what age I myself became conscious of this connection I cannot recall, but I do know that it dawned as a sort of fourth dimension, at first obscure and speculative.

In the beginning this speculation concerned itself with a very few of the older people. I find far back in my memory a gallery of portraits, a rather limited gallery, of men and women who came under my observation in that early period when this new thought, that they might represent my own future, was dawning. Those are the grown folks of my earliest recollections.

I think that I first took note of men who attracted me; such men as Uncle Frank, Mr. Myron Kinsley and Charles Cragin. They were in charge of the factories and, while this meant nothing to me, they seemed surrounded by an atmosphere of masterful activity and accomplishment.

Uncle Frank was tall and stood so proudly erect that as a child I never dared speak to him unless he spoke to me. He came to Oneida as a boy of ten years, brought there by his mother, Laura Burgess Smith, whose gaunt figure seemed as unbending as her son's and whose countenance always looked so uncompromisingly stern that we were glad she was no longer one of the Children's House mothers as she had been in earlier years. We called her respectfully, "Miss Laura Burgess."

Mr. Myron Kinsley had broad shoulders, great physical strength and the energy of two men. All of this energy was devoted to the work of building up the Community businesses. He wore a long, black beard. His father, Albert Kinsley, left a prosperous farm and an excellent social position in northern Vermont to join the Perfectionists at Oneida. That was in 1848. He brought with him Myron, then twelve years old, a brother Martin, and two sisters, Jane and Sarah. Albert Kinsley was a man on whom my father relied for advice and action and he served as one of the "Four" in whose name the communal property was held.

Charles Cragin died when I was seven years old; hence I remember little about him except that he seemed always hurrying around on important business and talked with a confident and competent tone in his voice. He was handsome and likable and the only Community man I remember who wore no beard.

Mr. Homer Barron kept the store and had in his possession sugar and raisins and a hundred nice-smelling eatables. I liked him and his job. He was another of those sturdy Vermonters who came to Oneida when a boy and throughout its existence remained a convinced believer in the Community's religion and manner of life. It was such men as he who made possible the material prosperity of the Oneida Community and the harmony in its communal life. He worked at many and varied tasks, accepting cheerfully whatever position was assigned him and with no reservations or resentment when men younger or of less breeding were placed above him.

Then there was Mr. Erastus Hamilton. He had been, from the earliest days, my father's first assistant—a sort of apostolic deputy. When converted to Perfectionism, he was a successful architect in the city of Syracuse. He had a rather domineering manner which would have rendered him a not too agreeable administrator had it not been for the intense sincerity of his religion and his susceptibility to the spiritual leadings of John Humphrey Noyes.

As spiritual overseer, Mr. Hamilton came frequently to the Children's House. I remember how his head shook and his voice trembled when he reinforced Papa Kelly's words of spiritual wisdom. His admonitions were general in character. He added obscure but nonetheless impressive references to the heavens and the Primitive Church. I knew from Papa Kelly's deferential attitude that Mr. Hamilton belonged to the upper hierarchy. I thought of him as one descending from a spiritual anteroom which lacked the warmth of my father's holy of holies. He brought only a "rod and staff"—admonition and correction—and appeared to prize goodness and obedience more than he did us children.

Dr. Theodore Noyes seemed the exact opposite of Mr. Hamilton. He was my half brother, thirty years older than I, and the only legitimate son of John Humphrey Noyes. His place was probably nearer the throne than Mr. Hamilton's, but he brought to the Children's House a spirit of benevolence. I remember his delightful chuckle of tolerant amusement in the presence of our moral crudities. He had studied medicine at the Yale Scientific School and, recalling his rather diffident questioning of the children, I am tempted to believe that he was more interested in our mental and physical development than our religious orthodoxy. When he visited us in sickness, he brought the same sympathetic and hopeful atmosphere which we credit to the old-fashioned family doctor. I am reminded of the picture formerly to be seen in many physicians' offices, which shows a dear old doctor attending a sick child. Dr. Noyes had the same confidence-inspiring beard, and he used to feel our pulses with the same "you-can-leave-it-all-to-me" expression on his face.

Mr. Woolworth was another impressive person. He was fine-looking, tall and straight, with a massive head and, what I especially remember, a wonderfully friendly smile. I do not know what he did, excepting that he had a part in the highest Councils, was one of the Community's elder statesmen, and that his attachment to my father went back to the days of the Putney Community. I always felt a sense of pleasure when I happened upon Mr. Woolworth.

Mr. Charles Joslyn was always an enigma to me. He seldom spoke to a child, but would stand on the South Walk watching us play. His smile, which, owing to a much bearded face, developed mostly in his half-closed eyes, was neither censorious nor definitely approving. We never knew what he thought of us. If some child performed outrageously or approached as though to speak to him, the smile would close his eyes still further, he would chuckle noncommittally to himself and walk away. Mr. Joslyn was the music master of the Community. When he led the orchestra, playing one of his own compositions or arrangements, we acquired great respect for him. I understand that he was a leading writer of editorials for the *Oneida Circular* and did most of the Community's legal work.

Mr. Pitt was a "character." I have heard men who considered him lazy say that he "wrote for the paper," with a note of sarcasm in their voices. On the other hand, a certain old member who was no special friend of Mr. Pitt's told me that it was wrong to call him lazy, that he did get out of unsuitable jobs as much as he could, but that in his chosen field, writing for the paper, he toiled unremittingly and long hours. Mr. Pitt had a luxuriant head of white hair, a massive white beard, and a pair of great blue eyes that looked us children through and through in a way to raise all the doubts we ever had as to the condition of our souls. Like Mr. Joslyn, he seldom spoke to us, but we did not expect it. For my part, I thought his mind was too much absorbed in the contemplation of Perfectionism to talk to anybody but my father.

2

There were other men whose orbits occasionally took them into our little sector of Community life, but, before I have prolonged these descriptions too far, I ought to say a word about certain women whose part in the scheme of things seemed equally important with that of the men.

I have mentioned Miss Libby and Miss Chloe who, as mothers of the Children's House, were always with us. Miss Libby was efficient and unsympathetic. Miss Chloe was sympathetic, but a rigid disciplinarian as well. I think her severity attributable partly to her New England upbringing, but even more to a genuine love for our souls and a Spartan determination that no softness on her part should let us slip down to perdition. She had a way of rapping our knuckles which hurt very much.

Aunt Sarah Dunn stood high in Community Councils. She was a practical doer and helper. In every sickroom she was the adviser and comforter. That was, of course, before the days of the R.N.'s, but the women assigned to nursing in the Community were selected for their sympathetic quali-

A GROUP OF COMMUNITY MEN

A GROUP OF COMMUNITY WOMEN

ties and their knowledge of simple alleviations and remedies. They were women with a passion for nursing. Mrs. Dunn was the most competent and sympathetic of these and became what might be called dean of the nurses. When I had the mumps I remember feeling better whenever she stayed in the room with me.

Her sister Jane, who died at the age of ninety-six, long after the Community broke up, was the purchasing agent for the household. I thought of Miss Jane as the person who kept us properly clothed.

We saw, usually from a distance, "Lady Allen" and "Lady Thayer" and several other Ladies (this must have been a title brought from New England), who represented a female dignity that I recognized but could not understand. They wore fancy lace caps, long dresses and old-fashioned hoopskirts when the other women were wearing short dresses and pantalettes.

I have never found anyone who could explain these exceptions to the short-dress fashion of the Community and I am left to conjecture that it was another example of John Humphrey Noyes's tact and common sense. It may be that in these three or four elderly women he ran up against violent prejudices which he was unwilling to violate. As a matter of fact, the short-dress costume was invented by the Community women themselves and, I am told, no formal rule ever made its adoption compulsory. Conformity, as with many details of conduct, was enforced by public opinion or desire for the approval of Father Noyes.

3

This brings me to "Mother Noyes." I regarded her as, next to my own mother and Aunt Harriet Skinner, my best friend. I was the child of her husband by a woman thirty years younger than herself and she might have hated me. Instead, she lavished affection on me and on my half brothers and sisters. It was a "treat," as we used to say, to go up to her room. When we were older she taught Humphrey and me to paint, and we each drew and painted a pack of playing cards under her supervision. (The Community considered cardplaying a harmless amusement. There was, of course, no gambling; no thought of gambling and no money to gamble with.) I can still see our Jack of Hearts which resembled one of the Alice in Wonderland Knights, and our King of Spades who looked like my father. They and the green-backed, much-varnished cards are a part of my cherished memory of Mother Noyes.

4

Did I ever have an ambition to be like my father? I wonder. Certainly when as a boy of fifteen I became better acquainted with him my respect, which was very genuine, stopped far short of any desire to follow his career. I have searched my memory for evidence of my estimate of him when I was six. The most that I can recall is that he seemed a great man, or better perhaps, a great power. I was told that he was my father, but he seemed the father of all of us, just as God is the Father of all of us, and my love of him, like my love of God, was rather impersonal.

I think that he himself must have cultivated a feeling of general paternity and that, either purposefully or otherwise, he cast aside most of his natural partialities. I do remember that on one or two occasions when I was allowed to go to his room after meeting, he took me in his lap and caressed me affectionately; once he gave me a cooky. I also remember his playing a game with Humphrey and Holton and me. He had a wonderful collection of tops of many colors and sizes. These he started spinning all at once and let us throw handkerchiefs at them to see who could stop the most tops. As a matter of fact, I think he was really fond of his children, but for everyday affection I turned to Uncle Abram.

Chapter VI

"Lucifer, Son of the Morning"

I

LIFE in those early aeons comes back to me not as a progressive journey toward maturity, but as disconnected layers of experience within each of which my reactions were on the same mental level. My child-memories are, so to speak, stratified. Throughout each stratum I see the same child with the same outlook on life, while between them the intermediate steps in development are lost.

When I try to define for myself the characteristics of those memory periods, my mind continually reverts to Papa Kelly's evening meeting as a sort of common denominator. Papa Kelly and his meetings were realities which persisted through all my life in the Children's House, and my attitude toward them was, on the whole, an accurate index of my mental progress.

During the early days of our attendance at meetings, we smaller children were ranged in the front row; hence very near to Papa Kelly. Physically as well as metaphorically, we sat at his feet. We revered him and believed unquestioningly all that he told us; all that we understood. When he talked his eyes were usually on someone in the front row, which led us to think that his words were intended mainly for us. This, however, I now believe to have been an illusion. The Mr. Kelly I knew in later years seldom looked squarely at the person to whom he was speaking, which convinces me that his appeals for obedience, truth-fulness, and a "soft heart," his lurid descriptions of Satan prowling about seeking whom he might devour, and especially his dogmatic expositions of God's plans for the universe, were really intended for the older children in the back rows rather than for five- and six-year-olds who could absorb little more than how hard it was to be good, and how sure were God's punishments if we failed.

I can still remember the solemnity of our emergence from the South Room after meeting. We were awed and subdued and feeling, if not thinking, eternal verities. An unnatural quietude went with us to the boys' sinkroom and lasted until we had washed our hands and faces; perhaps for a longer time. I do not mean this ironically. Ten minutes is a long time in a child's life.

So the front row in meeting symbolizes the mental and spiritual simplicity which characterized the stratum of child-hood I have so far described. Papa Kelly was in his heaven and the little world he ruled seemed good. I carried to the playground and school and wherever else our roamings took me a simple faith that people were what they seemed to be and that realities were obvious.

Between that period and the much later time when, being ourselves "older boys," we sat in the back row and relieved the tedium of meetings by catching flies between a moistened thumb and forefinger, an intermediate stratum of experience and psychology supervened. During this interim I listened to Papa Kelly with respect and much belief, but outside of meetings my mind was opening to new and strange possibilities. I did not unfrock him or lose my respect for the grown folks or my love for the Community-world in which I lived, but I questioned. Papa Kelly had become a man—a very good man, but only a man. Dick and I discussed privately both him and his pronouncements. We became more critical.

2

One day we found one of his belongings—I think it was a cap—on the floor of the South Room closet where we all hung our outdoor wraps. What I especially remember is Dick's calling him "Old Kelly." He said, "Old Kelly is just as shiftless as we are." Shiftlessness was one of the deadly sins in Papa Kelly's code; we were warned against it in preachments and accused of it in criticisms.

I got a thrill out of Dick's disrespect. A year before it would have been unthinkable, but now I was pleased to find myself an accessory to so bold a declaration of independence. "Old Kelly" meant "who's afraid," and the criticism of his shiftlessness was merely retaliatory, but the sauciness of Dick's attack on him who had been the source of all authority and wisdom announced a general emancipation from slavish acceptance of grown folks' dicta and formulas. It ushered in—so the incident registers in my memory—the age of investigation and revaluation. From that time I remember increasing interest in the world outside.

Hitherto this had seemed somewhat unimportant like the frame around a picture. In the geography books I had seen colored maps which suggested that there were large areas beyond our hills, but my attention was chiefly taken up with the funny shapes of the subdivisions. Similarly, my contacts with Outsiders had aroused only childish curiosity regarding details of men and things.

3

When I began to take a livelier interest in the Outside my first impression was that everything there was immensely bigger and more powerful than in our world. Perhaps this was suggested by the Ontario & Western freight trains which emerged from the hills to the south, rumbled down the long trestle at no great distance from our playground, and disappeared in the swamp woods.

Dick and I got as near to the track as our "bounds" would permit and as the great cars thundered past we discussed where they came from and where they were going. The engineers, looking out the cab windows, became heroes. Theirs must be lives of romantic adventure; theirs a Gargantuan world where things and actions were on a scale quite beyond our experience or imagination.

I did not become discontented with life as it came to me; the days were too full of interesting things to be done. It was only that in my picture of the world there was forming a background which suggested even more exciting possibilities. And with this came doubt as to the finality or completeness of the picture of life presented to us by our elders.

I remember arguing with my brother Holton, who had more faith and steadfastness than I, that Outsiders knew more than our folks. He was sure that our folks were better and knew more. I think I had in mind the tough-looking, smoke-begrimed engineer who looked down on us from his monstrous puffing engine and I insisted: "He's bad, but none of our folks can run an engine." Dick went further. He drew a marvelous picture of the *Great Eastern*, a ship as big as our Community home. In a flight of imagination he informed us that his father had told him that the *Great Eastern* was run across the ocean (I have forgotten in how many days) by men twice as big as any we knew.

4

At the age of six boys' bodies grow by the food they eat and their minds by experience, but their imaginations, their subconscious selves, their souls—call them what you will—grow through revelation. Somewhere within their consciousness lies highly explosive emotional stuff. Touch it off and lo! scales drop from their eyes and their vision attains new distance or new color or both, and the color of those dreams never quite fades out.

I must have been out on the South Walk very early one morning, for the sun was rising behind the east hill in a blaze of glory. Red, angry clouds with fiery edges concealed its face, while crimson outriders seemed rushing toward the zenith; behind them the eastern sky was turned to gold. Some man beside me—I think it was Dr. Noyes—waving his hand toward this glory, exclaimed, "Lucifer, Son of the Morning!" He may have quoted further, but all I remember is the effect of those words.

"Lucifer, Son of the Morning!" I do not suppose I rationalized one complete idea, but my soul was swept by a new emotion. I sensed grandeur, magnificence, immensity; a loftier world, more powerful beings, more magnificent lives than my childish mind had ever before conceived. "Lucifer!" A beautiful godlike name, and there he was "Son of the Morning," a prince with unbridled freedom of the skies.

Always God had been in the sky, but it was an everyday blue sky, without form or romance. God was everywhere: in me, on the playground, more especially in the South

Room. He could not seem magnificent; only an undo-with-outable element in our daily lives. Of course He was important. He could punish and reward; we knew that.

But this Lucifer, charging up from the unknown limitless east, with his clouds of red and gold, *he* was a charioteer, a gorgeous, reckless, irresistible driver of cloud horses and a rider of the winds.

I must have asked someone about him, since I early learned that he was not a good god. Still, for a long time I cherished glorious Lucifer secretly and even to this day a spell of color, magnificence and daring surrounds that name. I fear that after that morning I did, at times, compare my Lucifer with the hallowed but, to a child, somewhat drab gods of my father's Pantheon—Christ, Paul, Principalities and Powers. Not that I lost respect for the Community's religion, but new thoughts were planted in my mind. I longed to ride in the chariot with Lucifer, Son of the Morning, and I suspected that in the great outside, now immensely greater than I had ever dreamed, there were realms of grandeur and opportunities for adventure quite beyond experience in the Children's House and perhaps beyond the knowledge of our grown folks.

Chapter VII

Boyhood

I

THERE is, I believe, a very definite line separating child-hood from boyhood; a line to be crossed only when accumulated accomplishments or some outstanding accomplishment have convinced the child that he can do the things grown folks do, without their aid, and care for himself without their protection. Certainly my own boy-memories have a quality radically different from my child-memories. They partake of different coloring. The soft shades of a cared-for, planned-for and, in the main, thought-for childhood are replaced by the bold primary colors of initiative and action.

When very young I am sure there existed in my mind a subconscious impression that happy days came to me through the benevolence of my elders; which irked me no more than knowledge that the sunshine and blue sky were not my very own. But when I became a boy I looked on time and space as mine. They seemed mediums in which to enjoy and multiply the things I myself could do.

In many lives, I have no doubt, this change is gradual; to me it came suddenly. Memories of my early life divide themselves definitely into the time before I swam across the "deep-hole" and the time after I accomplished that feat. Before, I was a child; thereafter, I was a boy.

It was in the spring of 1877 that Mr. Clarence announced, "Every boy who swims across the creek before winter will be given a coconut." Oh, joy! A whole coconut! At rare intervals we had tasted small sections of coconut, but to have one all our own, white meat, milk, shell and all, seemed too good to be true. How we splashed and churned the waters of our swimming hole—and dared. Before the season ended eight of us had qualified for coconuts. Some may have dog-paddled their way to the other bank, but all had crossed the deep-hole, unaided.

I shall never forget how nearly Bert came to drowning in a last attempt to be the ninth. With the courage of a Spartan, but not sufficient athletic prowess to overcome his age handicap of a year, he made a last desperate effort and failed. In midstream his strength gave out. Fortunately, at the point he had reached a tree hung low over the water and, grasping this, Bert hung on until Mr. Clarence rescued him.

The coconut part of the affair was a dismal disappointment. In the Community library there is to this day a book —I saw it recently—entitled *Zigzag Journeys in Europe*. On its flyleaf, written with a pencil, are the names of eight boys followed by the legend, "Swam across the deep-hole— 1877." I still dislike that book. I even think that a distaste for the word "zigzag" has, on its account, been with me since 1877.

It is a melancholy story—not the *Zigzag Journeys*, but how we got the book. Mr. Clarence called us together, the Eight, and congratulated us on learning to swim. Already we could taste the coconuts. I have forgotten most of the moral and didactic discourse with which he prefaced his unexpected suggestion, but I remember well the words that dashed our hopes: "You are each entitled to a coconut, but don't you think it would be more profitable to put together the cost of eight coconuts and buy something of lasting value? With that money we can buy a good book which all can read and which will last. The coconuts would soon be gone."

I need hardly describe our dismay. We wanted coconuts and we didn't want a book; but we dared not exhibit our spiritual crudeness to Mr. Clarence.

I remember exactly where he stood when he made his proposal that we swap our coconuts for a book. Behind him was the tall black-walnut bookcase which, along the west wall of the South Room, broke its otherwise continuous wainscoting. In this bookcase could be seen the backs of the Castlemon series of adventure stories, *Frank on the Prairie, Frank on the Gunboat,* and other "Franks"; also, of somewhat less interest, the Rollo travels in Europe. Below was an entire shelf of girls' books which we despised or at least affected to despise.

After Mr. Clarence's talk, there followed a significant silence which he chose to overlook. I think instinct told us that opposition would only convict us of a false sense of values, and bring us under criticism without accomplishing anything in the way of coconuts. That is why *Zigzag Journeys in Europe* is in the Community library today.

2

I remember when Mr. Clarence joined the staff as Papa Kelly's assistant. We feared him as we had never feared Papa Kelly. He was a youngish man with a red beard too severely cut to look youthful and too short to add any touch of benevolence to his unsmiling face. He was a just man, and fanatically religious, with no sense of humor or sympathy with wayward youth. Like the modern scoutmaster, he or-

ganized games and "tramps" (long walks) and rallied secretly
reluctant boys for berrypicking, asparagus cutting, or other
work profitable for their development.

He invented the order of the "O. & F." (Obedient
and Faithful); an organization revered by naturally law-
abiding children, but secretly distasteful to the rank and file.
When deprived of our O. & F. badges, we lost freedom of
action and other privileges. And how easy it seemed to lose
those badges! Around the South Terrace Mr. Clarence built
a wire fence within which culprits, temporarily suspended
from the O. & F., were confined for periods, carefully graded
to match the heinousness of their offenses. How well we all
remember that fence! Its green posts encircled the terrace
like a row of sentinels and between them strands of gray
wire symbolized our moral quarantine. I say symbolized
because it was in no sense an effective barrier. The wire was
not barbed and any boy could see how easy it would be to
slip through, but the spirit of Mr. Clarence electrified its
gray strands until they appeared as dangerous as a barbed-
wire entanglement.

Yet to do him justice, not all of Mr. Clarence's activities seemed negative. I think we would all give him a long
credit mark (that is what he used to hand out to us as reward for meritorious conduct) for the thoroughness with
which he equipped our various sports and for his O. & F.
tramps. Those were glorious expeditions he arranged to the
Cascades or the Twin Gullies: twenty or thirty boys and
girls off for a day of freedom, with our luncheons packed
in little tin knapsacks strapped on our backs. My memory-
picture of those tramps is a pleasing miscellany of building
dams, wading in cool water which ran swiftly over smooth
ledges of limestone, climbing trees, catching minnows, making whistles out of willow withes and, yes, puppy romances,

carrying Althea pickaback across the stream and swapping
the yolks of my eggs, which she coveted, for the whites of
hers.

The origin of our knapsacks was typical of Mr. Clarence's legalistic mind. We had to earn them. During one entire autumn we worked an hour each day in the Playhouse
nailing packing cases for the canning department. In return
that department made the knapsacks.

3

So now I was seven years old and had swum the deep-
hole, thereby laying the foundation for that measure of self-
confidence which distinguishes a boy from a child. The
change meant more than that, more than a simple access of
self-confidence; there followed a period of rapidly changing
outlook on life. During the ensuing winter the yeast of
egoistic ambition fermented in my soul, and in varying degrees I believe in the souls of at least seven other small boys.
We still wore the livery of childhood, the simple pants-and-
jackets and brass-toed boots of the Children's House, but
in our minds had been born a conception of ourselves as
real boys.

I am sure that Dick and I stepped out into this new
area of anticipated power and prowess together. Through
many discussions we built up our new egos to match the
possibilities we saw ahead. Enthusiastically and imaginatively
we lifted ourselves and each other by the bootstraps, and that
to very considerable heights. I remember one of Dick's en-
couraging pronouncements, "Someone told me" (that was
his formula for adding to the reality of ipse-dixit state-
ments) "that any boy is stronger than any woman."

Quite aside from these flights of imagination, there was

a very realistic side to our new ambitions. We worked hard
for recognition by the "four big boys"—Ransom, Amos,
Eugene, Deming. They were heroes in our eyes and they
knew it. At times they stooped to try us out in their own
field, always, however, with a fickle and decidedly patronizing friendliness which our admiration and ambition overlooked. Their approval registered our progress toward boy
stature.

Ransom, Amos, Eugene and Deming put our class of
boys through a series of informal initiations, which ran the
gamut of speed tests, strength tests and courage tests. In
the Playhouse below the terrace was an "exercising bar," a
homemade affair consisting of a round wooden bar supported
at different heights by iron pins thrust through holes in two
upright supports. On this we struggled to match the big
boys' feats, to "chin" ourselves as many times as they, to
turn "flapjacks," and to swing over and over the bar hanging by a back-crook of the arms. It was only after many
weeks of failure that I finally succeeded in turning a flap-
jack, pulling my body up between my arms and thus to a
sitting position on the bar. That was a great day—like passing a difficult examination. The boy who could turn flapjacks was a long lap ahead in the Ransom-Amos-Eugene-
Deming recognition.

Then there was climbing to the cupola of the Playhouse. Twenty-five feet above the floor a trap door gave
access to the cupola where the big boys had fitted up a
snuggery of their own. Its privacy was guarded by the difficulty and danger involved in its attainment; i.e., climbing
a dangling rope the entire twenty-five feet, then stepping
off onto a slender beam from which a ladder led up to the
trap door.

It was a tough tryout for a small boy. When, after negotiating the climb for the first time, I looked at the beam for which I must exchange the comparative security of the rope and then down at the dizzy distance to the floor, I half regretted my ambitious attempt to perform a big-boy stunt.

Hanging on the wall of the South Room was a wonderful steel engraving picturing the adventures of Christian as related in *Pilgrim's Progress*. This became for me a picture of life and I found athletic giants to pass and Apollyons of fear to fight in my journey toward the Promised Land of self-reliant boyhood.

I could tell of our hair-raising climb up a crude ladder, fifty-five feet, in a pitch-dark ventilating flue, from the basement to the roof of the New House; of being dared to approach nearer and nearer a water hole until the ice broke and let the last competitor in; of April plunges in the frigid creek; of speed races and weight liftings and having our fingers pinched to see who could stand pain the longest. Those struggles to add accomplishment, force recognition and enlarge my ego were immensely interesting and important to me at the time. Such tales, however, would differ little from the doings of other boys and to multiply them here would add little to the story I am trying to tell.

4

All fathers are called on to tell their children stories about "when I was a little boy." One such story became very popular in my own family and was called for, over and over again, by each child. I must always tell it in exactly the same way. They knew it by heart. If I changed a word, they interrupted me passionately, for the Muskrat Story grew to be a family saga. It ran thus:

"When Father and Cousin Richard were little boys, they thought they would try to catch a muskrat. So they went down across the creek beyond the New Yard. There they found a muskrat's runway. Now, a runway, you must know (the children were especially jealous of any change in this phrase), is a sort of little hallway where the muskrats run up to the hill and back to the creek.

"We set a trap in the runway, and covered it with leaves. The next morning Cousin Richard could not go down to look at the trap; so Father went alone. He came to the runway, but could not find the trap. Then he looked farther up toward the hill and there—a-crashing and a-thrashing and a-smashing in the leaves was—a muskrat!

"Father was so excited that he ran right through the creek with his shoes on!" (To my children that was the most exciting part of the story, "through the creek with his shoes on.") "He ran home and found Cousin Richard and shouted: 'We've caught a muskrat! We've caught a muskrat! We've caught a muskrat!' Then both of us ran down through the New Yard and"—again—"right through the creek with our shoes on. We killed the muskrat and skinned it and put the skin on a 'stretcher' and, when it was dry, sold it to Pete Charles who sold it to another man who sold it to another man who made it into a muff just like Mother's." "No! Not like Mother's!" The children pretended to be outraged by the suggestion that Mother's muff was made from the skin of a lowly muskrat.

5

After that first catch of Dick's and mine, we trapped muskrats along the creek, and skunks in Spring Grove. Skunk trapping had the advantage of frequent expulsions

from school on account of malodorous clothing. Ruddy occupied a position of special authority in our "trapping company" because his grandfather Hamilton helped write the
Trappers' Guide, a booklet published in the interest of the
Community's trap manufacturing.

A certain ravine still bears the name "Otter-wood
Gully" as a tribute to Ruddy's wisdom. We were scouting
for larger game, as always impersonating Bill Lawson, Dick
Lewis and other hardy woodsmen of the Western trapping
stories. Like them, we were "running a trap line" and looking for "signs." On the steep side of this ravine we found
several long, smooth streaks in the clay. Ruddy examined
these carefully. "Otter slides," he announced with a positiveness reminiscent of his grandfather Hamilton.

We set traps for the sliding otter, and after many days
of alternating hope and disappointment came upon a cow
slipping and sliding down the hill. Observing the marks it
left, we could not hide from ourselves the fact that these
were the same as our "otter slides."

Trapping had a commercial lure. We sold the animals'
pelts for money, real money, the first we had ever possessed.
Pete Charles, a Negro, who in the later days of the Community worked about the kitchen, taught us how to skin
our catch and stretch the skins on boards. Pete was a trader.
He sized up Community boys and mixed a rather magnificent air of worldly wisdom with a friendliness which
stooped to our simplicity. In the end he always took the
skins off our hands at less than half their value, assuring us
volubly, "That's more than I'll get for them."

6

One of our enterprises suggests a falling from grace, or at least an unsanctified attraction for the most material element in the world's system of selfishness—money. The Community made its own cans for preserving fruits and vegetables. In the process, little round tin disks were punched from the tops and these, being bright and about the size of a silver dollar, suggested money.

Which boy first collected a stock of these tins from the floor of the tinshop or the backyard of the canning building, I do not remember. My only recollection is of the sudden rage for buying and selling with tins as legal tender. We bought services and other boys' turns on the velocipede, and we bargained for each other's "tents," always paying with tins. One enterprising child, whose parents had given him a stick of licorice, made licorice water and sold drinks for a few tins.

The end of this financial era came dramatically. Grosvenor, whose father was superintendent of the fruit department, discovered among the piles of "scrap tin" several barrels of the little round disks. He must have taken a few others into the secret, for I remember that Bert was a very rich man for a day. Soon, however, others learned of the barrels. After that, inflation of the currency proceeded so rapidly that, like the German mark in 1923, our money steadily lost its value. Within a few days the financial wreck was complete and the Children's House became again communistic.

Chapter VIII

School, Work and Meeting

I

M Y first memory of the "big school" in the Seminary building goes back to the time when I was still a scholar in Aunt Susan's class. One of the older children took me down to the Seminary to participate in a grab bag organized by Mr. Warne, the schoolmaster. I remember a great thrill when I was privileged to reach into the pillowcase and pull out a package which turned out to contain two pieces of candy.

Later, when I began going regularly down across the road to Mr. Warne's school, a great ambition was gratified, but the glamour soon wore off. Each morning the games or budding enterprises of a boy's new day were cut short by the bell in the Seminary tower. How reluctantly we dropped bats and ball, or slid down out of trees, and proceeded toward the schoolhouse at speeds proportioned to our distance from it; for we early discovered that it was unprofitable to be late.

On the other hand, our school periods were short, confined to forenoons, and Mr. Warne was an unusual schoolmaster. He spiced his pedagogy with frequent unique and interesting breaks. One day it would be a short lecture on butterflies, insects' feet or a fly's proboscis, and every child was given a chance to squint at the specimens through his microscope; again, he would tell humorous anecdotes and illustrate each by original blackboard pictures—I remember a fat man, "Mr. Pussyfront," talking to "Mr. Someone-else" who was ridiculously thin, carried a cane, and wore a stovepipe hat. Then there would be days when he read to us for half an hour. There was the story of a Negro boy who studied trichinosis in a doctor's office. A mischievous monkey, Sponsy, furnished most of the plot of the story.

Mr. Warne obtained from the printing office cases of type which we set in sticks and he blocked in galleys. We had no press. The printing was accomplished by running a roller over the paper. We were very proud of the long sheets of printed matter produced for our own and our parents' delectation.

Best of all were our "walking-schools." Often, when we had resigned ourselves to the multiplication table or the boundaries of states, Mr. Warne would announce a walking-school to Parson's Gulf, or Quiet Valley, or Run-Down-Hill. Young as we were, Mr. Warne was able, by anecdote and imaginative suggestion, to interest us in scientific aspects of the things we saw. On those walks we absorbed much information about the birth and the life history of plants and insects and trees and woodchucks and fungi and lichens and even stones.

On one of those walks we found a really gigantic tree in the Olmstead woods, a tree that five boys, taking hold of hands, could not encircle. Mr. Warne said, "We will name it Gog." Then he had us all sit down on the flat stones round about while he told us the story of Gog and Magog; how thirty-three great giants, living on the island of Gog, defied the pagan gods until Alexander the Great killed all but two, Gog and Magog; and how he finally captured those two and imprisoned them in the innermost recesses of the highest mountains of the Caucasus, where they remain to this day;

their escape being prevented by twelve trumpets blown by the north wind.

Our imaginations were so stirred that when we discovered another big tree we insisted on naming it Magog. After that, when Mr. Warne announced a walking-school and asked, "Where shall we go?" there was sure to be a chorus of "Gog and Magog!" "To the Gog and Magog woods!"

On another occasion he told us of the Blarney stone, which Irishmen kissed to insure, for their tongues, permanent eloquence, and suggested that we name a certain granite boulder we had found at the edge of a wood the Blarney stone. We all kissed it and thereafter made many expeditions to kiss our Blarney stone. In recent years I have endeavored to rediscover that stone. I believe I have located the woods, but so far have failed to find a stone deserving such distinction.

Mr. Warne was fond of children, especially boys. Richard, Humphrey, Dorr, Ruddy, Pierrepont—he called us his five boys and in many ways he petted us. Even with his five boys, however, he never spared the rod and spoiled the child. He was a disciplinarian and reacted promptly against mischief, deceit or disobedience. His smart raps with a ruler —one, two, three—left many a sore hand. I am sorry to say that he was often guilty of that maladroit Victorian exaggeration: "It hurts me more than it does you."

2

Mr. Warne came originally from the West—St. Louis, I believe, where he had been a college professor. We all owe him much and I regret that he lived to regard his "five boys" as nuisances. He had a quick temper, which became more

MY CLASS
Mr. Warne's five boys (and two girls)

SEWALL NEWHOUSE

PAPA KELLY

irascible as he grew older and we, at the harum-scarum age of twelve or thirteen, used to throw gravel at his window on dark nights knowing that it would result in an exciting chase through the shrubbery. When we played ball below the terrace and fouls flew into his garden it was always a race between him and us. If he got there first we were minus a ball.

I still recall with affection his ascetic face with its Roman nose, and the square beard which grew only on the end of his chin. He walked with a quick, nervous step. When he died there were found in his apartment, which for years had been barred against intrusion, huge collections of fossil stones, pinioned butterflies, botanical specimens, and microscope slides on which were preserved diatoms from every section of the country. Strangest of all, in his wardrobe hung thirty suits of clothes, evidently the collection of a lifetime. These were so nearly alike in color, cut and shabbiness that they could not be told apart.

3

The Community evidently believed that children should work. Every day, except Sunday, we made chains for an hour after lunch; slow-working boys made them for a longer time since each had a "stent" of one hundred chains. The girls and the younger boys picked over links; untangled them for the chainmakers. The Community manufactured steel game traps and to each trap was attached a fourteen-inch chain. We children thought we were making all the chains used and considered ourselves important factors in the business, but I suspect we overestimated our contribution to the industrial prosperity of the Community.

The chainroom was in the basement of the Mansion House. It was a large room with walls of unplastered masonry and cellar windows high up near the ceiling. Mr. Jones, who punched out spool-silk labels, sat in one corner on a huge dry-goods box. He was thus elevated to bring his work nearer one of the windows. The process of cutting labels was then very crude. A hole in a hardwood plank was fitted with circular knives and Mr. Jones, with his mallet, drove sections of printed sheets through these holes, thereby producing finished labels.

Mr. Jones must have been a spiritually-minded man; otherwise he would not have joined the Oneida Community, but in my childish inventory of the grown folks I figured him as a liability. He had a terrible temper; also he was deaf, always carrying about with him a large tin ear trumpet. Both temper and deafness, as well as the piratelike cut of his snow-white beard, were associated in my mind with a rumor that Mr. Jones had once been a sailor. The story ran among the children that his deafness came from standing too near exploding cannon. He never exhibited temper in the chainroom, so far as I can remember, but sat on the elevated platform, his ear trumpet beside him, pounding, ceaselessly pounding, thick bundles of paper. And yet, either the unhopeful way he looked down at us, or the savageness of his mallet blows, or unconscious suggestion from his reputation, led me to expect that someday that mallet would be thrown at us.

I do not know why Mr. Jones punched silk labels in the chainroom when all the other processes of silkmaking were carried on in another building. This was primarily a children's room and, as I remember it, somewhat crowded when we were all at work.

4

Chainmaking was an art. We sat on high stools around a thick-topped, hardwood table, with one foot in a strap treadle and a pointed implement of flat steel, called a "twister," in the right hand. In front of each was a vise worked by the treadle. The operation consisted of seizing a malleable iron link, slipping it through the eye of a previous one, giving it a squeeze in the vise and evening the end by several quick snaps of its steel jaws. Skill in chainmaking was largely a matter of skill with the twister; as the eyes of the links passed each other, a deft twist brought them tight together.

We were very competitive, hence concentrated upon our work. Hands and feet flew unceasingly until, one by one, we were able to call out "stent done," then snap free our vises, throw off our work-aprons, wash our hands (more or less clean in proportion as inspection threatened) and off for the afternoon's play.

At times we experienced a pretaste of life's bitter disappointments. With "stent done" and half our companions already on the playground, we would be called back to rectify bad work, or because a checkup failed to confirm our count of a hundred chains. Those disciplinary holdups were especially irritating when an expedition had been planned with several others, and, working frantically at the vise to satisfy Mr. Leonard or whoever was inspecting, we pictured those others starting for the Island Woods or Parson's Gulf without us.

Visitors to the Community were generally shown to the chainroom. They always admired the nimbleness and enthusiasm of the small-boy chainmakers and we listened eagerly for their remarks. There was, however, a fly in our

ointment. The way a certain boy's "false motions" attracted
the visitors and elicited their applause became a sore point
with the rest of us. He was not one of the faster chainmakers, but he appeared to be. In spite of the fact that
Papa Kelly, anticipating twentieth-century motion study,
severely criticized "false motions," this boy's twister flew
dramatically in a thousand unnecessary arcs and angles and
his vise clicked hysterically. Yet the visitors always, inevitably, crowded around him.

5

Perhaps the darkest spot in our daily routine came with
the Children's Meeting. Every evening at five o'clock we
were called in from play to sit on little wooden chairs in
the South Room while Papa Kelly read from the Bible and
gave us serious talks about our souls and the way children
might please God. At times the tedium was relieved by singing; Miss Alice would come in and lead us in singing Moody
and Sankey hymns—"Pull for the Shore" or "Only an
Armor-bearer." We enjoyed Miss Alice's singing. As a matter of fact, her voice was so promising that she and another
girl were sent to New York City where they spent three
months studying under a first-class singing teacher. At
other times we all joined in reciting "The Lord is my Shep-
herd, I shall not want . . ." I remember my love of the
words and the rhythm; but a childish doubt as to the safety
and cleanliness of "He maketh me to lie down in green
pastures." On the other hand, "My cup runneth over" suggested something cool and sweet like soda water.

Occasionally Papa Kelly, aroused by some overt sin or
evidence of spiritual shiftlessness, became the Prophet Kelly
and spoke in thunderous tones until Jonathan Edwards' hell

yawned at our feet. My soul still bears the scars made by one or two of his dramatic revelations of eternal fire and brimstone. I have especially in mind a criticism of Ormond, my half brother. I suspect that he was incorrigibly mischievous, but not really wicked. He may have been one of those cases now called "problem children." I hesitate to characterize him because we saw little of those older boys and my memory of Ormond in Children's House days is confined to an emotional impression that he was often in trouble. Children were not encouraged to emphasize relationships among their companions. I remember suffering over his sins and misfortunes, but suspect that this was largely sympathy with my mother's sufferings.

Papa Kelly had evidently reached the end of his patience with Ormond's disobedience. He proceeded to liken God's mercy to a ball of yarn and added: "There is a limit to that mercy. Every evil act unwinds a certain length of yarn. When the ball has been completely unwound, the sinner is lost." How well I remember his conclusion, uttered solemnly to the assembled children: "Ormond's ball is nearly unwound!" The horror of my brother's situation remained with me for days.

Such early American reproductions of hell-fire were rare. In general Papa Kelly smiled hopefully on us and read chapters like the thirteenth of First Corinthians.

Occasionally other grown folks attended the meetings, sometimes as listeners, oftener to "say a few words." Mr. Erastus Hamilton once gave us a talk on unselfishness, ending with a story substantially as follows:

A certain man determined that no one should share any of his belongings. He kept his wife in his pocket. She, being like-minded, kept her children in her pockets; the children kept their playthings in their pockets so that no other children might touch them. In addition [I hardly know where this fitted into the story] the King's son hid his money in a fish's mouth.

There may have been more of the story, but the general effect was to emphasize the futility of selfishness.

However, neither school nor work nor meetings greatly interfered with our happiness. I think we regarded these as necessary evils, in the same class with having faces washed and hair brushed. We were told that the grown folks put such trials upon us for "our best good," and we endured them with varying degrees of patience, the least serious-minded keeping one eye on the clock and the other on a window from which could be seen our land of promise.

Chapter IX

"Scrapes"

I

IT occurs to me that I have, throughout this chronicle, suggested a childish religiosity not warranted by the facts. Our lives were not devoted to "the things of the spirit" to any unusual extent; nor did conscience guide our conduct at all times. If we absorbed much religious information and were, through meetings and preachments and the spiritual aspirations of our adult background, impressed with the immanence of heavenly agencies, we carried little of our religion to the playground. We were Biblically educated, but not morally precocious.

My memory tells of more than one "scrape" sinfully planned and painfully repented. (I always thought that Papa Kelly invented the word "scrape" as a badge of dishonor to be pinned on culprits.) There was, for instance, that unfortunate affair known for a long time thereafter as the "Woodshed Chamber Scrape."

We called the great attic of a service building that stood back of the kitchen wing the Woodshed Chamber. Of course, there was beneath it a woodshed, but this was incidental; we boys thought of the whole building as the Woodshed Chamber. It was a huge, sprawling, wooden structure, at least a hundred feet long and fifty wide. On the ground floor were a half dozen service rooms.

First came the dairy where long, cylindrical cans of

milk were sunk almost to their brims in vats of cold water,
and where the pervasive odor was of buttermilk. Miss
Jerusha Thomas was the presiding genius of the dairy. She
was excessively homely, the homeliest person we knew. I
remember that when old Jim Perry came down off the East
Hill and attracted our notice by having his picture taken
at the Oneida Fair as the homeliest man in Madison County,
we all thought that Miss Jerusha Thomas ought to marry
Jim Perry. We knew that marriage was an error of "world's
people," but thought of it as a sort of mechanicosocial join-
ing like the pieces of a jigsaw puzzle.

Beyond the dairy were various storerooms for apples
and potatoes, interesting only because the doors were locked;
and, just before you came to the open woodshed section,
the "store." This the Community maintained primarily to
serve the kitchen but, there being no other grocery in the
vicinity, Mr. Homer Barron kept it open at certain hours
to accommodate neighboring farmers.

Up from the woodshed ran a rough flight of stairs.
Above, the attic was one large room darkened almost as
much as lighted by small cobwebby windows at either end.
Barrels and boxes and crates and old furniture were piled
to the roof. Among and between these ran winding passages
and unexpected dark spaces seemingly arranged on purpose
for hide-and-go-seek.

Exploring in the Woodshed Chamber, we discovered
that beyond the farthest row of barrels, where the slanting
roof approached the floor, ran a passage large enough for a
boy to crawl through. Soon we made another discovery, that
in places the piles of barrels could be moved, and this led to
our forming a very secret society of four or five members.
With great labor and much secrecy we hollowed out of the
pile a sizable "tent," which could be reached only through

the before-mentioned passage. The entrance to this we concealed with boxes and other miscellany. It was an ideal hangout for a gang of boys. We did not smoke there as Stalky and Beetle did in the *Wuzzy*, because we had never learned to smoke, but we found joy in the knowledge that we were beyond the reach of authority; beyond Mr. Clarence's reach. In addition there was the excitement of eluding the watchfulness of other boys who tried to spy out our secret place.

Having completed our tent (the real fun is always in the building), we would perhaps have soon tired of its dusty darkness if we had not made a third discovery. The rough floor boards were not nailed down, and a little shifting of barrels enabled us to slide one board over another. What luck! We were looking down into the store and it did not take us long to decide on invasion of that room of temptation. Cautiously one boy crawled through the opening; then we all followed him and climbed down into the store.

We made directly for a certain barrel containing brown sugar. We knew where it was located because Mr. Homer Barron used to give us lumps, if we did not visit him too often, satisfying any misgivings he might have as to the propriety of the gift by a brusque, "Now run along." Now we helped ourselves freely. After that the Woodshed Chamber meant something more than hiding. We became increasingly liberal with ourselves, and at all times kept brown sugar on hand in our tent.

This life of secret sin ended as such affairs usually do—in disgrace and punishment. Overconfidence or sharing our secret with other boys destroyed us. Either Mr. Barron noted the too-rapid exhaustion of his stock of sugar and became suspicious, or some of our new members talked unguardedly.

One day, after we had worked industriously in the barrel and had mined a lump of the soft, sticky sweet as big as my head, we were swarming up the framework of the building, passing our prize from hand to hand, when Mr. Homer suddenly rose from concealment. To understand how startled we were, the reader would need to sense the respect for authority with which we were brought up. It was not so much what Mr. Homer said; his words were scathing, but every child knew that he had a weakness for children. Our minds leaped instantly to Papa Kelly and punishment.

It is odd, but my memory of that punishment confirms a conviction that we were seldom physically punished, and more, that it was always administered without temper. A full day must have intervened between discovery and our whipping. We foregathered, I recall, at the Playhouse under instructions from Papa Kelly, and devoted the time before his arrival to preparing ourselves for the ordeal. Someone suggested the insertion of boards under our "pants-and-jackets." This was found impracticable, so we experimented with beating each other "to toughen ourselves." In the end, we were all properly whipped and forbidden to go to the Woodshed Chamber for a long time.

2

Then there was the near-tragedy in the back parlor. When Grandfather Worden, who was grandfather to both Dick and me, visited the Community, our mothers obtained a special dispensation that we might visit with Grandpa. The visiting was not very exciting, but we enjoyed being all dressed up and eating with "company."

Grandfather, I remember, was strong for peace; also, I judge, for safety in general. He lectured vehemently, to a back parlor full of relatives, on the wickedness of war; and, while I do not recall any direct reference to the dangers of ocean travel, the double-barreled plan he proposed certainly suggested that he classed the sea as another of mankind's enemies. His proposal was that all the guns and cannon and other muniments of war be thrown into the ocean as a start toward building a bridge across it.

Dick's sense of proportion must have been outraged. He blurted out, "But, grandpa, all those things wouldn't even start a bridge across the ocean." I remember that Grandpa looked at him astonished, but his reply was directed only at our mothers and aunts and cousins: "All the soldiers of the world could be set at work digging dirt and the battle-ships could carry it to the bridge."

It was not, however, Grandfather but Grandmother (a step-grandmother) who spoiled for Dick and me that joyful day of freedom from Papa Kelly's oversight. In spite of the fact that the blame was ours, I think we took back to the Children's House an unreasoning resentment toward her.

All the grown folks had gone—I have no idea where they had gone—except Grandma. She sat by the window knitting. At that time there was, among the boys, a rage for crossbows, and the natural complement to crossbows was the allurement of targets. Unfortunately—at the time we thought it a piece of good fortune—there stood on a pedestal at the far side of the back parlor a plaster statue of Venus. This appealed to us as a God-given opportunity. Our projectiles were shingle nails.

I cannot understand why Grandmother Worden did not protest when we started peppering that statue of Venus with shingle nails but, so far as I can remember, she did not; just went on knitting by the window. The shooting must have continued for some time and our marksmanship must have been good, for the statue, still in existence, looks as though Venus had had smallpox. We were enjoying the sport when, suddenly, a nail ricocheted and struck Grandma full in the face. She screamed. We rushed over to her in great alarm, assuring her remorsefully that "we didn't mean to." Other people came in. At first they were preoccupied with Grandmother's injury (by a miracle that missile which broke her glasses did not touch her eyes), but they soon turned their attention to us.

It is an understatement to say that we went back to the Children's House in disgrace. I remember waiting—a long anxious waiting in the seclusion of the South Room— for the arrival of Papa Kelly, and I also remember Dick grumbling, "She shouldn't have been sitting so near where we were shooting—she ought to have known better."

There were other scrapes and, in the long aeons of boy-hood, many times when we stepped over the chalk line of permissible adventure, but the fact that we were, in general, allowed such freedom and such wide latitude for roaming convinces me that our violations were not more frequent than wise guardians considered inevitable. Someone believed in allowing boys much opportunity to develop themselves.

Chapter X

The Outside

I

I AM not certain at what age I first became conscious of the outside world's hostility toward the Community. Certainly throughout what I have called childhood there never entered my head any suspicion that we were regarded with unfriendly eyes, or that our isolation was other than a measure of protection for spiritual pearls-of-great-price. I had, I think, a vague feeling that the Oneida Community was a sort of oasis wherein the "heavenly powers" were developing a holiness unattainable in the spiritual desert round about.

It must have been when I was six or seven years old that the truth was forced upon me. I remember the gloom of that day. The trees were bare, the sky overcast, and in the air was the chill of autumn. A rumor had run through the Children's House that some agency—I think it was called the "clergy"—was about to launch a campaign for our destruction. With this, but in what connection I cannot imagine, there went a story that a clairvoyant medium or fortuneteller had foretold the complete wiping out of the Oneida Community.

I remember crossing the South Terrace, walking slowly, listening to the wind in the trees, staring now at darker clouds coming over the west hill and again at the familiar outline of the Mansion House, the only home I had ever known, and wondering—wondering, with fear in my heart —whether such a thing were possible. I pictured our people, the men and women I knew so well, the only men and women I really did know, with their backs to the wall, fighting a losing fight against the ravening wolves of a wicked, anti-Christian Outside. I asked myself why—why did they want to destroy us? I had then no inkling of the Community's social heresies and doubt if I would have understood what it all meant if someone had tried to explain. Hence it came about, on that dreary autumn day, that I answered the question in the only way my limited experience made possible: "They are envious."

So, the hosts of envy and wickedness were about to attack our Garden of Eden! I thought of my mother and Uncle Abram and the boys and myself. Self-pity seethed in my heart.

As I stood there, utterly forlorn, my father came out the south door and walked in an opposite direction. Instantly, the sight of his broad back and vigorous stride reassured me. It was impossible! Father Noyes had firm hold on a stronger power than the hosts of wickedness. He would protect his people. My fear was gone.

That experience, however, did something to my psychology. It opened wider the door to reality. It reoriented my conception of the world and our place in it. After that, God and Christ and the Apostle Paul seemed necessary for our safety.

2

Another incident, which must have occurred somewhat later, enlarged still further my conception of the world outside our little oasis. Turkey Street, an Irish-populated village strung along the Seneca Turnpike a mile from the Community Mansion, housed those Outsiders who worked in the trapshop. Tradition says that Turkey Street acquired its name in the early days of the last century when the Seneca Turnpike was the main highway to the West. As the story goes, a flock of turkeys, being driven to Buffalo or Rochester, decided at this point that they had gone far enough and to emphasize their determination to go no farther they flew up into the roadside trees. After futile efforts to dislodge them, the driver sold the turkeys, still in the trees, to local residents. From that time the place was known as Turkey Street.

On this particular day, Humphrey and I had visited the trapshop at Turkey Street. We were walking toward home, feeling rather pleased with ourselves because Jack McQuade, the burly Irish foreman, with the red shoebrush mustache, and tobacco juice oozing from both corners of his mouth, had taken pains to show us all the machines and processes of trapmaking. We had not gone far when a loud yelling attracted our attention; looking back, we saw a mob of Turkey Street boys running down the road toward us, their actions suggesting hostile intent.

When they came nearer, they jeered; called us "Christ boys" and "bastards." One little boy, wearing a cap so big that it covered much of his dirty face, ran in front of us and dared us to fight. We were disconcerted. Community boys were forbidden even to speak to "outside" boys, and here were the lowest specimens of the species bent on forcing us to more forbidden action.

I cannot, at this distance of time, appraise our fright (we were unquestionably frightened) because of the horror evoked by the swearing of the rabble. "God-damn" and "Jesus Christ" hurled at us by boys of my own age froze my blood. How dared they? Deliberately courting damnation! An older boy, called Tom, grabbed my arm and thrust his face in front of me. He sneered, "God-damn goody Community boys."

My memory does not include any physical attack by the Turkey Street gang, nor does it, as one might expect, stress my quite understandable alarm. All other emotions I may have felt have faded from the picture save only surprise and horror at the unbelievable exhibition of human depravity we had encountered. Turkey Street became for me a nightmare, and Tom the type of a lost soul. "Children of Belial" was my thought. (For some reason Belial struck my childish imagination as more besotted than Satan.) It was a new and shocking idea that boys, small boys, could so blacken their souls.

3

In spite of this disagreeable experience, perhaps because of it, Turkey Street acquired a strange fascination for me, and Turkey Street seemed determined to destroy the illusions of a Community childhood. We of the Children's House, I am sure, preserved our belief in the goodness and honesty of grown folks several years longer than do most children. It was another expedition to the trapshop, and again with Humphrey as my companion, that first shook that belief.

Halfway up Christian Hill we stopped at a spring whose waters were impounded for neighboring householders by a headless barrel sunk in the ground. Looking down into the water, we were astonished to see a sparkle of gilt jewelry. We were greatly excited; jewelry was a rarity in the Community. Finding that we could not reach the bauble, we tried to get it out with the aid of sticks, and were struggling, arms and heads deep in the barrel, when the sound of a man's voice brought us to the surface. "What are you boys trying to do?"

It was "Tip" Thomas, a neighborhood character, who manufactured bucket pumps, whenever he felt like working, in the old wheelbarrow factory. I remember his hawklike nose and his black silky beard and the oily voice with which he conducted the ensuing negotiations. Confidingly we pointed out the bright thing at the bottom of the spring and asked him to help us get it. "Yes, yes, boys," he crooned, "I'll help you. It looks like a brooch-pin, doesn't it, boys? Certainly, I'll help you." He rolled up his sleeve, talking patronizingly to us all the while. "You certainly are nice boys. What are your names? How old are you?" And more of the same kind of ingratiating conversation.

He leaned far into the barrel and a moment later came up with a cameo breastpin in his hand. Together we inspected it; Humphrey and I wriggled with delight. But Tip had ceased his friendly conversation. He held the pin at a little distance, studying it with one eye closed and his mouth pursed as though trying to remember something. Thus for a moment only. Suddenly, he exclaimed, "By golly, if that ain't my gal's pin!" Then, without another word to us, he slipped it into his pocket and walked rapidly up the hill.

As soon as we recovered from our surprise, we ran after him. We urged, "That's our pin. We found it." But Tip Thomas strode on, paying no heed to our passionate protests. We did not know at the time that he had no daughter, but instinct told us we were being cheated. In the end we had to give it up.

Our feelings were outraged. Moreover, we could hardly believe that a grown-up man would cheat. We found it difficult to reconcile our conceptions of adult integrity with the perfidy of Tip Thomas. Walking home, we discussed the matter heatedly. Humphrey said, "We've got to look out for Outsiders, even though they look honest and speak friendly."

So my "knowledge of good and evil" progressed still further, and the world outside became more and more a reality; a disturbing reality, but, I suspect, increasingly interesting by contrast with the simplicity of our utopian isolation.

Chapter XI

The Community at Work

I

IN addition to our own naïve enterprises, a new field of
exploration began to interest us. Like most children, we
had in earlier years taken for granted all the ordinary ac-
companiments of daily living—clothing, shoes, furniture,
houses. When, however, it dawned on us that all these things
were created by the labor of men and women, the how and
where of their creation fired our imaginations. We began to
investigate places like the half basement of the office building across the road where old Mr. Van Velzer sat on his
shiny leather cobbler's bench surrounded by tools of every
description. The Community, having drawn its membership from many walks of life, found it possible to provide
for most of its own wants through home labor.

Mr. Van, as we called him, punched holes in leather,
sewed together strips, and drove little wooden pegs—
thousands, it seemed—into the thick soles of shoes. Never
since then have I listened to a more satisfying sound than
the "plump" of his little broad-nosed hammer as it finished
its stroke against the solid leather, sending, at a single blow,
peg after peg into place. Mr. Van was friendly. He took
pains to show us his machinery and often let us drive home
a peg already started in its hole.

With one or two assistants, Mr. Van made all the shoes
for the Community. He was a North Vermonter who joined

in the early days of the Oneida settlement and, being a specialist in an important department, was one of the few men who never changed jobs. Besides his shoemaking, Mr. Van was one of the association's star actors. He played a leading role in many Shakespearean dramas.

The fact that I do not remember attending any Shakespearean performances as a child leads me to believe that they belonged to an earlier day. I recall a Dickens play, *Pickwick,* in which Mr. Lord made love to Miss Phoebe; also a melodrama wherein Mr. Frank Tuttle, the villain, whispered hoarsely to his accomplice, Orrin Wright, "Heist, Heist, De Pu-is," the score reading, "H'ist, H'ist, Dupuis." It may have been a symptom of the changing spirit at Oneida that during those later years the Community turned from Shakespeare to lighter plays and comic operas such as *Pinafore, The Doctor of Alcantara,* and *The Pirates of Penzance.*

2

Then, there was Mr. Aiken in the tailorshop, two floors above Mr. Van—a tall, fine-looking man, silent and dignified. We never got very near his work. Miss Conant, who sat by the window, always sewing, seemed to take an interest in us, but sewing had no such attraction for boys as did Mr. Aiken's operations, cutting cloth with shears as long as one's arm, or ironing with a huge self-heating affair which Miss Conant called a goose.

In general we were not allowed in the kitchen basement. Eating between meals was frowned upon by our guardians. But occasionally we did wander in there lured by the great range, glowing red under its array of kettles and steamers. We stood fascinated before the noisy, machine-driven potato washer and the apple parers that turned out long snakelike coils of skin. If possible we slipped into the bakery where a deft colored woman plunged her pink-palmed hands deep into the huge pan of bread dough and brought up a sticky handful, cut it neatly with a broad-bladed knife, and began the interesting process of kneading and patting it into a loaf for the waiting oven.

Another interesting place was the laundry down by the Mill. I could stand indefinitely watching the jerky gyrations of the homemade washing machine whose thrashing scrubbers, swinging on long wooden arms, slid alternately down into the sudsy water among the clothes. Its noise and violence made the washing machine one of the most alluring of all the Community's home industries. Miss Olive had charge of the laundry. She appeared willing to have us around, but boys were not welcomed in all the departments. Often the people in charge seemed afraid we would touch something we ought not to and, while they might speak to us pleasantly, they were, quite obviously, glad when we left.

This was notably the case at the tinshop where Mr. John Leonard worked. The tinshop, a little old wooden building, stood back of the Woodshed Chamber and on the very edge of a stagnant brook where grew that highly-prized remedy for poison ivy—"celandine" (otherwise jewelweed). Mr. John was a little man. His words were few and his motions brisk, and he kept a suspicious eye on us all the time we were in his shop. I don't know why he worked in the tinshop. I have been told that he was an unusually expert cabinetmaker; that he made the showcase which still stands just outside the Big Hall and has been the object of never-failing interest to three generations of children.

Through the glass top of that showcase could be seen curios brought by members and visitors from all over the world. There were ancient coins, rare geological specimens,

shells from the South Seas, and a mastodon's tooth, copies
of the Koran and Talmud, an autographed letter from
Horace Greeley, and many objects of beauty. I remember a
carved ivory ball and a sandalwood fan. We children hung
over the showcase, discussing what articles we would choose
if someone offered us a choice.

At the tinshop we watched great sheets of tin or gal-
vanized iron go through the rollers and come out as gut-
ter pipes. Mr. John Leonard soldered the edges together.
We tried to please him because we did want to watch the
spluttering solder and see the completion of an article whose
usefulness we understood. That was the magic of creation.
Mr. John was not fond of boys, and we knew it. At the
most interesting point of the process he was likely to say
shortly, "You had better go now. You'll get hurt." Occasionally, when he was away, we entered the tinshop through
a back room where his brother, Mr. Stephen Leonard, kept
honey. Then we experimented with the tools and cut up
pieces of tin with the shears.

Mr. Stephen was different from his brother. He
liked boys. When he came from the beehives over beyond the
gooseberry patch, with gloves on his hands and a netted
frame covering his head, we used to follow him to the honey
room. Often he would say, with a smile in his eyes even
more than in his voice, "Here, boys, try this"—"this" being
a large spoonful of grained honey.

Even dentistry enlisted our interest; not the torture
chamber where Dr. Dunn worked over people's faces, but
another room in which could be seen jars filled with shiny
white teeth, bundles of soft red rubber strips, and "plates"
going through the various processes. Bert used to smuggle
us into this room when his father was busy elsewhere. He
raised himself appreciably in our opinion by pretending to

a knowledge of the making of false teeth and he would open the vulcanizing oven with a knowing air to see how things were progressing.

3

From the earliest days the Community had a predilection for doing all work possible in "bees." The custom came from New England, but it fitted especially well with the social enthusiasms and the theory of equality upon which the Community was founded. Those bees often took in the boys and girls of my age. I remember an early morning exodus of what seemed the entire Community family to the fields below Burling Street for a strawberry-picking bee. Burling Street was our name for a certain narrow strip of woods which bordered our lawns on the west and through which meandered a secluded path. The name came down to us from an older class and I have never heard an explanation of its origin.

It must have been very early in the morning, for the dew on the strawberry vines was white like frost and felt nearly as cold to our fingers. I remember the high spirits with which men, women and children straggled down to "Seymour's strawberry patch." I thought, "Outsiders never have such fun as our folks." My father was in the crowd and I saw him work down a row of strawberries as vigorously as the others.

One time when a carload of peaches had come unexpectedly to the fruit-house, as we called the canning factory, there appeared in the dining room at suppertime a great poster reading, "Rally round the flag, boys, rally once again, rally in the cause of—PEACHES!" The wording must have been influenced by the hurrahs of the Civil War, then scarcely a decade past. We boys rallied with the rest. We felt very important and helpful, rushing around the fruit-house with empty boxes for the workers.

At such times everyone rallied. Community members, old and young, joined the regular employees at the fruit-house and the great workrooms were scenes of lively activity. If Mr. Henry Allen, the superintendent, announced that the peaches were so ripe they would not keep, all hands worked on until the last peach had been peeled and bottled.

The habit of work in the Oneida Community and the tradition that all kinds of work were equally honorable persisted. When I was a boy I supposed that all adults worked. I have always been eager for play, but childhood in the Oneida Community planted in my mind a conviction, from which I have never been able to escape, that play is good only when earned by work.

Chapter XII

Oneida Communism

I

M Y father was the center of life at Oneida. He was a
zealot; perhaps today he would be called a fanatic.
Reading his early letters, one can follow the logic which led
him irresistibly to the conclusion that the demon selfishness could not be slain in a world that worshiped riches.
He preached the communism of the Primitive Church and
his followers accepted his logic. For more than thirty years
the three-hundred-odd members of the Oneida Community
lived together like a great family, holding all worldly belongings in common.

I would regret it if the Oneida Community were to be
confused with that modern "communism" which denies
God and makes material considerations paramount. The
Community adopted communism only that the members
might live the unselfish lives ordained by Jesus Christ. This
communism was nonpolitical and noncontentious. My father
aimed at a system under which the individual would forget
self and strive for the happiness of all. It was thus he interpreted the spirit of the Primitive Christian Church.

A review of my early psychology confirms a suspicion
I have long entertained, that the desire for exclusive ownership of things is not a primal human instinct. Unquestionably acquisitiveness bulks large in the life of today. It is
reckoned one of the important forces behind progress and

a necessary support for civilized society. And yet, may it not be itself a product of our particular form of civilization? Did primeval man have anything he called his own except food which he devoured as fast as he could?

The Community must have exorcised the spirit of acquisitiveness very completely, since throughout my childhood the private ownership of anything seemed to me a crude artificiality to which an unenlightened Outside still clung. We children struggled for the use of things we desired, but ownership was never seriously considered. For instance, we were keen for our favorite sleds, but it never occurred, to me at least, that I could possess a sled to the exclusion of the other boys. So it was with all Children's House property.

To be sure, each boy had his everyday clothes, also his special hook on which to hang them, but I thought—if I thought about it at all—that this was arranged for the sake of orderliness and convenience. When I went away from home or had my picture taken I proudly wore one of the Community "best suits."

There was one best suit we all coveted. It was known in the Children's House as the "youth's suit." The coat was a cross between an Eton jacket and a regular coat, while the knickers had a smarter cut than the pants we ordinarily wore. That youth's suit approached the smartness of the clothes we had seen on certain well-dressed boys who visited the Community with their parents.

Mrs. Van Velzer, up in the dressing room, was the custodian of best suits, and selection was a matter of fit. Photographs of Community children, of which many are still to be found in family albums, show little tots in the same Scotch plaid dress and five- or six-year-olds in the same white blouse and velvet knickers.

The status of adult clothing in the Oneida Community

differed little from that of the children. At home the men's garb was simple and serviceable; I remember many linen dusters. The women's costume was even more simple and designed with the added purpose of discouraging vanity. The short dresses and pantalettes worn by Community women were a scandal to orthodox females in the days before Amelia Bloomer exploited bloomers. Visitors to the Oneida Community always came with a lively curiosity to see the short dresses and short hair of the women. For short hair was another Community fashion and, like the dresses, was aimed at discouraging feminine vanity.

"Going-away clothes" for grown folks, as for children, were common property. Any man or woman preparing for a trip to Wallingford or New York City, or even to Syracuse, visited Mr. Aiken or Mrs. Van Velzer and was fitted out with one of the suits kept in stock for that purpose.

It was not clothes alone that were communized. My father believed that there was inherent selfishness in exclusive personal relationships. This basic principle impinged on us only when boys took themselves "out of circulation" by too much special fraternization with each other. The partiality for which Papa Kelly separated Dick and me was one aspect of that special love which the apostles of communism sought to extirpate.

2

All of which suggests a novel question: Why did not our elders take measures against the competitive spirit? Why did they not seek a substitute for that antisocial, or at least anticommunistic element in their training of future communists? Neither Papa Kelly nor Mr. Clarence ever frowned on competitive games. They taught us such. Ball games, foot races, all kinds of athletic contests were encouraged, not to mention spelling bees, cards and dominoes.

Those Perfectionists adopted communism of property to eliminate material self-seeking; they dressed in simple clothes, tabooed jewelry, and the women cut their hair short, to eliminate vanity; they arranged that every member should take his or her turn at the humblest kind of labor to eliminate the selfishness of pride and power; they abolished marriage to do away with selfishness in love. Why, then, did their carefully worked-out program for bringing up Perfectionist children permit them, at the character-forming age, to cultivate such an egocentric passion as personal rivalry?

Lenin, who was, I think, much like my father in carrying theory recklessly to its logical results in practice, struggled to prevent the competitive spirit from getting a start. He exhorted youth to play games for health and refreshment, but forbade a competitive spirit.

When I visited Moscow a few years ago, my Russian friend and guide took me to inspect a great institution where thousands of young men and women were being trained as teachers. We visited the gymnasium. There I saw some fine-looking fellows playing basketball and as I watched them I tried unsuccessfully to persuade myself that their savage struggles were engaged in and the goals "shot" without any feeling of personal rivalry.

As we looked on, the umpire announced a decision evidently displeasing to one side. There followed an outburst of language on the part of a dark-haired forward which I did not understand, but which—no one could mistake it— was as fine an exhibition of "roasting the umpire" as I ever heard at a country ball game. I smiled, and suggested to my Russian friend, "No competitive spirit here; anyone can see that." He looked embarrassed, but ventured only, "Very unusual."

3

I am in doubt as to whether my father's logic stumbled at this point or whether he was wiser than Lenin. He may have decided that the competitive passion was ineradicable until age had created a mature spirituality. Or, he may have been governed by practical considerations. Having eliminated economic self-seeking, he may have concluded that some urge should be cultivated to insure efficiency and industry. Or— this seems like him—was it a very human desire to leave color in the day's work that life in the Community might be interesting?

We are all born, I believe, with competitive instincts. I remember a story my aunt Cornelia was fond of telling, of how, when I was a very small boy, she interfered in a quarrel between Dick and me. She insists that I burst out crying and wailed passionately, "I want to be headest!" It seems to me probable that the craving to be "headest" in some department of activity will be the last passion suppressed; perhaps never profitably suppressed. It may be that in the next stage of social development, when Anglo-Saxon individualism has run its course and necessity has introduced a new economic system, personal rivalry will prove a satisfactory substitute for the pursuit of wealth. Perhaps competition for accomplishment will prevent that slowing down of material progress so greatly feared by economists.

4

In the Children's House we were taught selflessness and had no training in personal conflict of the kind which seeks supremacy by throwing down or wounding a fellow. We believed that only bad boys, outside boys, attacked each other; we felt superior to outside boys. We rather pitied them. We knew that "out in the world" things were different, but in that world were Sodom and Gomorrah.

We lived, in the south wing, like a great family of brothers and sisters. We felt surrounded by a larger family of grown folks who seemed also brothers and sisters. On them we relied as a bulwark for our protection. If, at times, they presented the aspect of a clinic for detecting our spiritual delinquencies and applying remedies, we believed that, in the main, they were striving to insure our healthy development into men and women like themselves.

It may seem strange—it does seem strange to me when I look back at the abnormally religious atmosphere which surrounded us—that we led such normal lives. The answer probably lies in the character of the people selected as our guardians. They were neither indulgent nor were they sadists. They seemed anxious about our souls and felt responsible for our health, but they never persecuted us, nor did they hover over us as doting parents do. Within certain spiritual boundaries and rather general limitations of time and space, they left us to ourselves. In addition—this may seem a paradoxical blessing—none of those fathers and mothers of the Children's House had, I am convinced, any great affection for us individually.

5

I have searched my memory for evidence that during my childhood in the Oneida Community I sensed its very unusual sexual arrangements. If any incident suggesting a relation so interesting between a man and a woman had then attracted my notice, I am sure I should recall it with unusual detail; but I find no trace of either incident or suggestion. The fact is that the stern way our guardians frowned on our immature peccadilloes naturally led a child to feel that they had outgrown such weakness and would condemn even more sternly sexual lapses on the part of grown folks.

It seems possible that the diffusiveness of sex association enforced by the Community system eliminated those "special loves" most likely to catch our attention. There was no flirting or courting in public and few indications of partialities between the sexes that could not be accounted for by joint occupations. Even in those later days when Earl and Chet were telling us of the Community's unorthodox practices, I do not remember that they pointed out any specific cases.

And yet there has survived in my memory an impression, a dim recognition, that the relation between our grown folks had a quality intimate and personal, a quality that made life romantic. Unquestionably, the sexual relations of the members under the Community system inspired a lively interest in each other, but I believe that the opportunity for romantic friendships also played a part in rendering life more colorful than elsewhere. Even elderly people, whose physical passions had burned low, preserved the fine essence of earlier associations; child as I was, I sensed a spirit of high romance surrounding them, a vivid, youthful interest in life that looked from their eyes and spoke in their voices and manners.

6

When I study the timetable of my early life, I am not a little puzzled by the extent to which, as a child under ten years of age, I sensed the spirit—I had almost said the theology—of Perfectionism. To be sure, I was exposed to many

Bible stories and Bible talks, but so are Sunday-school pupils
everywhere. I am inclined to believe that my father's genius
for dramatic characterization is largely responsible for this
precosity. The illuminating definitions and homely formulas
he invented to represent spiritual truths made many an ab-
stract principle available as a guide to everyday living, available for the least subtle-minded of his followers, and even
for children. Perhaps those picturesque phrases played the
same part in opening my mind to spiritual ideas that Mr.
Warne's storytelling played in the realm of scientific facts.
They sank into my consciousness and meant something real
to me.

Consider, for example, his emphasis on "ascending fellowship" and "descending fellowship." I am sure that I
understood the import of those words as soon as I learned
the meaning of ascending and descending, and I grasped their
implications, particularly their limiting possibilities, before I
was ten years old. My father laid down the rule that for
spiritual health everyone should maintain a substantial balance between his ascending and descending fellowships;
meaning, of course, that contacts with those of lesser spiritual
attainment must be cantilevered, so to speak, by a greater
weight of association with one's superiors.

Once, after I had observed him sitting very still in his
great haircloth chair with eyes closed and forehead wrinkling
vigorously, Grandfather Ackley told me that my father was
communing with the Apostle Paul, his ascending fellowship.
He explained that only through such communing could he
qualify himself for helpful fellowship with his flock.

My father, unlike many religious enthusiasts, never
claimed to be a Christ; nor did he even try to approach that
status. The Community believed that his inspirations came
down what he called the "link and chain": from God to

Christ; from Christ to Paul; from Paul to John Humphrey Noyes, and by him made available for the Community.

The problem of balancing ascending and descending fellowships played an important part in the social life of the Oneida Community. The words were easily understood and the validity of my father's formula appealed to all. At times men and women discussed earnestly with each other and with themselves as to whether their own relation was ascending or descending; a query whose answer might bring them face to face with the dilemma of self-denial or an uneasy conscience.

Papa Kelly introduced a finer line—"horizontal fellowship." Perhaps this intermediate relation was given especial attention in the Children's House because, while adults were assumed to be able in general to classify their associates as ascending or descending fellowships, the spiritual grading of children was more difficult. My recollection of criticisms, of which there were many in Children's Meetings, includes, as one of the most frequent and serious charges, "too much horizontal fellowship."

I am not sure but that one feature of my father's management which has always puzzled me can be explained by reference to this principle of ascending fellowship. Why, in this separatist Community, was there no censorship of outside reading matter—no *Index Expurgatorius?* Miscellaneous news items from the daily paper were read to the family in the evening meetings. The papers themselves and many current magazines were available in the reading room, and the Community library was kept fairly well up to date. Surely, he left Community members exposed to disaffecting literature in a way that much less sectarian organizations fear to expose their votaries. Perhaps my father relied on home talks, criticism, and much reading of the Bible to combat possible disaffection. He must have distrusted the enforcement of intellectual isolation and trusted ascending fellowships and propaganda.

7

Another of John Humphrey Noyes's inventions explained the relation between spirituality and the seasons. It was not so much an explanation as a characterization which dramatized the spiritual stimulus of winter and warned his followers of the dangerous lure exerted by nature's physical ebullience in the spring and summer months. We all know that as winter deepens and the world grows cold and dreary, human beings tend to increase their intellectual and spiritual activities. Their thoughts turn inward. Their human sympathies are quickened. My father, appreciating the value of definite dates, located the high point of this movement as the 20th of February, the day when he first confessed Christ his Savior from sin. He called this the "High Tide of the Spirit."

From the 20th of February he recognized that the tide of materialistic enchantment gradually rose until around the 20th of August it had reached its limit. This he designated the "High Tide of the Flesh." I doubt if a more expressive phrase could be devised to warn earnest souls of the dangerous enticements Satan conceals in the lush fullness and joy of summer. Even the children got the idea.

Several years after the breakup of the Community, when my Children's House training had become somewhat overlain with worldliness, I remember being sensibly shocked by old Dr. Dunn's disrespectful reference to that which still seemed a sacred formula. The doctor was a storyteller and a wit. His was a dry humor, possessing something of the cynical quality associated with present-day "wisecracks." In the old days, he had been popular with the boys, partly for the sake of his stories dealing with the slightly ribald adventures of "Uncle Aaron" and "Uncle Roberts" in Northern Vermont before he joined, and partly because he used to produce from his pocket shiny red chunks of spruce gum long years before Wrigley invented Spearmint. His vocation had been the pulling of teeth and making "false plates." That was my impression; he also filled teeth. He had a flowing red beard, and cured warts on boys' hands by touching each with the end of his cane and burying it in the ground. In his later years, Dr. Dunn became a valetudinarian, always wearing a gray shawl and supporting one shoulder with a crutch. It was thus that he ambled out from the dining room onto the Tontine stoop the day I have in mind.

Milford Newhouse happened to be standing near by. He was a younger man but, like the doctor, something of a cynic, albeit a good-natured one. Milford was a star entertainer in the children's eyes. His greatest concert success was a song, "Don't Wake the Baby," in the course of which he twisted a handkerchief into the semblance of a baby and sang in a voice suggesting the muted cornets of an orchestra.

Now, he planted himself in front of Dr. Dunn and trumpeted in his assumed falsetto—the doctor was then quite deaf—"Well, Leonard! That was a bully dinner; better than the old good dinner days." (In the early years the Oneida Communists were poor. Once or twice a week they had special dinners with butter and other luxuries ordinarily denied. These they called "good dinner days.") The older man wagged his head solemnly, then with a twinkle in his eye but an unsmiling face, said laconically, "Yes, Milford, the High Tide of the Flesh."

I wonder whether the other boys of my age who were standing about felt as I did; just a little shocked, as though we had listened to blasphemy. It had never before occurred to me that a division of the year into the High Tide of the Spirit and the High Tide of the Flesh was not as basic as the periodical solstices or the precession of the equinoxes.

8

The Community believed in the curative possibilities of "criticism" and employed it for reducing fever and, in general, for stimulating the healing agencies of the body. It was a common thing for the Committee to repair to a sickroom and criticize the patient. Many cures were attributed to this treatment. It is even claimed that criticism and cracked ice ended an epidemic of diphtheria after all other remedies had failed.

I remember a later incident which showed the continuing hold a belief in the efficacy of criticism had on Community members. Mr. Ellis was an old gentleman whose mission in life in Community days had been the making of rustic benches and arbors. I recall that he once constructed a great flannel, mummylike animal with runners, on whose back we slid downhill in winter. Two or three years after the breakup of the Community he sank into a state of despondency, and one winter's night decided to commit suicide.

His first plan was to drown himself in the soft-water cistern, but, according to his statement afterward, he bethought himself of the inconvenience to the family; that was all the soft water they had. He then tried pounding his skull with a hammer, but this hurt too much. He ran head first into a brick wall; again too much pain. Finally he elected freezing to death. It was a bitter night and, after lying in the open for a time, Mr. Ellis felt uncomfortably cold so covered himself with some strips of old carpet.

In the end a searching party found him, still alive. He

was taken to the Community's Turkish bath—the Community maintained a Turkish bath before such were common—and there Mr. Kelly, formerly our Papa Kelly, and Mr. Stephen Leonard gave him a terrific criticism. Mr. Ellis always insisted that his life was saved by that criticism.

There was current in the Community another curious story which suggests how literally one member, at least, accepted the spiritual value of criticisms. Mr. John Lord had become an enthusiastic clarinet player in spite of the old rattletrap instruments assigned him, probably clarinets brought to the Community by some of the early joiners. He was also a salesman. He longed for a set of modern clarinets, and when traveling, frequently tantalized himself by dropping in at a music store and sampling the dealer's stock. One day in St. Louis Mr. Lord was overcome by a desire to own the set of instruments with which he had been experimenting. Thereupon his peculiar mentality hit upon a solution which testified either to an implicit faith in the value of criticism or unusual ability to rationalize his desires. He decided that if he bought the clarinets he could be sure of getting two very valuable things: a criticism and the clarinets. He bought the clarinets.

Chapter XIII

Recreation

I

ONEIDA Perfectionism, as viewed from the Children's House, was a happy religion, never a gloomy one, nor did Bible communism appear to demand ascetic living. The grown folks seemed almost as bent on being happy as they did on being good. Everyone worked; also everyone seemed to have time for play, or perhaps I should say for recreation.

At almost any hour of the day there came to our ears, from a window or faintly down a hallway, the sound of practicing, the tooting of horns, the scraping of a violin or five-finger exercises on some piano. As a result, the Community was often entertained by a good band or an even better orchestra. We children preferred the band, but the orchestra was a more general family enthusiasm. My father, I am told, although far from a musical genius, stuck doggedly to practicing the violin until able to play an acceptable second part in the orchestra. It is also related that after a protracted enthusiasm among Community members for thorough bass and musical composition, someone took from his room literally reams of paper showing his efforts to compose.

Dancing was not only permitted, but cultivated. Even the children were taught to dance. The first time I went to a family dance I sat in the gallery; my brother Holton was with me. Some good friend of the children had suggested that it would do no harm to let us look on for a while, and no one seemed to object. I was much interested in the proceedings. Mr. George Hamilton called off the figures from the stage and seemed greatly in earnest.

Holton was very much alive to the humorous aspects of the scene below. "See Mr. Inslee! He looks like a jumping jack! . . . And Aunt Betsy! See Aunt Betsy! Oh! Oh!" Holt doubled up, lowering his chin onto the gallery railing to conceal his grin of amusement. Mr. Inslee's technique was the same we had learned from Mrs. Newhouse—"one-two-three-'tis-four-'tis-five," alternating heel to instep, but his teetering on springy knees, his courtly approach to his partner and other women brought to him by the dance was something new in the experience of boys.

Later we were permitted officially to attend the dances. The Community favored quadrilles, but Virginia reels and country dances were sparingly interspersed. In later years, I remember ambitious young couples exhibiting polkas, schottisches, and the nineteenth-century slow waltz.

At first we children divided our time between exploring tunnels, under the heaps of benches and chairs which lined the walls of the room, and watching the snare drummer. Our next choice was Miss Tirzah at the piano. Her twinkling fingers high-stepping over the keys, her vigorous dashes from one end of the keyboard to the other, never lost their fascination and convinced me that she was a wonderful piano player.

A few children, of a musical turn, preferred Uncle Frank's violin playing. He was a talented violinist and looked wonderfully handsome sitting at the front of the stage, erect, and drawing from his Gemünder violin the well-known tunes.

I wish I could describe the spirit of those Community dances. The background was our great hall, where high above us—it seemed very high—the modest tans and blues of a frescoed ceiling were illumined by rows of gallery lamps which made colorful four small lunettes. From each of these looked down a classic maiden symbolizing one of the Muses. I thought they were angels.

In this setting, three score men and women formed for each quadrille. There was much hurrying around the room for partners and a rush of ambitious young people to get head-couple positions. It seemed to me that an atmosphere of joy and good-fellowship filled the hall. That was the Victorian age when ambition to go through the figures perfectly was keen. The Community dances ended at ten or ten-thirty, and always with the lancers. The figures of this dance were intricate and novices were not welcome, so it was a proud night for me when I was allowed to attempt the lancers.

2

Pantomimes, simple ones, were in great favor with the children. In *When I Was a Bachelor,* an especial favorite, Humphrey, dressed as a little man, was seen running around the room trying to step on cloth-stuffed rats pulled hither and thither across the stage by strings. I can even remember the tune Miss Marion sang while Humphrey chased the rats, and the words of the jingle:

> When I was a bachelor I lived by myself
> And all the bread and cheese I had
> I laid upon a shelf.
> The rats and the mice they led me such a life,
> I had to go to London to get myself a wife.

Then a mobcapped woman exhibited her seven mobcapped daughters to Humphrey, who selected the youngest. He toted my younger sister Irene across the stage in a little wheelbarrow to the singing of a second verse:

HUMPHREY AND IRENE
in "When I Was a Bachelor"

A COMMUNITY GROUP
in the quadrangle of the Mansion House

The streets were so broad and the lanes were so narrow,
I had to take my wife home in a wheelbarrow.

In the last verse, the "wheelbarrow broke" and "down came wheelbarrow, little wife and all."

Someone once asked me what was the effect on a Community child of a play filled with talk of bachelors and wives? Perhaps the words of the song itself will suggest an answer; that a wife was necessary to protect the bread and cheese. We children knew that in the world outside every man had a wife, but we thought of that wife as largely devoted to protecting the bread and cheese. She was her husband's housekeeper. If I pry further into what we thought about married couples in their relation to children, I am inclined to believe that the father stood in our minds as a provider and a protector of the family, in return for the housewifely labors of the mother. In any case, there was never any concealment from us of the universality of marriage outside the Community, nor do I remember any attempt to explain or defend our social variant. I think that we children accepted the negation of marriage as a principle inherent in the Community's relation with the Primitive Church.

3

Then there was play-acting. The Community's dramatic performances attained a local reputation at a time when such things were not common in the rural districts. Mr. Van Velzer's Antonio, Mr. Pitt's Shylock and Dr. Dunn's Falstaff were acclaimed by their contemporaries and became a tradition with succeeding generations.

"Entertainments" were also in vogue. Generally Uncle Abram and Mr. Burnham sang, and Mr. Seymour played the flute. Often Mr. George Hamilton did a humorous skit as the man with a cork leg. The orchestra played and we children would gallop onto the stage, wearing little red shoes, and singing, "See 'tis sow, sow doth the peasant." We enjoyed the publicity and the red shoes, but we boys slightly resented being paired off each with a girl.

When "excursions" were entertained, my brother Godfrey, then six years old and always our athletic prodigy, used to shin up a rope like a squirrel and disappear through a trap door in the ceiling of the stage, amid great applause from the audience. I must admit that some of us older boys secretly envied his prowess and the applause.

I remember being greatly embarrassed once when my mother and Miss Minerva, dressed in gypsy costumes, danced and sang. They had short skirts without pantalettes, and bare arms. To me, the exhibition seemed very worldly.

Outside entertainers were, I think, seldom invited to Oneida, and the few I recall indicate a jealous censorship. Once there came a glee club from Hamilton College, which sang dismal religious songs in a pleasing college tempo. One sang:

> Baptist, Baptist is my name
> And Baptist till I die;
> I was baptized in the Baptist Church
> And I'm on the Baptist side.

This was followed by a chorus, and then the Presbyterian sang the same propaganda for his church. Other sects followed.

Occasionally I saw a couple playing chess or checkers in the Upper Sitting Room, but in general group games were encouraged. Croquet on the North Lawn became almost a group game. The croquet ground was surrounded by benches and during the long summer evenings I saw many of the grown folks gathered there watching interestedly a match between well-known competitors. In the later days it was customary to play cards in the Hall after evening meeting, mostly euchre. I recall this because when old enough to attend the meeting I was allowed to play.

I must not forget picnics. The grown folks were much addicted to picnics. We boys often went along with the family and I have many vivid recollections of corn roasts, where huge fires blazed and of butternut cracks down on the Island. I remember an occasion when Ransom, Amos, Eugene or Deming, helped me climb a butternut tree and sent me out on limbs where they could not go, to shake off the nuts. That was a thrill. The greatest thrills are combinations of adventure and a little fear.

4

Community funerals were not at all like funerals anywhere else. The exposition of human agony and hopelessness at parting, then customary in outside funerals, was anathema to Mr. Noyes and his followers. The Community believed that faith should be demonstrated in all the relations of life. If it were God's will that a brother or sister be called to another field of activity, those left behind should accept the decree not only willingly but gladly. Although for a time there might be tears, no spirit of mourning was encouraged or tolerated. The attitude must be one of smiling Godspeed.

This was always the atmosphere of the simple funeral ceremonies held in the Big Hall at Oneida. The members would gather there quietly as for an evening meeting, and the exercises commenced with the singing of one of the victorious old hymns from the "Plymouth collection," such as "Rise, My Soul, and Stretch Thy Wings" or "How Firm a Foundation." Then some man, usually a Central Member,

read a comforting psalm and several of the faith-building sayings of Jesus Christ.

Following this each member, as he felt the call, would rise and say some kind of loving thing about the departed one. Perhaps a short story would be told illustrating one of the deceased's admirable qualities. Those not having the courage to speak in meeting could always show their feeling by a brief, "I join in that" or "I sympathize with what Mr. —— says." Then a final hymn, and the people would file out to follow the coffin on foot to the Community burying ground.

5

The Shakers from Massachusetts were frequent visitors at the Community. I remember Elder Evans and the Shaker dances, all the women keeping to one side of the stage and the men to the other.

An odd picture comes to me of Elder Evans and my father in friendly and earnest conversation. The elder was a tall, distinguished-looking man. I was struck by the fact that my father treated him as an equal and seemed to recognize some spiritual value in an Outsider. I have characterized the incident as odd because it is difficult to understand how so friendly a relation could exist between the Shakers and the Oneida Community. The Shakers were celibates and, aside from communism, their social theories and practices were at the opposite pole from the Community's. At the time I thought our hospitality a magnanimous gesture toward the Shakers. Today I must believe their visit a Shaker tribute to the essential honesty of purpose and spiritual consecration revealed by the daily living of the Oneida Communists. Is there not a subtle but inescapable sympathy and understanding between spiritual peoples?

Part III–The Breakup

Chapter I

Disintegration

I

O N that autumn day when Earl and Chester Smith appeared in the Children's House, there entered with them what Papa Kelly would have called a new "influence." They landed on the south playground from somewhere in the outer regions of space like meteorites, and we soon discovered that, like meteorites, their constituent elements were new and strange. In their role of an "influence," my memory registers them as a single entity. Their names were usually bracketed and their sophistications labeled Earl-and-Chet.

Historically they were just two small boys whose father had rejoined the Community after an absence of twelve years, bringing with him a wife and children acquired outside; but for us they came as disturbing yet, on the whole, stimulating emissaries from that world regarding which we were growing daily more curious. To say that they came from Lansing, Michigan, is to give a wholly inadequate impression of their background. They seemed surrounded by Lansing, Michigan, as with an aura; when they looked askance at our simple ways we felt the scorn of Lansing, Michigan; and it was not long before the opinions and doings of Lansing, Michigan, were, for me at least, authoritative revelations of life in that human Sahara which surrounded our little oasis. I became greatly impressed and somewhat intimidated by the hardihood of boys who had grown up in Lansing, Michigan.

Earl was a year older than I, Chester nearly a year younger. Earl was superior and vocal, while Chester said little and, although he seemed friendly enough, there was about him that quality of self-reliant brutality which marks a boy who has learned to hold his own in the rough democracy of public school or village street. At first their revelations were covert; their newly joined parents had, I assume, placed them under strict injunction to fall in with Community discipline, and under no circumstances get the family into bad odor by proving themselves undesirable additions to the Children's House.

As time went on they grew bolder. These outside boys from Lansing, Michigan, opened our eyes to new realities. They dubbed our ethics cowardly; they scoffed at our games and the way we played them; they jeered (guardedly) at our obedience to Papa Kelly and Mr. Warne; in physical encounters they exhibited a prompt and efficient sadism decidedly baffling to boys whose quarrels had represented only temporary lapses from a turn-your-other-cheek psychology.

In another field their sophistication had its effect on us. They stimulated new interest in girls and gave greater zest to the curiosity already awakening in our minds. The Community had been surprisingly successful in delaying its children's interest in sex. While young, boys and girls played together under constant supervision, and when we were old enough to roam, our expeditions, as I recall them, seemed masculine enterprises, too adventurous for girls. There were, of course, exceptions, mostly, as I remember my own experiences, daring invasions of privacies or, more rarely, furtive comparisons of sex. As a rule such sinnings were ill concealed and the sinners held up before their fellows in a five-o'clock meeting as "dirty children."

As late as my seventh or eighth year there was extant among the boys an apocryphal and fantastic story as to how children were conceived and born. In this connection, Earl dropped uncomfortable hints as to the legal status of children born in the Community. It was the first time I had realized that my birth differed essentially from births in the world generally, or at least that it differed in any way to be frowned upon by that world. In the end Earl was quite explicit: he and Chet were "legitimate," we were not. He made definite the nature of that intended insult which was only dimly sensed when the Turkey Street boys called us bastards. My mother said, "We consider you children more legitimate than any children in the world," and added, "You need never feel badly about that."

Dick and I, when away from Earl's immediate influence, were able to repair any damage done to our self-respect, even partially to rebuild our normal superiority complex toward worldlings. We fell back upon Papa Kelly's descriptions of the "wickedness of the world." Our discussions, however, led to a more critical curiosity regarding the lives of the grown folks, and thereafter we gave ear to rumors and stories which would have been little heeded in earlier days.

For instance, a romance which had caught and held the imagination of the children was the separation of Charles Cragin and Edith Waters. At the time, we were satisfied with the explanation that he had been sent away to Wallingford because he was in love with her. This seemed very sad, but impressed us then, I am sure, only as the parting of dear friends, much like the separation of Dick and myself for partiality. Now we interpreted it from the angle of sex. Again, some boy secured a literal definition of the word "celibate," whereupon the rumor that Mr. Warne was a celibate explained for us his preoccupation with teaching, gardening and science. I also remember that when we heard of the birth of a child, the question "Who was its father?" seemed of more interest than formerly when we had thought fathers were appointed.

2

I have perhaps placed greater emphasis than I ought on the influence of Earl and Chet. The fact is that before they came that spiritual unity which for more than thirty years had been the strength and glory of the Community was in process of disintegration. The most fundamental tenets of Bible communism were being questioned, and the leadership of John Humphrey Noyes criticized.

During the winter of 1878-1879, Earl's cynicisms were not the only intimations that some unusual disturbance was agitating the grown folks. We heard of many meetings, assemblies of all the family, mysterious gatherings of small groups. Men strolled back and forth on the South Walk, talking together earnestly, or I came upon them arguing in a hallway. Always when I approached they became silent and remained so until I was out of earshot. Our parents were evasive when asked about the "troubles"; but occasionally a child would confide that his father or mother had said, "Certain people are trying to make trouble"; or more explicitly, "Mr. Hinds is stirring up folks against Father Noyes."

There was little change in the routine of the Children's House. Mr. Warne held school in the forenoon, we made each our hundred chains after lunch, and Papa Kelly marshaled us for meeting at five o'clock as usual. The difference lay in the attention paid us. We felt instinctively—at least I did—that the Children's House no longer occupied the important place it had always held in the interest of our elders.

Nor was there officially any relaxation of discipline. The rules remained, but they lacked their earlier finality and, most demoralizing of the changes, Mr. Clarence had lost much of his ability to terrify. His words of admonition or even command no longer seemed undebatable, and his grim visage became an object of secret ridicule rather than fear.

How much our weakened respect for authority was due to growing older, how much to a loss of that spiritual unity upstairs which had furnished effective backing for Papa Kelly and Mr. Clarence, and how much to Earl and Chet, is hard to appraise at this distance of time. I remember that the Lansing boys scoffed at Mr. Clarence's threats behind his back, and I have a dim recollection of Earl's openly defying him without either Mr. Clarence or fire-and-brimstone from heaven descending upon the culprit.

3

And then came Professor Mears of Hamilton College. It was early in 1879 that I first heard of him, and fifty years have not sufficed to cleanse the name Mears of a sinister significance. At the time, I placed him in that gallery of wicked men where my childish imagination had placed "Boss" Tweed, Samuel Tilden (although our elders never voted, their sympathies must have been enthusiastically Republican), and a man named Holden who, in 1876, absconded with Community funds and was caught by Mr. Myron Kinsley after a detective-story chase.

Professor Mears—so the story ran—was attacking the Community. I had heard before of threatened "crusades of the clergy." I had come to look upon crusades as harmless and on the whole rather flattering attentions paid our true religion by hypocritical representatives of the Antichrist. The clergy were a sort of species or genus—pedantic individuals who mostly lived in Syracuse. But Professor Mears!—our men looked worried whenever they spoke of him and my mother's expression, when I asked about him, was, in Community language, prayerful. He was said to be organizing meetings of protest in central New York, writing scathing articles for the newspapers, trying to persuade the legislature to pass laws against us, and in general raising a storm which could not be disregarded.

I remember my very definite mental picture of Professor Mears: the shoulders were broad and truculent, the head large, the face made coarse by a mottled redness, predatory by a huge nose, and pharisaical by a long smooth gray beard. He crouched behind our east hills where lay Hamilton College. At times he rose and called savagely across our valley and over the West Hill to the clergy in Syracuse, upbraiding them for their timidity and urging attack.

It might be inferred that between Professor Mears's hostile activities and the reports of internal strife which reached us, we children lived through those troublous days in an atmosphere of dread; and yet my memory reserves for a later time anything more poignant than occasional stirrings of uneasiness. I think that, in spite of Earl and Chet, we had confidence that our elders would see the danger through.

4

During the spring of 1879 we became aware that the grown folks' quarrel was a serious matter, and for the first time sensed the possibility of a radical change in our lives. The routine and regulations of the Children's House were little altered save for a welcome relaxation of discipline, but our confidence in the future was shaken. We lived in an atmosphere, whenever boyish preoccupations permitted us to live in any "atmosphere," of uncertainty and insecurity. When tempted to worry I tried to squeeze some juice of cheerfulness out of the thought that with the breaking up of the Children's House restrictions there might come opportunity for adventures beyond our hills. I suggested this to one of the older boys—Ransom, I think, but it may have been Amos, Eugene or Deming.

"If the Community breaks up we can go to Oneida [the village of Oneida] as often as we want to, or to Syracuse, and we can do anything we want to."

The reply was, "You won't go to Oneida because you won't have any money. You can't go anywhere or do anything without money."

"I'll earn money."

"You don't know what you're talking about. You don't know as you can earn enough money to get things to eat."

This was a new idea and a disheartening one. Dick and I discussed it seriously. His final verdict was:

"Maybe *he* can't, but you and I will earn enough money."

We acquired a new interest in "hired men." I remember haunting the horse barn, drawn there by the lure of conversation with George Ayres, the Community's garrulous Negro hostler. Good-naturedly he answered our queries about things outside, but he could not resist the temptation to twit us slyly about our birth and bringing up in the Community. And yet when we engaged in a stone-throwing competition with his son, "little George Ayres," he was surprised to find that we could throw farther than his boy.

My increasing respect for Earl and Chet during this

period is an index of my progressive realization that all was
not well with our social status, or, at least, would not be well
if the Community broke up; for by this time there were
plenty of people, inside and outside, to tell us that it was
about to break up. I remember spending hot summer afternoons naked at the high-bank swimming hole, mainly to be
with Earl and Chet. Neither of them could swim as well as
the other boys, yet this deficiency, which ordinarily would
have lowered a boy's social standing, left their superiority un-
diminished. We were secretly proud to rub elbows with them.
Had they not lived outside? And more, was there not always
Lansing, Michigan, as a land of promise for their future?

Here let me say parenthetically that there was no hero
worship in our lionizing of Earl and Chet. We had never seen
them do anything we could not do, or, at least, that we did
not think we could do. It was merely that they seemed competent Outsiders at a time when we suspected that our paths
might lead outside.

5

If our routine was little changed by the turmoil about
us, my memory records a decided change in the relation of
adults to the Children's House. Frequently now, after a childish quarrel or angry dispute, a father or mother would invade
the playground and assail, with accusations and threats, some
persecutor of their offspring. Such attacks provoked in me a
resentment I had never felt for Papa Kelly's criticisms or
punishments. Most of the responsibility for his severities I
transferred, if not to the heavens, at least to agents of the
heavenly powers who foregathered somewhere upstairs and
who were really interested in the souls, if not the activities
and ambitions, of children. At other times, I listened to
mothers arguing with Miss Chloe or even with the uncom-

promising Miss Libby over fancied injustices put upon their children.

There was noticeable among the older boys a new courage in their dealings with grown folks: a courage amounting to disrespect, and in some cases forthright defiance. I particularly remember a disgraceful encounter between Harry Kelly and old Mr. Jones, he of the tin ear trumpet and snow-white beard. Harry, a boy of sixteen, was putting me through some kind of painful hazing. He had me down, I remember, on the South Walk when Mr. Jones happened along and ordered him to desist. Harry refused in disrespectful language, whereupon Mr. Jones undertook to use force and in the scuffle which followed was either pushed or knocked off his feet.

It was a great scandal. We children were shocked, but not as shocked as we should have been and would have been a year earlier. Mixed with our condemnation for Harry's disrespect, there was, I fear, a new admiration for his courage. I remember that he was sullen and defiant when brought before Papa Kelly. I also remember our astonishment that he was not severely punished. I tried to explain this to myself by recognizing how much stronger he was than the head of the Children's House, but I must have known that in earlier days the moral backing of higher authorities would have given Papa Kelly courage to make the attempt and that, in case of resistance, a stronger man would have been sent to aid him. All of which tended to break down our lifelong reverence for grown folks. When Humphrey pointed out Mr. Towner as a bad man, I could accept it in spite of my mother's denial and a traditional belief that all Community men were good men. Humphrey also told me that Mr. Towner was a seceder, which meant little to me except that he was some kind of troublemaker.

6

In those days I spent much time with my mother. Departmental oversight must have been greatly relaxed or new freedoms were granted at the age of nine. She was reticent as to the internal dissensions, but talked with me more freely about the crusade of the clergy who had now actively joined forces with Professor Mears. She called them all hypocrites; said the churches were insincere, full of scandal themselves, like the Tilden-Beecher scandal, and given over to un-Christlike practices and beliefs; that they had substituted formalities for true Christianity and thought more of outward morality than holy living. In fine, I got the idea that it would be only decent if the churches, themselves given over to the worship of Mammon, would let alone people who were trying to live as Christ commanded.

One of the most unfortunate results of the dissension upstairs was the poison of a secondary partisanship which now began to separate children who had all their lives regarded each other as brothers and sisters. At first the cleavage was evidenced only by group whisperings, but as the year advanced there came about, in sympathies if not in physical association, a definite sorting up into youthful loyalists and seceders.

Dick and I continued to stand together. I think that both his mother and mine belonged to a middle party which I have been told played a leading part in the final settlement. We condemned the seceders, but discussed secession only as a remote possibility. We did not really believe that the enchanted world in which we had lived all our lives could pass away. And yet there were times when a creeping suspicion sobered us. What if . . .? Dick shook his head solemnly. We went back to a discussion of ways to earn money and rebuilt our courage on optimistic plans for the future, if the worst should happen.

Dick was my superior in supplying data to back up theses which in his case sprang from his brain, full panoplied. I remember suggesting that we go out West and trap, like *Frank on the Prairie*. Dick's reaction was instantaneous. His face lit up and his eyes sparkled as always when new ideas were being born. "No, we'll go to the North Woods and trap. They get two dollars for a deerskin and five dollars for a beaver." Then he had a better idea: "We'll go to Canada. They say all Canadian trappers get rich."

That "if" became a subject of speculation among all the boys. We talked of "going out West" and "down South"; we argued the relative advantages of the United States and Canada; and one boy, whose father had been to the Centennial a year or two before, was continually enlarging on the glories of Philadelphia.

During the year, Eugene, a boy five years older than I, began associating with us. It may have been our militant optimism, or it may have been the greater unsettlement of mind and expressed uneasiness among his natural companions that induced this boy of fourteen to stoop to Dick and me. At first his attitude was patronizing, but in the end he accepted us and was accepted by us as an equal.

Together we collected old material from down back of the Arcade and built a shanty in an obscure location beyond the orchard. There we constructed a brick oven in which we melted down pieces of lead pipe and molded sinkers for fish lines and slugs for crossguns. We talked much of supporting ourselves and our relatives by this industry and others suggested by Dick's fertile mind.

Chapter II

The Beginning of Retreat

I

ON the 23rd of June, 1879, something happened so unthinkable, so perturbing, that the very framework of life seemed falling about me, as the timbers of a house are torn apart and scattered by a cyclone. My father disappeared; departed secretly from Oneida and no one seemed to know whither he had gone. I saw tears in my mother's eyes. She would not discuss with me the cause of this startling event or its probable results, saying only, "I don't know. We'll not talk about it, Pip, until we know." Dick told me that his father said, "Perhaps it is for the best," and Earl scoffed, "He's run away."

As a matter of history, John Humphrey Noyes, after maintaining his unorthodox communal system in defiance of public opinion for more than thirty years, after defending it against attacks by the clergy and the law courts, decided suddenly to leave Oneida. He had, it seems, definite information that certain men inside the Community were about to ally themselves with the outside crusaders.

It was not the leaders who threatened thus to join the enemy, but younger men who had sat in the secret meetings of protest and listened to indictments of Mr. Noyes just as long as their excitable natures could stand talk without action. I can easily believe that the threat of actual treason alarmed Mr. Towner. Neither he nor Mr. Hinds aimed at destroying the Community, but were attacking a leadership that a somewhat disaffected generation had come to look upon as dictatorship.

2

On that evening when the struggle inside the Community seemed to have reached a dangerous crisis, it is recorded that my father called into council two of his loyal supporters and asked their advice, and that Myron Kinsley and Otis Kellogg advised his departure with great positiveness. They urged, "You should go away immediately! Tonight!" They argued, "Tomorrow it may be too late. Tomorrow the Community, your children, all of us, may be dragged into a publicity that could blight many lives."

While he hesitated, weighing the wisdom and righteousness of this advice, the two men laid their plans. Late that night, Mr. Otis Kellogg hitched two horses to a buggy and stationed himself at a little distance from the home grounds, while Myron returned to my father's room for further argument. It was after midnight when the two men left the Mansion and made their way to the place where Mr. Kellogg awaited them.

They drove thirty miles to Holland Patent. There my father took a train to a St. Lawrence port and crossed to Canada by ferry. I have never doubted the sincerity of those two advisers, but I have suspected that they unduly stimulated my father's alarm. I am not sure.

3

Any estimate of the factors making for the breakdown of Oneida communism must take account of the emergence

of a new generation who knew not the John Humphrey
Noyes of early salvation-from-sin days. The majority of
these young people had none of the religious devotion which
the original members brought to Oneida in 1848; hence
for them my father's heresies lacked effective religious sanctions. Among the younger men, too, that scientific enthusiasm which, during the latter part of the nineteenth
century, was challenging old beliefs, undermined respect
for his spiritual, not to say mystical, leadership.

As a matter of fact, the foundation for the great schism
was laid back in 1876 when my father attempted to transfer his leadership to his eldest son, Dr. Theodore Noyes. His
abdication was formally announced to the world in the
Oneida Circular, May, 1877, and soon thereafter he retired
to Wallingford in order that Theodore's authority might not
be weakened by a divided loyalty. Unfortunately, this son
had little of his father's talent for leadership. His was a
philosophical and benevolent nature. He had no stomach
for meting out criticism and shrank from the personal administration of discipline. To make matters worse, he had
come back from Yale a frank agnostic.

The older members were disturbed and somewhat bewildered by this call for loyalty to a new non-religious leadership, but few were actually alienated because the change
had been ordained by Father Noyes. Their loyalty to him was
well-nigh indestructible. The disillusioned minority, however, became increasingly vocal in opposition to customs and
restrictions which seemed to them no longer sacred. Unfortunately, one of those social embroilments that always
arouse active personal resentment soon added its explosive
fuel to the smoldering spirit of revolt and the slow-burning
religious discontent.

Dr. Noyes's agnosticism was bad enough, but his natural diffidence, encouraged by a certain ambitious woman, led to a form of government highly offensive to men and women who had always regarded their great family as a democracy, guided rather than ruled by the inspiration of a spiritual Father. The doctor was persuaded by her that his was a different genius from his father's; that he could rule more wisely if he kept himself a little aloof from the generality. It seems more than likely that the stories which have come down to us exaggerate this woman's part in the doctor's unwise absenteeism, but the members at Oneida certainly suspected that many of the schemes and edicts which came from the absent leader were her work. Rumors of an even more daring segregation of the leadership were believed and the plans laid at her door.

It was not long before the surprised Communists found themselves regimented to such an extent that they were called upon to render written reports of each day's work or play in order that this ruling couple might know what was going on in the Community without personal contact or residence at Oneida. Even we children were given little pads, printed and lined, so that we could record each hour of the day. I can remember our enthusiasm over being able to do the same thing we saw grown folks doing.

Such a condition could not last long. Within a year rebellion broke out so violently that my father was forced to return to Oneida and resume his leadership. The episode, however, left many scars and a residuum of soreness that served Mr. Towner well in his campaign aimed to force John Humphrey Noyes to share his leadership.

4

Strangely enough, the dramatic exit of the Community's Father Noyes stilled, almost overnight, the rising
tide of strife among his followers. In its place an atmosphere
of anxious questioning filled the Mansion House. Loyalists
were stunned, and seceders disconcerted. Few of the malcontents had visioned anything more drastic than reorganization of one-man control and revision of certain elements of
the system; and fewer still could face the startling possibility
of dissolution without emotions more painful than regret.

A majority of the membership, still loyal to their leader,
questioned, grieved, and then girded themselves to fight the
"evil spirit of disunity." Anyone who has seen a flock of
sheep, upon the appearance of a dog in their pasture, turn
as one and, ceasing all other occupations, face the intruder,
can picture the spiritual reaction of the Oneida Communists
to this unexpected threat of destruction for their social
system, perhaps destruction of their home.

We children sensed a crisis. The black cloud of fear
which descended upon the Mansion House threw its shadow
over the children's wing and for a time sports took second
place in our interests. The worst of it was that we were able
to get little authentic information as to what was going on
upstairs. Our elders became secretive. We fed our fears on
the whisperings of children who had heard this or that from
some relative; from whom, they "mustn't tell."

For myself, it was a first effective introduction to the
idea of human instabilities. I felt bewildered. I do not recall
any immediate fear over the possible loss of protection from
the exigencies of a brutal Outside, chiefly because I did not
then realize how protected our lives had been. The occasional
evidences of outside roughness which had come to us, even

Earl and Chet's dramatic tales of hard-fighting boys, had met somewhere within me a congenital self-confidence which always insisted that I could manage in some way. Nor do I remember dread of being plunged into the un-communistic world with its struggle for existence. I was still but dimly aware that there existed any such struggle. No, the spasm that gripped my solar plexus (my father's passion for definiteness located the spiritual heart in the solar plexus) was more a nostalgia. Even those expeditions into the outside world, which my imagination had pictured, always started from the Community home as a base and ended with a return to that home. Half their allurement, I am sure, was the thought of fighting its battles.

5

Through the months of July and August, 1879, fear and uncertainty racked the nerves of our elders, of loyalists and seceders alike. Then one day my mother told me that Father Noyes had written a letter proposing that Community folk marry just like Outsiders. She added little in the way of explanation, but I thought her tone was one of relief. Later she said, with great earnestness, "We will never give up communism." She left me with the impression that the new regime would not greatly affect our manner of living or our happiness. I suspect that my mother hid from me her real feelings.

At seven o'clock that same evening, a solemn gathering of the entire membership discussed my father's proposal to abandon sex relations which for nearly two generations had been regarded as a sacred part of the true religion. The change was accepted with only one dissenting vote, and later an agreement was signed by all members. At ten o'clock Thursday morning, August 28, 1879, complex marriage came to an end. I have always revered the literal honesty with which that agreement to discontinue lifelong sex associations was lived up to by the former members of the Oneida Community. This has been, for me, eloquent testimony to the sincerity of the men and women who undertook the Oneida experiment.

During the succeeding months, many Community couples were married. Wherever possible, the men of the Community married the mothers of their children. I have vivid recollections of weddings in the Hall, many of them. Some were by simple contract. At others Mr. Towner officiated as a justice of the peace. For still others, Mr. Herrick, who, before he joined the Community, had been an ordained Episcopal minister in New York City, conducted orthodox church ceremonies. I especially remember the day when Mr. Erastus Hamilton was married to Miss Libby. This has stuck in my memory partly because Mr. Hamilton's marriage, he being a Central Member and a loyalist, impressed me as finality for the old order; partly because it was a double wedding, Mr. John Cragin and Miss Lily being married at the same time; and partly, perhaps chiefly, because wine was served to all present. I think it was my first taste of alcohol.

In spite of the new social order, our Children's House persisted. Its spiritual pressure was sensibly relaxed and its control further weakened by new regulations which turned each child over to its parents after the five-o'clock meeting. I ate supper with my mother and was under her care until after breakfast the next morning. Dick lived with his family in a different part of the house, in a wing called

Marriage License.

Lincense is hereby granted to *John Homer Barron* and *Helen C. Miller* to join themselves in marriage on the grounds stated in their application dated *March 5th*

For the Administrative Council,

George D. Allen Chairman

Oneida Community, *March 12, 1880*

ONE OF THE MARRIAGE LICENSES ISSUED BY THE
COMMUNITY AFTER THE ABANDONMENT
OF COMPLEX MARRIAGE

THE CHILDREN'S PLAYHOUSE

THE TRAP SHOP

Ultima Thule. I missed him evenings as I did the other boys with whom I had shared Children's House sleeping accommodations.

6

I found compensation, however, in a companionship with my mother which grew ever more precious as time and maturing understanding revealed her qualities. She was a courageous woman; in general, cheerful or at least hopeful through all those times of uncertainty, when she must have visioned disagreeable possibilities. Not that she could always conceal from me her anxiety regarding the future. Often when she talked of possible changes in our lives, her eyes would wander to a crib where lay my little sister Stella, not yet three years old. Then a lump would come in my throat and I felt like crying.

In that sympathetic relation with my mother I can discover the first stirrings of a new emotion. To a child's egocentric conception of life was added a feeling of responsibility for others. I told myself that I would care for my mother, come what might, and my heart warmed to the privilege of defending her against the world's attacks. I presume I bragged. I remember assuring her that she needn't worry, that I would soon be a man and would make her rich. My own temptations to worry were mostly night-shadows. They rarely survived daylight, out-of-doors, and the boys. It comforts me to believe that I brought to her from the playground waves of enthusiasm and an impervious, if unintelligent, optimism which brightened those anxious days.

I once asked her whom she was going to marry. I remember my mother's serious face when she answered, "Perhaps no one. Your father is already married; so is Ormond's father." At the time—I must have been thinking only of myself—this did not seem any great hardship. In fact I had seen enough in Dick's family, and in others, to arouse a suspicion that their new fathers or stepfathers were more strict than Papa Kelly.

The winter of 1879-1880 was a season of alternating fear and hopefulness, fear that the carefree life of the Children's House might be nearing an end, and recurrent hopefulness regarding the possibilities of an unknown world.

7

The year that followed the social revolution of August, 1879, must have been a troublous one for our grown folks. I have tried to recall my own state of mind, but with meager results. I am surprised at this. Through all this struggle to reconstruct a past so far away as childhood, I have found my memory more thickly strewn with emotions than incidents. In fact, many of the incidents I have related were rescued from the limbo of forgotten things by starting with some well-remembered emotion—the reaction to a word, a color, or even an odor, and following this down into my consciousness until it brought back an associated incident.

I find it hard to account for the scarcity of emotional memories during that year of uncertainty. There must have been many reminders of our social instability and I was a boy by no means insensible to emotional disturbances in those about me. Perhaps the recent adoption of marriage by the Community tempered my fear of a more destructive revolution. On the whole, however, I suspect the persistence of a prolonged immaturity. I am sure that I grew up more slowly than most boys. At the age of nine I was still so immensely preoccupied with the present that suggestions of future trouble could not compete on anything like an even basis with current sports and enterprises.

Other boys of my class may have realized more clearly than I what the rumors of a breakup might portend for themselves and have been correspondingly more disturbed. I think they were. I remember bitterness in Humphrey's tone when he spoke of Mr. Towner; also the interchange of reckless taunts between him and Earl. When Earl called Mr. Hamilton "Three-fingered Jack" (two of his fingers had been cut off by a buzz saw), Humphrey countered by calling Mr. Towner, who had lost an eye in the Civil War, "One-eyed Captain."

To the reader these may seem harmless words, but for children brought up on a literal interpretation of the Sermon on the Mount, "calling names" came very close to the edge of sin. If we called a brother "thou fool," we knew we were in "danger of hell-fire." Even "bywords" were anathema to Papa Kelly. We may have occasionally and in secret practiced "by George" or some of the other "bys" heard at the barn or brought us by Earl and Chet, but we knew them to be wrong. When—and this was rare—we heard a woman let slip, "good gracious" or "land sakes," or a man ejaculate "by golly," we got all the wicked thrill of a good "damn."

Eugene occasionally held forth to Dick and me on the coming disaster. Sitting in our smoky cabin beyond the orchard, waiting for the lead to melt, he would tell of Mr. Towner or Mr. Hinds visiting his father's room and of loud talking heard through the closed door; or how some woman said to his mother, "Father Noyes made a mistake taking the Towners into the Community." He was filled with gloom about our future. He took Dick to task for saying, "Aw, they won't break up the Community."

"They won't, hey?" Eugene stood up as straight as he

could in the low cabin and orated: "They'll never stop till they've broken it all to smash. My father says so. You boys think you're smart. Just wait until you see it smashed; then you'll believe what I tell you."

Being unable to think of an effective reply, I said to Dick more than to Eugene, "What do we care?"

Eugene's discouragement aroused in me a superficial opposition. I tried to conceal my own uneasiness from him and from myself as well by boastful air castles—boyish, unreal assertions of what I would do in a world about which, of course, I knew little. Always, however, when we emerged from the shanty bent on consuming our own product of "slugs" or "sinkers," Mr. Towner and Mr. Hinds were forgotten and dark forebodings evaporated.

That winter, as I remember it, was filled fuller than ever with skating, sliding, catching on bobs, trapping and other winter enterprises. Our enlarged freedom gave greater latitude for exploration. Over in Patton's Woods we constructed a shelter among the thick firs, where we lived the dangerous life of the Western stories; walked backward so that our tracks in the snow would fool pursuing Indians; took turns as lookouts in the top of a tree to give warning of approaching enemies.

Spring came and with it the always exciting epidemic of inundating freshets. Those memories are treasures of boyhood; racing along the edge of a raging, roily flood to find the biggest ice jam; then hair-raising attempts to ride the great cakes of ice when the jam went out; and another race, sopping wet, along the bank to follow the crunching mass hoping to see it carry away a bridge below.

When the ice was gone, we settled down to fishing for suckers. I remember sitting with a fishpole in my hands, gazing at the swirling waters and nursing an uncomfortable feeling that my future was painfully insecure. The lawless flood, gnawing at and often overleaping the banks of Oneida Creek, must have brought to the surface all the fears that had been buried in my subconscious mind during the previous months. Perhaps the melting snows of a dying winter rushing madly on to oblivion in the sea suggested the irresistible march of those unseen forces threatening my Eden. Even so, memory does not emphasize fear so much as it does a sort of creeping homesickness.

8

Aside from that lone memory of fishing by the flood, I do not recall any great change in my mental state, nor for that matter in the life around me. Married folks sat together in Big Meeting and ate at the same tables in the dining room, but so far as I could see this did not affect their old cordial relation with other members.

Most of the grown folks were making, I believe, an honest effort to adjust themselves to the new system and thus preserve their communal life. An Administrative Council had been appointed, with Mr. Erastus Hamilton at its head. As nearly as I could make out, he had become the Community's new leader, but I have since been told that he and the Council kept in constant communication with my father, who was still the real head.

I remember an unusual amount of social activity during that period. Either the Council encouraged this, or the membership sought to forget dissension and bridge a difficult season of adjustment by frequent entertainments, dances and dramatic productions, these latter on a more ambitious scale than ever before. The opera *Pinafore* was staged with elaborate costuming, wonderful scenery (it seemed so to me), and endless drilling and rehearsing. The result was so successful that after two or three performances for the family, the opera was repeated in neighborhood towns.

Behind all this social activity, which must have lulled others besides myself into a feeling of security, a ferment of discussion was going on between realistic loyalists and seceders. The fate of the Oneida Community no longer hung on the outcome of personal strife; it was being settled by the inexorable laws of human nature and human association.

Every serious student of social problems has discovered that possessiveness in sex and family relations make economic communism unattainable. To put it the other way about, the family, monogamy, is the main support of economic individualism. For the sake of family, millions endure the chaos and misery of our competitive regime. On August 28, 1879, the Oneida Community, by adopting the family system, had taken a first step backward, away from communism. They expected, or perhaps only hoped, that the movement would end there. They did not know that this change made the dissolution of their community inevitable.

Chapter III

Joint-Stock Looms

I

LATE in the month of June, 1880, the final blow fell. A year of hopeful experimenting had convinced the leading men of both parties that communism of property was unworkable for a large group divided into small families. They had discovered that family interests insidiously undermined attachment to group interests, and that family selfishness grew apace until it destroyed the spirit of self-abnegation so essential for communal living.

The story that came to the Children's House was very explicit; the Committee had proposed that the Community give up communism. We children were greatly excited and Eugene became so gloomy that Dick suggested we build a cabin of our own. If I am not mistaken, we did at that time build a "tent" in a large maple tree down on the Island. There among the practicalities of building operations we forgot Eugene's pessimism and, if at times the seriousness of the situation intruded, Dick easily transmuted disaster into opportunity by suggesting magnificent programs of action and accomplishment.

Bert must have been a partner in this enterprise, for I have a clear recollection that we were sitting in the cramped quarters of a tree-tent discussing future possibilities when he bragged, "My father is a dentist and can earn lots of money." Dick was not to be outdone: his father was superintendent of the trapshop and would get a big salary. I presume I tried to keep up my end of the competition of earning fathers. If so, I must have dragged in Uncle Abram, who was superintendent of the carpenter shop.

It was one thing to maintain a brave front in boyish discussions, but anxiety for the future of my mother, my sister and myself was then, I am sure, taking definite form. From that time until the actual change six months later, fear struggled increasingly with self-confidence. I got along fairly well in the daytime. Earl's exultant "No more Papa Kelly!" found ready response in me, superficially. But when I was alone the thought would come, "No more of Papa Kelly and the Children's House, but—perhaps no more of the old life and associations." This would bring a lump to my throat and I would gulp hard to down it.

At night doubts assailed me and often cheerfulness was attained only by force. My mother read to me in the evening—Dickens, Cooper or Walter Scott. I enjoyed Dickens, but when Pip's troubles or the sorrows of little Nell had fanned into flame the embers of my own anxieties, I would urge, "Let's not read any more. Let's talk." Then I would strive to build up my mother's courage and in the process often rebuilt my own and went off to bed exultant, self-hypnotized into a conquering state of mind.

Not always, however, was I brave at bedtime. Frequently I would lie awake for a long time, long for a boy of ten, and pretend to be asleep so that my mother would not think I was weakening. I recall a picture that frequently haunted my wakeful hours. I must have seen it in an English book. In the dim light of a horrid attic a haggard woman was lying in bed and helplessly watching several emaciated children. Some were playing on the floor, while a baby girl grasped the tattered bedclothes, apparently begging for food. It must have been thoughts of my little sister that gave that picture its poignancy.

I also remember a nightmare wherein my mother, Stella, Uncle Abram, Ormond and I seemed about to be driven from home—pushed out into the world. That nightmare was so vivid that it has remained with me until this day. We were in a huge room. We five were standing together at one end, while facing us the entire membership of the Community pointed at us (physically or metaphorically, I am not sure which), repeating some formula of excommunication. For several years thereafter whenever I wakened in the night I used to see that picture and hear those words which condemned us to exile.

2

The sudden intrusion of difficulties and danger gave both speed and direction to my development. After all, the important thing in this experiment of human living is experience. Looking back, I see that until my tenth year childhood had brought me little experience in the sense I have in mind. Experience is struggle, struggle with objective obstacles or emotional problems. Suddenly and unexpectedly, I now passed from the green pastures of a protected childhood into that forest of problems wherein all active lives are spent. I tasted "experience."

In addition, I think I see in that first time of stress the beginning of mental habits which have conditioned all my intellectual life. While Mr. Warne's scientific information, as also Dick's and my explorations, had enlarged and colored the physical map of the world, neither had stimulated in me any particular urge to analyze my own relation to it all. Like a child in a roomful of toys, I had been satisfied to be

there and have so many things to absorb my time and attention. In 1879, I fronted a new problem; what would happen
to me and mine if we were thrust out into a hostile world?
For now I was beginning to be aware that in that world I
would meet with accusation, condemnation and sweeping
denials of all the principles I had been taught. Further, I now
suspected that gigantic oppositions might stand astride those
vistas of adventure which had inspired Dick and me in days
gone by.

This personal questioning led to a more general inquiry
into realities. My mind was immensely stimulated by the
serious problems I faced. I am inclined now to believe that
this necessity, at the age of nine, to find a new and authentic
basis for future activities did something to my mind; produced what nowadays is defined as a complex. The effort
to adjust myself to wholly new conditions started me in
pursuit of information about the world in general and human relations in particular.

Perhaps—and this is the kernel of my thought—that
early experience was the effective, brain-creasing cause of an
eagerness, which has followed me through life, for knowledge
upon which I could found hypotheses defining the universe
and my place in it. As I have grown older, the possibility
of such larger placement has, of course, become steadily
dimmer owing to the receding limits of the cosmos. But my
subconscious mind has never quite given up the attempt
to plot our world and then the infinite and make an X at
the exact spot where I myself am standing.

3

During the next two months all kinds of stories cir-
culated in the Community and many of them reached the

Children's House. According to one, the Community property was to be divided between seceders and loyalists. The latter (a substantial majority of the members) would join Father Noyes at Niagara Falls and there found a new Community. The records show that a paper was actually signed by one hundred and twelve members who desired to take this course.

In the end, majority opinion settled on reorganization into a joint-stock company. The details were worked out by a Commission, then discussed by the entire family assembled in the Hall. Even children must have been allowed, at times, to listen in, for I remember sitting in the gallery looking down on a hall filled with people engaged in earnest discussion, and hearing Mr. Alfred Barron say, with a gesture toward us, "When the Pips and Dicks are grown up . . ." He was evidently making a point in debate, arguing as to how their settlement would affect later generations. I remember only this fragment of his speech and my surprised recognition that the august Commission took us into account.

It was on my tenth birthday, August 18, 1880, that a Committee from the Oneida family laid their plans before my father at Niagara Falls. I have since read his letter dated August 19, 1880, which the Commission took back with them to Oneida. This shows the spirit which animated the final discussions leading up to the abandonment of communism; also the relation of my father to the settlement:

My reflections and, I trust, my inspirations lead me to accept the plans which Myron has laid before me, as being the best that we can agree upon amongst ourselves, and probably better than any we could expect from an outside arbitration. If the liberal and fair spirit which seems to pervade the new plan can preside over the carrying of it out in all its details, we shall achieve a victory more splendid than any that I dared to hope for. Of course the recommendation of the Commission must be followed by free thought and discussion on the part of the whole Community, and the proposed change ought not to be pushed through against the wishes of a considerable minority. But I hope for a breeze of unanimity in favor of this financial revolution like that which carried us through the great social revolution of a year ago.

On September 1, 1880, the "agreement to divide and reorganize" was signed by the Community family, and on January 1, 1881, communism of property came to an end.

While the Commission was writing "finis," my father gave an impressive demonstration of that genius for interpreting misfortune or disaster as victory, which heartened his followers through all the trials of their great experiment and which preserved their belief that such were merely incidents in God's inscrutable plan for educating his chosen people—preparing them for their eternal birthright. He wrote:

We made a raid into an unknown country, charted it, and returned without the loss of a man, woman, or child.

Could anything be more dramatic—a man now in his seventieth year, standing amid the ruins of his lifework, shouting "Victory!"?

Chapter IV

Last Days

I

DURING those months when the Oneida Community was
dying, the Mansion House buzzed with rumor, discussion and interparty negotiations. Heated debates in the
South Sitting Room, where, every day, the Commission
met, were echoed at general family gatherings, and members
who had seldom "spoken in meeting" asked pointed questions.
There was, however, less bitterness than during the days of
militant secession. As a matter of fact, loyalists and dissidents
worked together in a rather surprising spirit of unity, searching for some economic readjustment which would enable the
Community group to live together happily in the old home.
The leaders of both factions had to struggle, on the one
hand, with the impassioned rebellion of loyalists against this
"surrender to the world" and, on the other hand, with timid
souls who grew more timid as the end grew near. All the
rumblings of discontent and fear as well as the daily grist
of plannings and proposals were known in the Children's
House. Secrecy had been thrown to the winds and parents
discussed the issues freely before their children.

The problem of my own future separated itself from
the general questions raised in adult debate. I saw with increasing clearness the end of that material safety which had
surrounded my childhood; in addition, I was becoming uncomfortably aware that another area of trouble threatened,

whose dimensions I could only guess. The possibility of social ostracism grew more real as the weeks dragged slowly on toward January first.

Our elders, some of them, showed unmistakable symptoms of a similar anxiety regarding their future social status. I heard Mr. John Cragin, a man who had always seemed full of confidence and courage, say to my mother, "We are likely to be confronted with a difficult situation out in the world, especially among church people whom we have so long defied," and Earl assured us that we children would find ourselves in an even worse plight. Either he or some other kind friend helped me to the idea that, while our parents' offense was a thing of the past, we, the improperly born product of the Community system, would be continuing reminders of its unforgivable defiance of Victorian morality and as such would suffer the reproach of illegitimacy through all our lives.

I remember standing alone down by the Playhouse near the close of a glorious Indian summer day. A chilly autumn breeze was blowing across our playground where the slanting rays of a setting sun painted cold yellow streaks between the lengthening shadows of the trees. I was repeating to myself certain words a hired man had spoken to me that day— "Illegitimate!" "Bastard!" He was not an unkind man, but a worker at the carpenter shop who spoke with the frankness of his kind. There was even a cynical friendliness in his voice when he told me, "You Community boys will never be able to make your own way in the world; you will always have to stick by the Big House."

As I stood there, the yellow patches on the sward looked as cold as the long gray shadows; the world seemed cold and hard. Passionately I rebelled at a hostile fate that threatened me with undeserved ignominy—that would rank

me below the level of "outside" boys; and then this thought
tangled itself with those other possibilities of trouble ahead.
For that evening I must have been a very gloomy boy.

There were times, however, when we boys became enthusiastic over the money we would earn in the days of
"joint-stock," money all our own. We would get pennies or
even nickels for running those errands we had so often run
for nothing, at the bidding of men who seemed to think that
little boys were created especially to run errands. Furthermore, our parents' anxiety about the approaching day when
they would have to pay for everything they got was offset
by our vivid anticipation of being paid for everything we
did.

2

Present pleasures easily divert children from worry over
future dangers, but I marvel when I recall the courageous
way my mother reacted to the prospective change. Our room
was haunted by women in similar circumstances to hers,
lonely women who came seeking encouragement or companionship in misery. I remember a certain Miss Mary's tear-
ful questionings:

"Do you really think, Harriet, they'll pay us dividends?
Will we have enough to live on?"

"Certainly they will," my mother told her confidently.
"You needn't be afraid; the Commission is arranging to take
care of everyone."

I feel sure that in those days my mother faced another
painful uncertainty. She was deeply religious and her spiritual
life was founded on my father's theology. I think that human
beings can shift to new economic bases or adapt themselves
to disagreeable social situations more easily than exchange
their religions. My mother must have asked herself, "Will

the Community religion die? Will 'salvation from sin' and
that intimate touch with the Primitive Church and heavenly
powers which Father Noyes brought us, pass with him?
Will I find myself drifting and rudderless during the rest of
my voyage through life?" She had based her happiness in this
world and her hopes of the next on Christ as revealed by John
Humphrey Noyes. Could she now expect to find in any
church a religion to replace that rock of safety—Perfectionism—on which she had learned to rest with confident
faith.

At the time I did not realize the extent of her spiritual
conflict, but I remember her talking with me often, and seriously, about religion and my father's principles. She may
even have told me of her doubts and misgivings, but a boy
of ten, try as he may (I am not sure that I did try to understand her; only to comfort), can hardly regard spiritual
problems as rating at all with such secular difficulties as
were then threatening us and whose practical effects were
well within his mental range. I believed in my father's goodness and wisdom and his close relation with the heavens,
but Perfectionism had not yet involved—to use a medical
term—any important nerve centers.

3

Interesting things were then happening almost daily.
Announcements were coming from the Commission which
made increasingly real the pleasant prospect of owning things.
For instance, it was decreed that members could retain the
furniture and clothing then in their possession up to a value
of $30 and could buy beyond that sum. Thereafter I looked
at our bureaus and beds and chairs through new eyes; they
would be ours—Mother's and mine. Again, when word

reached the Children's House that to every child would be given $100 a year until the age of sixteen and at that time $200 in cash to help with further education, we felt like little capitalists, and the economic dangers of joint-stockism temporarily vanished.

The corporation bound itself to furnish living accommodations in the Mansion House, at cost, for members and their children; all were to have company jobs in preference to Outsiders, "other things being equal"; Mr. Warne's school, now Mr. Underwood's, was to be maintained and to be open to Community children free of charge; and last but not least, every member was allotted $60 in cash to start the new regime.

My mother's statement to her discouraged friend that "the Commission would take care of all" seemed fully justified when their complete plan was laid before the family. The assets of the Community were to be represented by twenty-four thousand shares in the new stock company, each with a par value of $25, and every man and woman would receive four and one-quarter shares for each year he or she had lived in the Community since the age of sixteen, plus half the property they brought in at the time of joining.

When a notice with details of this plan appeared on the bulletin board, my mother and I lost no time in figuring out our capital and probable income: $2,850 in stock! If they paid us six per cent, that would be $171 a year. Then $100 for Stella and $100 for me. A total of $371. It looked like a lot of money. My mother, I have no doubt, did some more detailed figuring, but for myself I remember only a new feeling that joint-stock might not be so bad after all. We were going into the new adventure with nearly $400 a year to spend.

About that time I had the measles. In the role of nurse
my mother was all cheerfulness, but during my convalescence
her absent-minded answers to questions tended to shake my
confidence in our financial strength. It was not her words;
she said, "We'll be all right," and I often heard her assuring
timid friends that the cost of rent and board would undoubtedly be arranged so that the incomes of all would be
ample for their needs. But by this time I knew my mother
better. I came to suspect that her confidence was founded on
the "goodness of God" about which she often spoke, more
than on the $371.

Either this suspicion or a certain mass anxiety which
surrounded us did undoubtedly turn my mind more and
more to anxious thoughts regarding our financial future. We
could not look to Uncle Abram for help with our expenses
since he had his own family to support, but he showed a deep
personal interest in our welfare and was a great source of
comfort to us. He had married many years before and in
1879 had resumed family relations with his wife, but he
came frequently to our room and interested himself in our
money problems. He was not, however, by nature an op-
timist. I remember that he shook his head sadly over the
breakup, and spoke savagely about Mr. Towner. I also remember his dodging my mother's analysis of her prospective
balance sheet with the emphatic but not very relevant assertion, "By jolly, they've got to take care of the women and
children."

I spent much time at the carpenter shop where men
made rough cases and beautiful cabinets with equal skill. I
was fascinated by the screaming buzz saws, and could stand
indefinitely watching boards dragged slowly through the
rolls of a roaring planing machine. It was all so creative.
Uncle Abram entrusted me with odd jobs and I got much

satisfaction out of his promise that after joint-stock he would pay me for shoving down the shavings and carrying out sticks.

Another thing that diverted my mind from worry was the rapid change of environment. My mother moved to a new room on the ground floor. It was in the children's wing and no one seemed to object to my making her room rather than the South Room my headquarters.

4

An event which temporarily lent a pleasurable color to the approaching era of private ownership was a grand auction in the Hall. Such items of personal property as had not been appropriated by individuals under the thirty-dollar rule, were exhibited there and the Commission announced that on a certain evening these would be sold to the highest bidders. For several days we boys haunted the Hall. We searched among the furniture for skates and sleds and other interesting articles of sport; also, I fear we laid profane hands on things we had seen all our lives but had never dared touch. I remember concentrating my activities on a certain sled. I was not satisfied until my mother had agreed to bid for it, and to make assurance doubly sure I told Uncle Abram how badly I wanted that particular sled.

The auction was a memorable occasion. Family groups whispered together, then one member bid, sometimes timidly, oftener in truculent tones which, however, may have concealed timidity. It was something new in all our lives. I am sure that the men and women there, bidding "56 cents—57 cents—60 cents," felt, as I did, a certain novel elation in thus wielding, for the first time, the age-old power of money to buy possession of things desired.

My mother bought the sled for me. Uncle Abram protested when the bidding ran, as he thought, too high, but
she stuck to it. I think she felt a considerable exhilaration trying out her new financial wings and pitting her resources
against the opposition of those others who would deprive
me of the sled. That auction was the last gathering of all the
Oneida Communists and it symbolized the end of communism.

The new life was rushing upon us. I remember once
hearing my mother say emphatically to Aunt Harriet Skinner, "No, I can care for him and I shall keep him." Whether
I had listened to the preceding discussion I cannot say. I am
certain, however, that I interpreted her words as refusal of
some plan to turn me over to the guardianship of the Noyes
family. In later years I found confirmation of this in a letter
written by my father late in 1880. He was living at Strathroy, in Canada, and his financial future must have seemed
very uncertain. It was a brave letter. After stating that he
placed his trust in God for the necessary means, he offered
to support and care for all his children as soon as he had
established a permanent home.

Part IV–Rebirth

Chapter I

The Plunge

I

JOINT-STOCK! Those hyphenated words became for Oneida Communists the designation for a revolution in their lives. For many years after January 1, 1881, events were dated as "before joint-stock" or "after joint-stock," and the tone in which the words were uttered registered approval of or regret for the change. My own feelings were mixed. I recall satisfaction over my new independence and moments when my imagination leaped over all obstacles to vision adventures in that larger Outside I had so long viewed from a distance, but underneath there ran a current of doubt and anxiety which at times forced itself to the surface. When in the evening I sat with my mother and watched my little sister playing on the floor, the uncertainties surrounding our future more than ever depressed me. Experience was making of me a realist. I could not conceal from myself how poorly a Children's House bringing up had equipped me for competing with the world.

On the other hand, there was a novelty about our new manner of living that lent a naïve interest to life. During those first months the atmosphere of the Mansion House was hopeful if not always cheerful. Everyone had a job of some kind, everyone who wanted one; and since board and rent were charged to accounts in the office, our financial problems seemed, for the time being, somewhat theoretical.

187

As for the new joint-stock company, the Oneida Community, Limited, it rose like a phoenix from the ashes of the Community. Time proved that it had unexpected vitality, but during those first few years fearful persons, especially unmarried women, listened apprehensively to predictions of failure. I happened to be where those predictions were coloring the atmosphere most darkly; for the fearful, both men and women, still haunted our room as they did in the earlier days of discussion and doubt. Perhaps under the circumstances timidity was excusable in people who, at the age of thirty or forty or even fifty, had never had any experience in providing for their own physical necessities.

2

A new respect for money and the attendant conviction that payment should always be made for exact value received led the directors to close our old family dining room and fit up an à la carte restaurant in the half basement of the New House (it is still called the New House although built in 1877). We children were especially enthusiastic about the restaurant. There we could order anything we wanted from a printed price list—butter pats one cent, two slices of bread for a cent, pancakes and maple syrup five cents. What joy! Cake and pie, which had been denied us except on special occasions, were now displayed on a side table and could be had for the asking (and the signing of a slip), when our parents were absent; sometimes when they were there. My own mother was rather indulgent. I can remember making almost an entire meal out of a huge piece of chocolate layer cake. Cream, too, was a novelty; I drank it until my stomach rebelled.

The éclat of this fiscal system of eating was enhanced by

the ambitious worldliness of the new rooms and equipment. The walls of the dining room were painted a luxuriant, unspiritual green, the tables were of polished oak, the chairs ornamental, and the dishes decorated with flowers. In the kitchen we saw food coming from bright copper steam chests. And finally when through eating, instead of carrying our dishes to the dishwashing room as we had done in the past, waiters took them away.

An amusing incident resulted from the old Community custom of "carrying away dishes." Some time after joint-stock, Dr. Dunn was dining at the Vanderbilt Hotel in Syracuse. Having finished his meal he rose and, from habit, started down the aisle carrying his dirty dishes. The diners in that then fashionable hostelry were greatly amused and Dr. Dunn correspondingly embarrassed.

The financial arrangements for our joint-stock restaurant illustrate the naïve economic ideas of men just emerging from lifelong communism. Its superintendent received the same salary as the president of the new company. Eating must have been rated a function as important as money-making, or else those people, trained to value character only, believed that the men chosen for president and restaurant superintendent were, from personal considerations, entitled to equal pay.

In those days "overhead expenses" and "depreciation" had not been heard of at Oneida. The kitchen committee added a rule-of-thumb profit to each item of food, and expected that the department would pay its way, even make a net profit. Great, then, was their disappointment when month after month the restaurant showed handsome losses, and louder and louder became the demand for a return to the old dining arrangements and a simpler system.

The life of that à la carte restaurant was short. Its

abandonment was hastened by a secession of the loyalists, stimulated partly by aversion to its daily reminder of money, partly by the desire of true believers to separate themselves from spiritual backsliders, and partly, I suspect, because the manager was anti-Noyes. Mr. Erastus Hamilton was responsible for this secession. Immediately following the breakup, he had instituted an imitation of the old evening meetings to which only recognized Noyesites were invited. Now, in partnership with Mr. Freeman and several others, he rented the former dining rooms and there revived as nearly as possible the Community eating regime. This culinary enterprise was called "F. & Co."—"F." for Mr. Freeman, "& Co." for Mr. Hamilton. In the beginning it was selective, as selective as the loyalist meetings, but when the à la carte restaurant was given up F. & Co. became a general cooperative dining room which has furnished board at cost for all the tenants of the old Community buildings down to the present day.

Both Mr. Hamilton's meeting and the new boarding-house made obvious the fact that my mother was not reckoned among the Noyes loyalists. She was invited to join neither. This did not worry me, because I was then reaching out toward the Earl-and-Chet companionships; but I think my mother suffered over it. My father's religion was still her religion. She told me that her exclusion was due to her friendliness with Mr. Towner and Mr. Hinds.

There was perhaps an additional reason for Mr. Hamilton's looking askance at my mother, and possibly at me. Her maternal uncles were able but worldly, not to say unscrupulous, lawyers. Two of them became mayors of large cities. The family name was Cook, and running through all my mother's criticisms in Community days were accusatory references to the "Cook spirit." Mr. Hamilton was a Perfec-

tionist of the complete-surrender-to-Christ's-representative
brand. As my father's chief deputy he had in the old days
run up against a streak of hardness in my mother which resisted his rather domineering management, and he probably
doubted her submissiveness to his new discipline, which now
had no effective backing.

I am not excessively proud of my own reaction to this
exclusion from the Noyes clan. I advertised it, hoping
thereby to help my standing in the Earl-and-Chet fraternity
which now included, besides a few of my Children's House
companions, a liberal infusion of outside boys from the
neighborhood. I knew that acceptance by the worldlings was
granted with reservations. I was illegitimate and, what was
worse, I once heard Albert Ross say:

"He's a son of old man Noyes."

I tried to make up for these shortcomings by open
apostasy and learning to be tough.

My mother often objected to my choice of companions
and I remember Uncle Abram's backing her up, forbidding
me to play with certain boys. It was not a happy period of
my life. The old basis of self-belief had disappeared, my status
in the youthful commonwealth was not secure, and underneath the superficial pleasure derived from playing with "bad
boys" ran that undercurrent of pessimism and doubt. At
times I wondered if my fate was to wander through life a
misfit and be looked down upon by everyone.

Dick and I were not so close as in the earlier days. He
had taken the name of his new stepfather and having thus
partially freed himself from the stigma of illegitimacy, could
play on equal terms with right-wing and left-wing boys. I
have no doubt that it was my pride, rather than any change
in him, that raised a slight barrier between us. I do not mean
that Dick and I lost our affection for each other. We were

no longer "partial," but still very much friends. I have a curious recollection of our sudden passion for what we called fighting, but which was, in reality, more a rough-and-tumble wrestling such as puppies engage in. Almost daily we furnished amusement for the other scholars during recess by our "fights." I am inclined to think that a subconscious urge to struggle out of the social and moral cul-de-sac into which a blind fate seemed forcing me rendered any kind of physical aggression a relief from my feeling of futility.

At this time I began associating more generally with home boys other than Dick. My trapping, for instance, must have been in company with Humphrey, since I remember an amusing misadventure that befell us. We had set our traps in a hole which we believed to be the entrance to a muskrat's den. The animal, when caught, crawled far into the hole and it was only after much prying and prodding that we succeeded in dragging it out. When it emerged, our muskrat proved to be a skunk. Nature took its inevitable course: our clothes were given the traditional burial in the ground, and we lost a day of schooling thereby.

The happiest period of my day was the two hours I spent each afternoon in physical work at the carpenter shop, for which Uncle Abram paid me four and a half cents per hour. I was earning money, but that was not all; the pay gave me a feeling that my work was useful, creative, like a man's work.

3

During the first months of joint-stock, our elders developed an exaggerated respect for private property, and an earnest search for opportunities to earn money. I remember an extraordinary business transaction in which Miss Jerusha Thomas exhibited this new passion of acquisitiveness in a way as unusual as her very unusual face. She insisted on measuring my hands, saying that she desired to knit me a pair of mittens. Then, after I had worn the mittens several days, she turned up with a bill for forty-five cents which my mother paid.

H. G. Wells, who visited us in 1906, says in his book, *The Future in America*: "I was told that in the early days of the new period there was . . . a jealous, inexperienced insistence upon property. 'It was difficult to borrow a hammer,' said one of my informants."

I myself have often heard old members say laughingly that when they borrowed a pin they felt in duty bound to return it.

Chapter II

Vineland

*E*VEN at this distance of time I can glimpse the color of that eager anticipation which took possession of me when my mother told of Grandfather Worden's invitation to visit him in Vineland. Here was the promised land of adventure my imagination had so often pictured in the old days. It would all be so new; so wholly "outside." Thereafter I would have a Lansing, Michigan, all my own. Vineland, in prospect, seemed like a door of escape, whereas the recent exchange of Children's House control for joint-stock freedom had merely pulled down the four walls of my house and left me there in the cold glare of an offended world's hostility.

While my mother was debating the issue, I gave her no peace. "Please, mother," I begged, "take me to Vineland." My Noyes relatives opposed my going and always regretted that expedition into the wicked world. But when Uncle Abram thought "the absence from Oneida, for a time, a good idea," it was settled; we would go to Vineland. I rushed out to find Dick and tell him the good news; also, I am sure, to parade my Vineland before Earl and Chet.

It is a curious fact that I recall vividly the emotional excitation of our railway journey to Vineland, but very little of incident. I was wide-eyed with anticipation. We were rushing out into the world from which those Ontario & Western trains came, and I was about to see all the wonders

I had imagined. The only definite picture I retain is of a trainyard where great engines, surrounded by whirls of white steam and black smoke, were shunting cars about. It seemed to me that there were a hundred tracks and a thousand cars.

We found Grandfather living in a small white house on a corner of the main street, Landis Avenue. He told us of Mr. Landis, the founder and patron saint of Vineland, and I remember installing him as Number One in the gallery of great men I hoped to meet on this excursion into the wide world. I never actually saw Mr. Landis; it was enough to live on Landis Avenue and feel connected, however distantly, with this creator of cities. I sometimes regret the prosaic disillusionments of maturity such as my later suspicion that Mr. Landis was nothing more noble than a real estate speculator. I do not think that I have since then ever found a Number One having the romantic possibilities of greatness with which my imagination clothed Mr. Landis in 1881.

2

Grandfather Worden was one of the original members of the Oneida Community. He had lived in that section of New York State which, in the early nineteenth century, was called by church people, "the burnt-over district," meaning the area that had been swept by the fervid revivals of Finney and others, and whose inhabitants had later listened to John Humphrey Noyes's call to "perfection." For many years Grandfather was a reader of my father's publications. He listened to his preaching and, becoming a convinced Perfectionist, joined the new Community in 1849. With him came his three motherless daughters, Harriet, my mother, then eight years old, and Susan and Cornelia. He left the Community in 1870.

My grandfather was a gentle soul. I told in a previous chapter of his quixotic plan to throw cannon into the sea as a start toward building a bridge across the ocean. When, back in 1849, it was decided to send someone to Putney, Vermont, as manager of the very considerable property left there by the Putney Community, my grandfather was chosen for the mission. His even temper and goodwill toward all men disarmed the hostility of Israel Keyes and Dr. Campbell whose militant righteousness had driven the earlier Community from the village, and he lived in Putney for several years, on excellent terms with the neighbors. Ultimately he liquidated the Community property.

His full name was Marquis de Lafayette Worden. He was the youngest of eight children and until his seventh year no one seemed able to think of a name for him. Finally, when the Franco-American patriot, Lafayette, toured this country, my great-grandparents, in a burst of enthusiasm, bestowed upon Grandfather the Frenchman's name and title. In my day, Marquis de Lafayette had become for all Worden relatives Marcus—he was "Uncle Marcus."

Grandfather was tall and lean and, when I knew him, wore a long, gray beard and walked slightly bent over, with a cane. Financially he must have been a wizard. From all I could learn, his earnings had been meager since leaving the Community and he had simply "saved" himself into a quiet prosperity. He was then living with his third wife. This new grandmother was just as saving as Grandfather, and when my mother and I landed in his story-and-a-half cottage, these two were living comfortably on very little a year.

GRANDFATHER WORDEN
(Marquis de Lafayette Worden)

3

This was my first adventuring in the Outside. I remember the mixed emotions with which I looked out upon boys passing our house, or the respectable and respected families in the houses across the street. There was a functional completeness about the postman and the milkman and especially the boy who brought the morning paper to our door, which made the life around me seem unapproachable. All appeared oblivious, if not actually hostile, to a Community boy like me. And yet I nursed a hopeful longing to break in somewhere. I was, at one and the same time, eager to find an opening into this charmed circle of accepted Outsiders and fearful of my reception if successful. Of course no one knew or cared who I was, but whenever a person looked at me, self-consciousness interpreted their glances as disapproving.

For a time I played alone in a vacant lot my grandfather owned, and the most exciting incident of the day was going up to the post office with him. He was extremely sociable and garrulous. It often took us more than an hour to make the one-mile round trip. He would stop and talk with everyone he met, and my memory still retains a picture of Grandfather turning and talking at a man who had torn himself from the endless conversation, talking until the victim was well out of earshot.

Presently, however, my urge to experiment with this new environment prevailed and I made the acquaintance of the younger Capper children who lived next door. Arthur Capper, now a prominent United States senator, was older than I and worked with his father in the printing office. When my mother heard that his father was a socialist, she was all for getting acquainted with the Cappers. Grandfather dampened her ardor by saying,

"He is not Mr. Noyes's kind of socialist."

My mother tried to entertain me at home. I think she was a little fearful of my reception socially; hence did not encourage me to branch out. On the other hand, Grandfather took me to call on some Worden relatives where there was an older boy, and later encouraged my fraternizing with another boy of about my own age, Percy Morgan, who lived nearby. Through this acquaintance I met other children, both boys and girls. Which reminds me that later I had a violent flare for Percy's sister Marion. I have forgotten whether this was reciprocated, but I remember a new emotion.

On the whole I suffered less from unfriendly comment than I had expected. My only clear memories of humiliation concern the few occasions when Percy and I quarreled. I was stronger than he and in the bitterness of defeat he would sometimes taunt me with my Oneida Community birth. Those taunts hurt cruelly, but were not of frequent occurrence. In general we were fast friends and almost as inseparable as Dick and I had been during Community days.

It was Percy's urging that led to my entering the public school. When I suggested this, my mother held back, but Grandfather came to my aid and, in his mild way, took her to task. I remember how, when she asked his opinion, he threw back his head and opened his mouth wide, holding that position for a few seconds, as was his custom, before delivering himself of grandfatherly wisdom.

"I wouldn't say so, Harriet." Another pause while he looked at the ceiling, with mouth thoughtfully open. "The boy ought to be in school."

4

So on a Monday morning I went off to the Peach Street
school with Percy, and for the moment fear was buried under
a flood of pleasing anticipations. I was about to become a
regular kid in a regular school. My first days in the Vineland
school were fully up to expectations; nothing untoward happened, and for the first time I had a chance to measure myself against that outside boy I had heard so much about. Les-
sonwise I found myself more advanced than most of my
classmates in arithmetic, spelling and geography. Grammar
was my humiliation. *Kerl's Common School Grammar,* with
its mechanical formulas and endless parsings, had never been
introduced to us by Mr. Warne; so I did very badly in that
subject. A certain dislike I have always felt for the word
"parse" was, I think, born of embarrassment in the Vineland
school.

Through Percy I became acquainted with several older
boys and either his friendship or their good nature postponed,
for a time, the rough initiation usually meted out to a new
boy. That breathing spell was my good fortune. I had time
to accustom myself to association with this new species and
to establish a certain measure of confidence in myself before
the inevitable trial came. Familiarity with the boys around
me stripped from them most of that aura of occult physical
superiority with which Earl and Chet had clothed the street
arabs of Lansing, Michigan.

It was not long, however, before certain of the older
boys began picking on me. They would shove me violently
against a lad of my own size with the command, "Lick him!"
and when I held back, they would throw me down or otherwise maltreat me on their own account. I remember a time
when I secretly wished that I had not rushed out into the

world so impetuously. I have no doubt that pride alone kept
me in that school. And matters grew steadily worse. When
my schoolmates discovered that I was not inclined to fight,
they made it their business to force me to do so. Even boys
smaller than I dared me and insulted me. When I recall my
feelings at that time I find nothing to be proud of except the
fact that I stuck to school.

I should like to think that in the end my own courage
rescued me from this ignominious situation, but I suspect
that Percy and his friends bullied me into fighting. My first
collision was with a Negro boy. I have an indistinct recollection of having provoked the fight myself. There was a rage
in the school for blowing putty balls from tin blowpipes, and
I think I hit the Negro boy with a putty ball. I remember
his rushing up and striking me. The circumstances were
probably as favorable for me as possible. Between the provocation of the blow and the fact that he was a Negro, my
fear was temporarily forgotten. We attacked each other with
approved public school technique. Nothing was barred. I remember Percy or some other of my well-wishers calling to
me, "Kick his shins; niggers don't like that."

The battle, it seemed a gladiatorial combat, must have
lasted a long time for when, at the finish, I found myself
lying on the ground receiving the final punch and kick which
the code permitted, my swollen eyes saw a circle around us
that looked like the entire school. I had been soundly whipped
before the whole school and that "by a nigger." I did not go
directly home, but crawled into the scrub alder of a vacant
lot to pull myself together and think it over. I remember
deciding that ability to fight was not an accomplishment, but
a necessity. There and then I resolved that I would learn to
fight.

When I got home my mother threatened to take me

out of "that awful school," and Grandfather inveighed against fighting. For myself, there was only one thing worth while in all the world—learning to fight. I have always reckoned that fight with the Negro boy a valuable lesson learned. That, and my other experiences in the Vineland school established, somewhere deep down in my consciousness, a conviction that he who will not fight must fight continually, and further, that willingness to fight can never take the place of preparation.

Percy encouraged my new ambition and offered to help, but I was not satisfied with what he could teach me. Together we appealed to Steve Montgomery. He was one of Percy's friends, an older boy, much bigger and stronger than we, and through many a hot afternoon he "roughed" us. I stood for anything, no matter how painful, so long as it promised to make me more proficient in fighting. I remember that Steve used to wade in and floor us, yelling, "Like this! Don't wait; go after them—like this!"

Romance would demand that I report a later meeting with the Negro boy at which I gave him a sound thrashing, but unfortunately memory suggests no such victory; in fact, it does not furnish any evidence of his continued existence. Disconnected details of fights in the schoolyard come back to me, but no vivid pictures of either successful or unsuccessful encounters like the one I have related. I must have achieved my lowly ambition to learn how to fight since I have a distinct recollection that during the latter part of my attendance at the Vineland school I lived on even terms with my schoolmates and had lost both fear and the feeling of inferiority which had oppressed me when I started.

Not that Vineland entirely destroyed in me the leaning toward nonresistance which an early inculcation of Christ's teachings grafted on Community children, but it

did start a backfire of what might be called intellectual courage. Incidentally, it laid the foundation for a new philosophy; namely, that life is a struggle; hence he who cultivates
a love of struggle will never lack for the raw material of
happiness.

5

Grandfather was outraged by my penchant for tough
boys. He protested violently against my associating with a
certain "rich boy" who, he informed me, was a criminal
and had been arrested for robbery. I remember the boy. He
dressed better than the rest of us, and although he attached
himself to our gang he was never a fully accepted member.
When we planned mischief he joined us, but if we became
romantic and chased around town hanging May baskets and
ringing the doorbells of our youthful sweethearts he lost
interest.

Finally my dear old grandfather lost his temper and
went entirely outside his part. My mother, having exhausted
her patience, appealed to him to stop my "running with bad
boys." Thereupon he worked himself into a rage such as I
had never seen him in before, and threatened: "I'll whip
you within an inch of your life." As a matter of fact, I do
not think Grandfather Worden would have ever volun-
tarily hurt a fly.

It ended in my being locked in a room upstairs. There I
nursed my resentment until I decided to run away, go West
and seek my fortune. I dropped out the window and started
up Landis Avenue, intending to leave my cruel family forever. At Third or Fourth Street I saw some boys I knew
playing ball and stopped to watch them. Soon I could not
resist the temptation to join the game. It must have been a
long game, for when it was over I had forgotten all about

my troubles and the fact that I was running away. I walked nearly home before I recollected the quarrel with Grandfather. My mother was so thankful to get me back that she said nothing about the escape, and Grandfather made no motion to punish me.

6

During the summer we visited Uncle Leander at Ancora. Grandfather, my mother and I traveled via a narrow-gauge railroad into the scrubby wilds of New Jersey. En route Grandfather gave an exhibition of that penny pinching which had turned the few hundred dollars he received when leaving the Community into a comfortable competence. On the train he told me to "scrunch down" in the far side of his seat. Then, when the conductor pointed at me, Grandfather waved his hand nonchalantly in my direction saying, "Oh, the baby." The conductor passed on. I was outraged and took him to task for calling me a baby. His answer has been one of the classics of our family legends: "Pshaw! I'd be willing to be called a monkey if I could ride free!" To do him justice, his ethics regarding railroad companies were the popular ethics in the middle of the nineteenth century.

We arrived at the Ancora depot as the sun was setting. There were no houses in sight; only the depot. Uncle Leander lived two or three miles away, the road running through dense woods. During that walk my grandfather's assumption of courage seemed hollow even to a boy. I remember that he brandished his cane and told my mother, "If robbers should come, I would strike them down with this." Fortunately, we met no robbers, and arrived safely at Uncle Leander's. His was a large, rambling farmhouse. After supper we sat around a cheerful open fire and my elders gossiped about Worden relatives scattered over many states.

I found living conditions at Uncle Leander's farm disconcertingly primitive and was glad to get back to the cottage on Landis Avenue. Vineland seemed another homeland, a sort of conquered territory from which I had driven the bogies of fear.

Chapter III

The Barn Fire

I

EARLY in the fall we returned to Oneida. I was feeling bumptious. I always supposed that "bumptious" was one of those Community words which had their obscure origin somewhere back in early nineteenth-century New England, but I find it in the dictionary defined as "conceited; pushing." I was both, and feeling iconoclastic as well. I not only looked forward to showing my old companions a few things about fighting as "world's boys" fought, but I intended to shame them out of the turn-the-other-cheek code of ethics; also, remembering our slavish Children's House respect for grown folks, I saw myself assuming the role of a David and defying some adult Goliath like Papa Kelly or Mr. Hamilton. I was especially eager to exploit my love affair with Marion. I had discovered the female of the species and, having in mind the half-smothered ferment of curiosity regarding sex which prevailed among the boys when I left Oneida, a ferment rendered ingrowing by the ridicule heaped upon anyone showing evidence of partiality toward a girl, I expected to dazzle them with my sophistication.

Once back at Oneida, realization proved not at all equal to anticipation; I was disappointed. My inflated ego found little on which to feed. Earl and Chet's parents had moved to a village a few miles away, and their gang, which I had hoped to rejoin on a new basis of equality, had disbanded.

Then, the Noyes guardians, owing probably to vainglorious exhibitions of worldliness on my part, forbade my brothers to play with me; and to complete my disillusionment I discovered that the companions left to me were either not greatly impressed by my Vineland attainments or were too much impressed. I was neither fish, flesh nor fowl. There was no admiring audience for my brave exploits and the danger of isolation soon led me to modify my ambitious program of toughness.

I do not mean that I returned to the Children's House psychology; those simple ideas of conduct and human relations were gone. What I had acquired was an exaggerated respect for physical force and a grim recognition of the limiting possibilities of Community principles and training. My ideas were still revolutionary, but desire for companionship was too strong to let me remain for any length of time offensively worldly-wise or truculent.

Unquestionably, I added yeast to the secularizing ferment already in progress among the Community children, but for myself the old environment and, even more, impingement of the old economic and social problems reduced the tempo of my campaign and the temperature, so to speak, of my ego. I had not been at home long before the old negative psychology began to encroach on my newly acquired self-confidence. In Vineland I had almost forgotten that social taint, but at Oneida, when I sought the company of outside boys, the ghost of illegitimacy rose again.

A resumption of financial worries also had a share in bringing me back to realities. My mother must have paid Grandfather for our keep in Vineland, since, when we returned home, I remember serious discussions as to whether the $371 were going to see us through the year. I think we were surrounded by people with similar worries, for suspicion was rife that the businesses were not doing well. My recollection of those autumn days pictures a gloomy Mansion House. I particularly recall evenings with my mother when we seemed very much alone in the world, and the wind roaring in the Quadrangle outside our windows sounded sinister and hostile.

2

Late in the month of October, the Community was startled by a midnight fire in the printing office down at the Arcade. It was extinguished by a watchman without serious damage, but it left a cloud of apprehensiveness hanging over us. Oil-soaked rags indicated that the fire was of incendiary origin.

In the days that followed, the most alarming and absurd rumors were credited. Callers brought to our room their fears that the Mansion House would be attacked next. I was proud of my mother. She maintained a quiet confidence, mixing advice to trust in God with heartening assertions of her belief that the menfolks were fully capable of protecting the buildings and would soon catch the firebug.

There was, nevertheless, even in her self-reliant cheerfulness an element of grimness that could not escape my anxious solicitude. I spent more of my time with her than ever before. For many months my mother had met the problems forced upon her by the breakup with a practical optimism. Neither her words nor her actions had suggested, to me at least, discouragement or even stoicism. She often said, "We have a good home, we have each other, and what is most important, we all have good health. God is good to us." Now, however, this new danger brought to the surface whatever of pessimism had lain buried in her consciousness.

I sensed this. I think that during those autumn days of 1881, my mother and I tried to conceal from each other our real feelings by little dramatic exhibitions of cheerfulness. She played lively tunes on the piano and sang the liveliest songs. On my side, I remember rushing in to her one evening and announcing with exaggerated enthusiasm a one cent per hour raise of my pay at the carpenter shop. We certainly pooled whatever optimism we had and it carried us, with reasonable morale, through the period which I have always reckoned as the low point, the emotional nadir, of my life.

As weeks passed by without discovery of the Arcade incendiary, there settled on the entire Community group a feeling of impending disaster. The number of watchmen on the premises was doubled. When men, even our strongest men, discussed the fire, there was an ominous note in their well-meant assurances. Memory is apt to be pictorial and my memory asserts that November, 1881, was a dismal succession of dark, rainy days, low-hanging clouds and thunderstorms. This picture may be only a reflection of the gloom in my soul.

And then came the catastrophe. One night my dreams were invaded by a cry, a man somewhere in the darkness yelling, "Fi-er! Fi-er!" Once awake, the cry sounded even more terrifying as it grew fainter and fainter in the distance. When the lamp in our room was lighted, I saw my mother dressing feverishly. She told me to dress, but to stay with Stella while she found out where the fire was. I shall never forget the ghastly terror of those minutes—they seemed like hours—while, alone with Stella, I awaited my mother's return. The accumulated apprehensiveness of the weeks just past was transmuted into horror.

It turned out that the fire was in the horse barn. We were greatly relieved, but I remembered that the burning barn stood just across the road and not more than a hundred yards from the Mansion House. My mother dressed Stella; not until then would she permit me to go to the front of the building, where I could see the fire.

It was a spectacular blaze, a huge barn filled to the roof with hay and all on fire at once. I was not allowed to go nearer than the North Lawn. From there, with other boys, I watched the roof fall in, a terrifying roar, and then a great column of fiery sparks rushing far up into the darkness. The spectacle was so gorgeous that, being boys, we at times lost all sense of disaster and went wild with excitement over each outburst of soaring flames.

Between the crashes we talked of the poor horses and were sickened by the thought of their agonies. We knew most of them by name.

Holton wandered restlessly among the crowd repeating the question:

"Don't you hope they saved Barnard and Prince?" (These were two huge bay-colored Clydesdales we all loved.)

And I heard Grosvenor anxiously asking someone:

"Was Judy saved?"

Whatever joy we found in the spectacle was gone when Ransom, coming out of the darkness, reported:

"Only two horses rescued and one of those, Jenny Snow, badly burned."

Circulating among the crowd we learned that another fire was discovered at the fruit-house—Arcade—just before flames appeared in the barn. Pat Maloney, our watchman, was the hero of this smaller blaze and he had a lacerated hand to prove his heroism. He told his story over and over. Pat was greatly, and it almost seemed permanently, excited. When he lost his men listeners, he was glad to repeat the tale to an audience of admiring boys. He told how he smelled smoke, and all the details of his fire fighting, and then when he had the Arcade fire out, how he looked up and, "By God, the whole barn was on fire."

For years thereafter November 9th, "when the horse barn burned," was a sinister date with all of us.

3

Whether I went to bed again that night I do not know. All I remember is a cold gray dawn, the smoldering ruin, and a pervasive smell of burnt horseflesh; twenty-seven horses were burned. The incendiary, with a fiendish determination to make destruction certain, started the fire in a chute which communicated with the hayloft above. There never was a chance of saving the barn and Pat nearly lost his life trying to rescue horses. I picked my way among the smoldering heaps of debris and dead horses in that part of the ruins where the flames had been extinguished. All the world and the future smelled of destruction—of charred wood and burnt flesh.

To my surprise and lasting admiration, our men appeared neither alarmed nor discouraged. They went about cleaning away the wreckage with the most matter-of-fact efficiency, and I heard them discussing, cheerfully, plans for a new barn and the hiring of necessary horses until such time as more could be bought. Their spirit told me of the difference between a man and a boy. Further, as I recall now the calm courage with which most of those men met that disaster, I think I know more about how the Oneida Community survived its many economic difficulties and the savage attacks by press, pulpit and public opinion for more than thirty years.

When, a little later, Dick, Eugene and I foregathered in

the shanty, which we had not occupied for some time, the odor of charred flesh still lingered in our nostrils. Eugene shook his head hopelessly:

"I tell you, there is an enemy of the Community hiding somewhere in the neighborhood and he is determined to ruin us."

Other boys joined us and Dorr reported a suspicion that Pat Maloney set the fire:

"They say that he talks too much about it and tries to explain too much where he was all the while."

We boys talked ourselves into a blue funk and then talked ourselves out of it. We agreed that if the Mansion House burned down, we could live in our shanty and, planning how it could be enlarged to hold our families, we arrived at a constructive state of mind. By the time that council adjourned, we were filled with enthusiasm for starting the battle of life. I remember Dick rolling up his sleeve and telling me to "feel of that"; "that" being his biceps. He closed his mouth tight and gave his head one of those jerky nods which always suggested that, after much thought, Dick had arrived at a firm conclusion. He said:

"You know, we are really almost as strong as the men; we can work with them."

Oddly enough, it was I who first went to work with the men. While the fire was still smoldering, Uncle Abram, Fred Marks and other Community men began measuring the ruins and figuring on the materials for a new barn. A few days later carloads of lumber arrived on the railroad siding and a flock of carpenters I had never seen before appeared on the job. It was like a war enthusiasm. With the aid of Uncle Abram, I persuaded my mother to let me leave school and be the workmen's errand boy. For several weeks I worked ten hours a day on the barn, the same as the men.

I climbed ladders, walked dizzy beams, slid down studding, carrying hammers, nails and saws to the carpenters. For the first time I got close to the rough life of physical toil. I enjoyed it with a vivid feeling of helping to create and a mounting desire to grow older as fast as possible so that I could do things like the men around me.

4

They caught the firebug. His was a queer story. He was a young man in his early thirties, who, having been brought to the Community when a child and reared in its isolation, was suddenly flung, like the rest of us, into a world he knew little about. He was vain and empty-headed. The new liberty meant to him liberty to dress foppishly, drive a span of black horses which he rented from the company, and with these two advantages break into outside society. In this he was temporarily successful. A rather handsome but evidently gold-digging type of young woman in the village of Oneida became engaged to him, and I think they were married. She had evidently heard the local tales about the wealth of the Community and, between these stories and the fine clothes and the horses, she believed this young man to be rich.

The black horses were his undoing. As a result of trying to keep up a style far beyond his means, he soon found himself in financial difficulties; and when Mr. Kellogg refused to let him rent the horses, his bubble burst and his ladylove left him. His crime was no sudden explosion of rage. Social disaster evidently brought on a season of brooding followed by a monomania for revenge. He carefully planned one fire, and when that failed he laid more ambitious plans, including an ingenious scheme of escape, which failed. He served seven years in the penitentiary.

Whether this young man was a case of congenital abnormality or whether his actions could be laid at least partially to the sudden plunge from a cloistered communism into the glare of worldly possibilities would be an interesting speculation for psychologists. I heard both theories discussed at the time. His father, who brought him as a child to the Community, was himself expelled after a short stay because he was found to be abnormal.

As I look back on that period of my life, it seems to me that the barn fire cleared the atmosphere of Oneida as a thunderstorm at the end of a rainy spell sometimes clears up the weather. Between the time of the burning of the horse barn and my trip to Niagara Falls the following spring, my memories are of a busy Community, whose members, emerging from the nervousness caused by our fire scare, had, through some kind of reverse suggestion, shaken off much of the questioning timidity which marked the first months of the new social order.

Chapter IV

Readjustments

I

JOINT-STOCK proved a disappointment to the men who had been most instrumental in breaking up the Community. Many of them, in the old days, had held prominent positions and had exercised a considerable influence on Community affairs. Their attacks on Father Noyes had been aimed, as I said before, not so much at destroying communism as obtaining for themselves a share in the management. Now they discovered that a large majority of the stockholders were loyal to Father Noyes. He was still their leader, and within a year the former malcontents found themselves entirely outside the area of power and policy-making.

The first board of directors was a typical Community compromise. The political affiliations of stockholders had not been put to the test of an election and the old "spirit of agreement" manifested itself in a division of directorships which recognized personalities rather than any theoretical stock representation. Of the nine directors, four were Noyesites, three were Townerites, and two belonged to a small group which, during the struggle over dissolution, had played a useful part as liaison between the contending forces.

The initial board was, however, a last gesture from the past, an exhibition of reasonableness made before the realities of money-power had penetrated communistic souls. One year of joint-stock changed all this. By the time the next annual election came around the Community had sensed the political possibilities of stockownership and when the votes were counted on January 19, 1882, it was found that the Noyes party had six directors, the Towner two and the middle party one.

James W. Towner, whom I knew in later life, was shrewd and inclined to political scheming, but endowed, it always seemed to me, with a singular dignity of soul. In 1882 he evidently saw the handwriting on the wall. Having no taste for the leadership of a hopeless, nagging opposition, he decided to leave and before the end of that year he led an exodus of fifty or sixty of his relatives and friends to southern California. There they bought land when California land was cheap and most of them lived in comfortable circumstances for the rest of their lives. Mr. Towner himself became a prominent judge of the county court.

Thus, the quarrel among our elders was over, at least for the duration of my father's life. His patriarchal headship was gone, but the corporate organization created as a substitute for communism, with its share-holding and share-voting, quite unexpectedly made him more absolute than ever. From 1882 until his death in 1886 there existed only one effective party. The officers and most of the directors of the company were of his selection, and any important move, whether business or social, always awaited his sanction. Sometimes he summoned to the Stone Cottage at Niagara, for consultation, one or another of his representatives on the board of directors. Even men of the opposing party were occasionally invited to visit him and, so strong were the habits of a lifetime, that they went, I think gladly. In general, however, his views were conveyed to the Oneida management by letters.

2

A pleasing result of this political truce was the passing away of partisanship among the younger generation. So far as we could see, the administrative machinery which governed this new organization was fixed and its management came to interest us less than did the restraints put upon us by its managers. We were now free to regard all officials of the company as the common enemies of boys. Did not those graybeards make rules which limited enterprise, and were they not continually interfering with our sports? We must not climb trees on the lawn, or play ball except in the farther field. If we opened a small hole in the hedge for our sleds to pass through, the president and secretary of the company rushed down the hill to forbid us. When we played "Escape" in the cellar or climbed out through an attic ventilator onto the tin roof of the Mansion House, Gaylord Reeves, its ubiquitous janitor, chased us. There was, of course, no Children's House and no Papa Kelly in immediate control, but Mr. Reeves and the "officers of the company" proved more lynx-eyed than he had been. Broken windowpanes or other damage to property brought demands for cash payments in place of the criticisms of former days.

In this altered environment we returned to our group life of play and school and work. We adventured on a more ambitious scale as befitted older boys. I had a feeling that I was growing older very fast. If the storm which swept away my past left no permanent scars, it certainly made new creases in my brain and some of them very deep. My respect for grown folks, as grown folks, was gone. My belief in the impeccable lives and spiritual authority of all Community men and women had been shattered, first by their own charges and countercharges against each other, then by the jibes of Outsiders with whom we now associated freely, and finally by my own more critical observation of their conduct.

3

This crumbling of authoritative sanctions left me doubting and for a time bewildered. Was my father just an insane fanatic, as his enemies asserted? Was his belief in the "second coming of Christ" and "salvation from sin," his claim of special "inspiration" through Paul and members of the Primitive Church—were all these only the vagaries of a disordered mind? My mother said no. Vehemently, she defended him; scathingly, she characterized his critics:

"Mr. A. says that? He was always shallow and pleasure-seeking. . . . G. R. S.? Oh! He was, even in the Community, inclined to atheism."

And at another time: "Fred L. is just insincere. He knows better. He is trying to curry favor with Mr. Noyes's enemies."

The most serious questionings that beset me had to do with my own birth. Could it be that the finger of scorn which at times was pointed at me had a substantial basis in reality? Was the Community wrong, and were children born outside of marriage not merely to be looked at askance by the Christian world, but, in very fact, morally illegitimate?

On the other side, my self-protective instinct is strong, and this stimulated active mental gymnastics aimed at rescuing my self-respect. It is my nature to scramble vigorously out of any Slough of Despond in which I may have stumbled or been pushed. The shock of the breakup still colored my emotions; there still haunted my consciousness a feeling best described as a plant pulled up by the roots, but I do not think that I allowed myself to be really unhappy for any length of time.

I was genuinely religious. I may have become uncertain about the theological soundness of the Community religion, but this could not have been a disturbing factor at the age of eleven. I believed in God and Christ and the hereafter, and nothing had happened to threaten the validity of those beliefs. The knowledge that obscure theories and theologies had attacked our theories and theologies which themselves had been, for me, equally obscure, affected me little. The fact is that I had always regarded "salvation from sin" as an attribute—perhaps I should say a prerogative—of grown folks rather than children; also the exact bearing of the "second coming of Christ" had on my own life was vague in my mind. As for Father Noyes's "inspiration," that might still be true; my mother thought it was.

4

After all, we were boys. We roamed more widely than ever and found much compensation for theoretical troubles in exploring the limits of our new freedom. We made the acquaintance of neighboring farmers who let us ride on their wagons and watch them at milking time. They even let us try our hands at milking. Then we discovered two cheese factories, and ingratiated ourselves with Mr. Bullock, the cheese-factory man, in order that we might hang around his ill-smelling establishment until the gorgeous yellow cheeses were turned out of the cylinder.

Mr. Bullock had a dark, saturnine face, with bushy eyebrows and a savage black mustache. He swore loudly and always wore rubber boots. There was a story that once, having forgotten the partitions between the cheeses, he found himself in possession of a great, round, yellow column of the soft substance, fifteen feet long. This stuck in the cylinder.

Over at Willow Place Pond we watched the ice being cut and helped float long rafts to the loading platform. I remember Dick's stepfather discovering us on the pond. He called to Dick:

"What are you doing here? You know better than to go on the ice without permission."

As Dick walked slowly toward him, Uncle Frank asked me pointedly:

"Does your mother know you are here?"

He was my uncle by marriage, but I said to myself (not to him, I am sure; the grown folks tradition was still too strong for that), "He is not my boss." Probably I made a motion as though to walk off the ice, but returned as soon as Uncle Frank was gone.

5

With Uncle Abram my relation was far different. He administered punishments which I have never forgotten and he thereby rebuilt my respect for authority. My mother was too maternally weak to establish such discipline as my head-strong pursuit of boyish objectives demanded. When she became worried over the frequency with which I brought home wet feet, I was able to silence her protests with the assertion, "I couldn't help it; the ice broke." In despair, she finally called in Uncle Abram who, taking me aside, ordered, with very significant emphasis:

"Pierrepont, from now on keep away from dangerous places in the ice; don't get your feet wet."

After that I kept away from the dangerous holes in the ice for a long time. Then one winter's day a stretch of that thin clear ice we called hickory ice brought disaster. We boys were trying to see who could skate last over this ice and I forgot all about Uncle Abram's warning. Once more I started across it. Suddenly, my skate caught in a crack; I stumbled; my feet went up in the air, and I sat down hard. All that could be seen above the ice were my head and feet.

When I got home I was, of course, very wet, so I sneaked down to the Turkish bath, hoping my mother would not see me. Someone must have told her of my mishap and she, in turn, must have sent word to Uncle Abram. Presently, he appeared in the bathroom. Very severely he said:

"When you are through with your bath, come to my room."

I suspected what this meant and delayed my bathing as long as possible. When I arrived at Uncle Abram's room in the North Tower, my mother was there; also two long red whips cut from a certain bush on the lawn. Uncle Abram said:

"Pierrepont, do you remember what I told you about getting wet? Take off your coat!"

That was an old-fashioned whipping. When the first whip had been broken so many times that it was too short for use, Uncle Abram reached for the other. By this time my howlings had softened the heart of my mother. She implored:

"Isn't that enough, Abram?"

But Uncle Abram brushed her aside, saying sternly:

"Don't interfere, Harriet."

Then he broke the second whip on my back and shoulders.

Modern educators may take exception to that whipping. I am myself convinced that the two or three severe punishments administered to me by Uncle Abram between the ages of eleven and thirteen not only fitted the occasions, but were invaluable for my education. Memory assures me that a boy of that age, when pressed by desire or urged to adventure by other boys, has very little respect for mild measures, but immense respect for physical pain. Uncle Abram taught me that there were in life positive limitations.

Chapter V

My Father Again

I

I HAVE no recollection of the negotiations which resulted in my visit to Niagara Falls in 1882. Whether my aunt Harriet Skinner, whose affection for me was not, I feel sure, always regarded by my father as "inspired," interceded for me, or whether he was determined to treat all his children impartially, I never knew. I do remember, however, that all my brothers and several cousins visited Niagara before I did.

The Stone Cottage, my father's new home, stood on a terraced bluff not far from the great gorge and overlooked both American and Canadian falls. It was an attractive Gothic house, built massively of stone, with a veranda on three sides. A huge stone barn was attached to the house by a long, low shed, also of stone. The original owner was an Englishman who evidently cherished aristocratic or artistic ambitions, for the driveway encircled a garden, in the center of which stood an ornamental fountain, then dry, surrounded by the remains of a concrete basin which must have once held water. Five acres of orchard and garden surrounded the house.

I was to stay there three weeks. Two memories of quite different character have always associated themselves with my first visit to the Stone Cottage. One recalls my father standing beside me on the veranda with the mighty cataract in full view and its all-pervading roar in my ears, and saying with great solemnity, "We are living near Nature's greatest exhibition of power." The other is a memory of Dick Brett, the handyman about the place. I had not been there an hour before he took me to the orchard and showed me a bluebird's nest in which were four eggs.

Dick Brett was a tall, rawboned youth of nineteen or twenty, the son of a Canadian backwoodsman with whom my father had spent the months at Strathroy before the Stone Cottage was bought for his permanent residence. The entire Brett family, including two or three boys and at least five girls, had followed my father from Strathroy to Niagara and were living in a cottage on the far side of the immense Bush estate, where they looked almost directly down on the Canadian falls.

Mimie Brett, about whose alluring femininity my brothers had woven much colorful romance, had figured prominently in my pleasurable anticipation of that visit. The possibilities of sex were evidently being taken with increasing seriousness by all of us. The story of Humphrey's puppy-love affair with Mimie had encountered at Oneida, not ridicule, as would have been its fate in earlier years, but only the envy of boys not privileged to visit Niagara Falls. I remember waiting impatiently for Mimie to visit the Stone Cottage, or for someone to take me over to the Bretts'.

The older girls, Emily and Carrie, came but were too old to be interesting. Twelve-year-old romanticism in general floats above physical sex. Perhaps a psychoanalyst would insist that biological urgings were behind my enthusiasm for the twelve-year-old Mimie Brett, but, if so, memory assures me that such enticement was not reinforced by any admixture of expectation. In fact, I am not sure but that my

anxiety to meet the young lady was stimulated to a considerable extent by a spirit of competition with Humphrey.
When I finally became acquainted with Mimie, I discovered
that she had really been smitten with my brother and was
not particularly impressed by me. If I am not mistaken, I
soon dropped down to her younger sister—I have forgotten
her name—perhaps it was Lois.

2

It is not, however, the Bretts but my father who remains the outstanding figure in my memory of that visit.
When I recall that my anticipations of Niagara had, in the
main, surrounded the much-advertised cataract and Mimie
Brett, I think this a tribute to his personality. For the first
time I made his acquaintance as a man.

I listened with genuine interest to the "home talks" he
delivered every evening to the assembled family and other
old Community members who had taken up their residence
in the neighborhood. Those evening meetings were much
like the old evening meetings in the Big Hall at Oneida, except that home surroundings and the smaller gatherings
made their atmosphere less formal. My father would sit with
eyes closed and forehead wrinkling for a long time before
he spoke, and at frequent intervals would relapse into a similar silence during which he appeared to be seeking "inspiration" for further words. He had one peculiar habit that followed him through all his life. When meditating deeply, he
rubbed his thumb so forcefully against a certain spot on his
vest that the cloth was soon worn through, and even leather
patches sewed on that spot needed frequent replacements.

He laid emphasis, as I remember it, chiefly on not let-
ting a worldly spirit get into our hearts. I was surprised that

the catastrophe at Oneida had not changed his outlook. He seemed strong in his faith and just as sure as ever that he had acted and was still commissioned to act as an agent of the heavenly powers. From that day to this, the founding of the Oneida Community has been closely associated in my mind with some spiritual—perhaps I should say mystical—mandate which my father neither could nor desired to resist. There was about him an unmistakable and somewhat unexpected air of spiritual assurance.

Those three weeks rebuilt in me much of the old respect and even reverence for my father, which had been sadly tarnished by the events of the previous two years. He seemed still the prophet of Perfectionism. In his presence the disagreeable things I had heard from his critics temporarily lost their effect. He seemed a great hero and his lifework an epic. I remember his taking me by the hand and saying, "The Oneida Community was planned by the heavenly powers, and still has a wonderful future"; and I remember a feeling that I wanted to help in some way. I think I was most impressed by my father's moral courage.

He had undoubtedly heard of my accession of worldliness, and probably distrusted my Cook ancestry, but this did not preclude exhibitions of affection on his part. I remember his taking me on his lap, big as I was, and fondling me as any loving father might; and this gave me great joy in spite of the aversion a boy feels for being petted. Not that he ever accepted me as a hundred per cent Noyes. I have been told that in his younger days, when he was building his association of Perfectionists, he brooked no opposition and no equals, and I have a suspicion that, remembering my mother's rather independent nature, he looked at me with the subconscious hostility an aging man often feels toward a son

who seems likely to insist on appraising the past for himself
and rejecting, or at least neglecting, the weight of his
authority.

3

On his lighter side, I was surprised to discover that this
prophet of spiritual perfection had a keen sense of humor.
(As a boy I had assumed that anything spiritual must be
solemn.) He saw the amusing side of many quite trivial
incidents, and I found his semisilent laughs, which shook
his whole body, very contagious. I remember his favorite
story, told with a certain naïve diffidence, as though he might
be going too near the profane; always, however, he ended
with an explosion of that side-shaking chuckle:

Attending one of the little backwoods schools of the last cen-
tury was an overgrown lout who could not master the alphabet.
His teacher worked hard to get him over this hurdle, and finally
thought she had driven a few letters into his thick head. So con-
fident of this was she that when the trustees visited the school she
put him on exhibition. Pointing to a letter, she asked:
"James, what letter is that?"
James looked blankly at the blackboard. The teacher urged
him:
"You know that letter, James."
But the longer she urged the redder and more embarrassed
James became. Finally the teacher gave up, exclaiming disgustedly:
"You ought to know! Now remember, that is A!"
Whereupon the lout broke forth impulsively, "Je-e-sus Christ,
is that A?"

Father always pushed forward his whopper-jaw and
dragged out the first words in imitation of a stupid bumpkin.
One day he took me down by the gorge to get a better
view of the falls. It happened that before I left home we
boys had a rage for walking on fences, and along the rim of

the Niagara gorge there ran a stone wall with a wide coping.
My nerves have never been greatly impressed by height, and
this wall looked like a perfect place to walk a fence.

I heard my father tell the story many times. He "looked
around and was petrified" to see me walking on the wall.
He dared not say anything, or show alarm, but sidled up to
me and when near enough dragged me down. Naturally I
did not understand his action. The wall was much wider
than the fences on which I was accustomed to walk, and
the danger seemed a figment of his imagination. I also remember that when he took me to Table Rock (which has
since then fallen into the gorge) he could not bear to have
me lean over the edge of the cliff. He held on to my coat,
and shortened my visit to Table Rock as much as he could.
I thought him physically timid, but later, when I myself
became a father, I was inclined to modify this opinion.

There were many relatives and friends living or visiting at the Stone Cottage, but I remember only Mr. Pitt, Mr.
Cragin and Aunt Harriet Skinner. Mr. Pitt seemed just a
little out of place in this new environment. In the old days
at Oneida, when he descended the stairs and emerged majesti-
cally on the South Walk, I could accept him as a sort of
lay figure in the furnishings of the Community's spiritual
center: a superbly silent man, but probably a helpful companion to my father in his moments of deepest thinking.
Now, however, when my father spent much of his time outdoors, talked familiarly with the neighbors and laughed at
children's pranks, I could not but feel that Mr. Pitt's great
blue eyes must watch his disproportionate secular activities
regretfully, perhaps with the same furtive accusation we
boys had always felt when he looked at us. What I am trying to express is a vague feeling that Mr. Pitt, with his great

head, long white beard and apostolic mien, seemed at Niagara Falls an artificial transplant from the sanctified past.

On the other hand, Mr. Cragin, who was one of the original members of the Community, appeared to be not only my father's practical man Friday, but more his confidant than Mr. Pitt. He evidently joined him in a cheerful acceptance of the new order. He was very friendly to me. He talked to me of simple things, but never lost a chance to magnify my father. I remember his saying with great earnestness, "Your father is a greater man than ever."

My chief memory of Aunt Harriet Skinner is of her evident anxiety that I make a good impression on my father. When he and I were together she hovered near. If I gave an unconscious exhibition of the "Cook spirit," she tried to put an innocent interpretation upon my actions. She was still a stalwart Perfectionist and communist, but the liberal atmosphere of Niagara Falls had greatly humanized her.

Chapter VI

Family Relations

I

W HEN I returned to Oneida I found our family increased by the addition of my half brother Ormond.
He was seven years my senior and, as I mentioned before,
his father was Uncle Abram. During the turbulent years
of 1879 and 1880, he had been sent to a boys' school at New
Preston, Connecticut, and after the breakup he was continued there by the directors of the new company.

I assume that Ormond was sent to that school as a
"problem" at a time when more serious problems were agitating our elders and making any patient attempt at solution
impossible. I have never been able, however, to discover why
a private-property-conscious board of directors kept him
there at the company's expense after joint-stock. They may
have shrunk from a return of the "bad boy" of the Children's House or—as I prefer to believe—those sincerely religious men, learning that the New Preston influence was
turning Ormond's ambition toward religion, decided, as they
might have decided in the old days, that an expense which
promised such spiritual profits was quite worthwhile.

As a matter of fact, Ormond came back from New
Preston very religious. My memory, however, takes greater
account of the incredible number of neckties he brought,
given him by the son of a Cabinet officer and others of his
wealthy fellow students. There were neckties of every color;

all of the broad Ascot style fashionable during the 1870's.

Hitherto I had known little of this half brother. Now he attracted me as a novelty, but his religious fervor bored me, and the fact that he joined Mrs. Bushnell's Bible class soon alienated my approval. The Bible class also led to serious arguments between him and my mother. Mrs. Bushnell had been, during early Community days, an ardent believer in John Humphrey Noyes's communism, but she turned squarely around at the breakup and her Bible class was a forum for vituperation against him. My mother would have none of her.

Ormond's mischievous nature could not be completely sublimated by religious enthusiasm. After the debacle which engulfed my father's position as primate, a considerable group took up spiritualism and they succeeded in interesting my mother. They made the mistake of inviting Ormond to a séance in our rooms. The medium presented the spirit of George Noyes, my father's dead brother, and offered a chance for questioning. Aunt Elizabeth Hawley, who in 1837 passed a certain confidential letter to Theophilus Gates, the publication of which in his magazine, the *Battle Axe*, is said to have precipitated my father's most radical break with society, took exception to the "communication" from him.

She asked, "Is this George Noyes?"

The table tipped, "Yes."

Aunt Elizabeth exclaimed, "I don't believe it is George Noyes!"

The table tipped, "Yes, it is."

After the séance, Ormond shocked my mother by telling her that he tipped the table with his foot.

2

Ormond was really a lonesome soul. He formed a great
affection for my brother Holton, and I am saddened when
I remember that at times I competed with him for Holton's
interest on evenings when Ormond had invited him to visit
our rooms. We lived in the Ultima Thule end of the south
wing. I am sure that on many occasions Ormond and I associated fraternally, but I have never ceased, in my adult years,
to regret that I did not appreciate his loneliness and act more
the part of an affectionate brother to him. My mother
showed him all the tenderness a mother feels toward an un-
appreciated child; she yearned over him.

Uncle Abram visited us often and tried, I am sure, to
be a loving father to Ormond, but his greater affection for
me could not be concealed. My mother recognized it and I
once heard her say to Uncle Abram, "You must love
Ormond; he needs you."

3

During those years my mother often took Stella and me
on visiting expeditions among the Worden and Cook relatives, of whom there were many in central New York. In
addition to her natural sociability there was, deep down in
her nature, a family clannishness which some laid to the
Worden and others to the Cook branch of her ancestry.
From whatever source this came, she certainly had a passion
for visiting relatives. We usually drove with a horse and
buggy—once I remember a cutter—on a zigzag itinerary
which took us over much of the country between Oneida and
Syracuse. First we would head for Canaseraga to call on
Kitty Sackett.

I had pictured Kitty as a pretty girl, and was correspondingly disappointed when we were ushered into a smelly
parlor by a thin, middle-aged woman, whose arid personality
and washed-out appearance fitted very poorly with her
name; so it seemed to me. She appeared glad to see my
mother. They talked for a long time about people of whom
I had never heard and my mother helped her get supper.
It was all so dull I was glad we were to stay there only one
night.

On the morrow we drove over the hills to Chittenango.
The beautiful Lily Barnes, who had once visited Oneida with
Uncle Josiah Cook and Aunt Christina, was living at the
hotel in Chittenango. She was not exactly a relative, but an
adopted daughter of that successful but somewhat dissolute
Buffalo lawyer, who supported her and her mother in what
Chittenango folks considered luxury.

We did not stop long in Chittenango, but drove on
into the hills toward Uncle Peter Groosebeck's farm. I think
we expected to visit with Uncle Peter and Aunt Susan for
a week, but by the fifth day the ruction between that bulky,
domineering aunt and my five-year-old sister Stella became
so unbearable to my mother that she hastened our departure.

Uncle Peter had a large farm and was rated a successful farmer. He looked as though his success had been the result of a life of hard work. His back was bent, his face
gnarled and grim; but I found him a friendly old fellow.
During all my visit he went about his work as usual, and
with few words showed me how I could help. I enjoyed
life on the farm; it was all so different. I rode on great loads
of hay, and in the barn helped the hired man shove the
dangling fork deep into the hay to be lifted. I fed the
chickens, hunted eggs, ran errands. There was at the far side
of the farm an extensive wood lot where I spent an entire

day with Uncle Peter cording up the wood he and his man sawed and split.

Aunt Susan Groosebeck was, as I have intimated, a very positive, not to say commanding, woman. She ran the house and everyone in it, including Uncle Peter—when he was there. Outdoors he was his own boss, but the moment he entered the house he became a vassal like the rest of us. Aunt Susan behaved decently to my mother because she was a visitor and a Cook. The old lady was immensely proud of her Cook ancestry.

Because Uncle Peter was deaf, she had acquired a habit of raising her voice, which added a savage quality to the scoldings and general tirades that burst upon us under the least provocation. She scolded Stella; she scolded Mother for her leniency with Stella; she often scolded Uncle Peter until he went to sleep in his chair.

I remember evenings when we were all assembled in the large living room, which served also as a dining room. There sat Aunt Susan, very straight and masterful, under the light of a hanging lamp, lecturing my mother on the bringing up of children. She never had any of her own. Uncle Peter, in the shadow and slumped far down in his chair, occasionally released a corner of his mouth from its task of retaining a large chaw of tobacco, in order to give my mother a quizzical smile which said plainly, "Pay no attention to her, Harriet! That's her way." If she turned her guns on him, he slumped a little deeper in his chair and usually maintained a grim silence. Occasionally, however, he would go back at her savagely—only a few words—and then leave the room before the exasperated Aunt Susan could get under way with a rejoinder.

For some reason she was nice to me, and I think my mother might have enjoyed her visit in spite of the old lady's tirades had it not been for the unaccountable spleen she showed toward Stella. I have forgotten the immediate cause of her antipathy. My impression is that it arose from no particular dereliction on the child's part, but was a complex such as some folks feel in regard to dogs and cats. She was just annoyed to have a child, with its unpredictable irregularities, loose around the house and always a threat to her immaculate housekeeping.

So we left our Groosebeck relatives sooner than we planned, quite to my disgust. I had become enamored of life on the farm. We drove by easy stages to Manlius Station (now Minoa), stopping at Fayetteville and Kirkville en route. I have forgotten the relatives we visited in those villages.

At Manlius we visited Charlie Worden's family. He was a blacksmith, and his two boys worked in the shop with him. Both Charlie and his wife Eliza were possessed of the old-fashioned spirit of hospitality. We all enjoyed our stay with them. I remember their snug little house on the main street; its rag carpets, black walnut furniture, wax flowers, and that odor I always associated with rag carpets and other fittings of outside homes.

The Community housekeeping must have been very thorough and more sanitary than was customary in 1870. I remember no disagreeable odors about the Mansion House except in the separate kitchen building, and I am sure that when I began visiting the Outside I was very sensitive to what seemed the "smelliness" of the houses. That was, for me, the greatest drawback to accompanying my mother on her explorations among the relatives.

Chapter VII

I Accept Fate

I

SURVEYING the memories of 1883 and 1884, I find myself affected by a curious feeling of disillusionment. Perhaps my aversion to dwelling upon this rather uninspiring chapter of my life is caused by the contrast between what seems to me now the drab spiritual quality of those years and the colorful childhood that went before. In the decade of the seventies our lives had been conditioned by proximity to an aggressively pursued ideal. No child could escape being profoundly affected by daily association with men and women who were eagerly and reverently trying to raise earthly living to the plane of the Primitive Church. In those years I did indeed enjoy an ascending fellowship. I lived in a society which was persistently, if fanatically, reaching upward to something beyond the material. Even Papa Kelly's daily Bible readings and Perfectionist preachments, though half understood by the youngest and boring to the oldest, turned our thoughts toward something greater than playground pleasures. Imagination, if not spiritually, was stimulated.

My bewildered alternations of depression and defiance immediately after the crash interest me, and the first years of struggle to adjust myself to a new world in which those about me no longer loved their neighbors as themselves were full of new discoveries, immature ambitions and minor tragedies that give them color in retrospect. It is my thirteenth and fourteenth years that seem, as compared with all that went before, bleak, a bleakness which extends even to our school. Mr. Warne had been able to idealize education for us, while Mr. Underwood, our new teacher, fed us, conscientiously, but unimaginatively, nothing but the pabulum to be found in textbooks. And yet I cannot consistently omit the account of those two years. They belong in this narrative and, after all, they were filled with very practical experiences which were to stand me in good stead later on.

2

Running through the memories of that period and conditioning all of them is my intimate approach to the toilers of the world. I became ambitious to be one of them. I longed to force recognition for myself by men whose efficiency and social completeness seemed immensely worthwhile.

By the end of 1882 I had progressed so far in carpenter shop technique that I was allowed to tend buzz saws and feed boards into the planer, which brings me two memories of painful experiences with machinery. Once or twice when I tried to force a water-swollen board through the crosscut saw, it jammed and suddenly shot back with great force. I was just tall enough so that the projectile always hit me in the pit of the stomach. I remember going out into the yard and sitting on a lumber pile with a ghastly feeling that my breath would never come back. I also remember being followed by a sympathetic but tough-minded carpenter who, when certain I was coming out of it all right, slapped my back good-naturedly with the humorous though hardly consoling suggestion. "It'll feel better when it gets done aching."

On another occasion, while slitting strips of wood, I reached over to pull one through and put my hand on the back of the rapidly revolving buzz saw. In those days the carpenters had a simple but effective method for sterilizing wounds. They took me over to the stove upon which was a gluepot kept always hot. One of them held me while another smeared the three lacerated fingers with hot glue. Then they wound a rag tightly around them. This sounds brutal, but it was really merciful. The hot glue destroyed incipient infection and kept air out of the wound. As a result, after the first excruciating pain, I heard no more from those fingers until they were well.

During the school term I worked only afternoons. It was then that, either on account of the pay I had attained, six cents per hour, which seemed very substantial, or the lure of sociability, Dick was attracted to the carpenter shop and I persuaded Uncle Abram to let him work with me. He was the same Dick of childhood days. Together as we worked we built air castles, in which he and I became boss carpenters.

I must not forget a triumph which encouraged our assumption of rapidly developing manhood. Eugene also worked at the carpenter shop. He was older, and much bigger than Dick and I. To relieve the boredom of work, he often bullied us as older boys will. When the men were not around, he would get one of us down on the floor and rub our ears, or would come up behind and slap us smartly with a stick. We endured this for a time, but finally took counsel as to some method of relief.

Near the center of the building was a trap door opening on the chute down which shavings were slid into the basement. To appreciate the anticipatory relish with which Dick and I contemplated our plan for revenge on Eugene, one should peep into that dark, dank basement, where the pyramid of shavings reached upward toward the trap door. Long serpentine wooden flumes led to sunken structures where old-fashioned turbine water wheels roared in the darkness and communicating gears ground out a peculiarly savage undulating refrain. The floor space was broken by many dark holes where unseen water gurgled and the walls of the basement were of jagged masonry. Altogether it was an eerie place in the minds of boys.

We decided—it was probably Dick's idea—that together we were stronger than Eugene. Having worked out every detail of our plan, we waited until he attacked one of us when the shavings hole was open. Instantly the other leaped on his back. Struggling desperately, we dragged him to the hole and in spite of his efforts and final protests, we shoved him, head first, down the slide. I think that Dick went down with him. The pile of soft shavings below insured that they would not be seriously hurt. Eugene did not trouble us any more.

To this day that old carpenter shop holds, for me, romantic associations. The three-story wooden building, now altered, is part of a greatly enlarged factory in which the Oneida Ltd. manufactures knives and knife blades. This old part was built by the early Community to take the place of the smaller mill in which Mr. Burt had sawed logs and ground grain. It stands exactly where his mill stood, astride a raceway along whose sides Dick and I trapped the muskrats that riddled its banks with their holes.

On the ground floor was a room for men who worked at the bench, and another room full of buzz saws, planing machines and lathes. On the next floor were stored reserve piles of matched flooring, clapboards and finished lumber. On the third floor, hardwood "tom-staves," special shapes, and all sorts of interesting half-made cabinets, pieces of furniture, and even boats.

Above this, the darkened attic offered a fascinating field

for boyish exploration. It was littered with forgotten experiments, machines with great wooden shives, and long timbers bent for some unknown purpose. Dick and I often went early to our work for the sake of odd "treasures" to be found in the attic. I remember scrambling hastily down from there when a rumble of machinery, in the room far below, announced that the time for work had come.

There is a certain window in the knife factory which looks down on the rushing waters of the tailrace. When I look out of that window today there arises before me a picture of Uncle Abram working at the bench while the buzz saws and other machinery hum and roar behind us, and I feel a little homesick in the present.

Chapter VIII

I Would Be a Carpenter

I

A LINE drawn to indicate the mental, cultural or, even more, the ambitional level of my life between the ages of twelve and fifteen would show a prolonged depression. I do not mean that my mind was less active or my ambition dormant. Both were changed in direction. Life had forced upon me a painfully realistic philosophy and, having as I thought finally got my bearings in the real world, I proceeded to devote my still immature mentality and all the strength of a rapidly growing body to the task of extricating myself from poverty and social humiliation.

By the fall of 1882 I had seized upon work, hard work, as the only weapon available for fighting those giants which the breakup had revealed standing threateningly in my path. I hoped that through work and the accumulation of experience I could rise to the position of journeyman carpenter and thus emerge from economic and social serfdom. For I knew that journeyman carpenters earned "twelve shillings" a day ($1.50), which seemed a substantial income. Boss carpenters who built complete houses earned two dollars a day, or even more. Secretly I aspired to becoming a boss carpenter.

Further, my association with workingmen suggested that if I proved my ability and willingness to endure hard labor I would gain their respect and could look forward to attaining social equality with men whom I admired and envied. They paid their way and asked no favors of anyone. Deep in my soul the words of Oren Morrison rankled, "You Community boys will never be able to make your way outside the Community." As a result, whenever I was assigned to Morrison as his assistant, I worked especially hard. Physically I gave myself no quarter, for I was determined that he should credit me with endurance and, in the end, competence.

I plunged into the struggle wholeheartedly and found a double reward in labor. Added to the joy of creation was the approval of those with whom I worked. When Frank Hyde and I completed the reshingling of a house or had given it a new outside covering of clapboards or had shored up a rotten foundation, the joy of creation was very real and when Uncle Abram praised my work I was happy.

One day Morrison and I were working on the side of a house where a torrid sun beat down relentlessly. Its heat was intensified by reflection from the bright clapboards and no breeze reached us. Suddenly everything turned black and I felt sick. Morrison helped me down the ladder. It was a near-sunstroke, but I felt amply repaid for the misery by hearing him say to Uncle Abram, "I told Pip not to work so hard; he's a good boy—a good boy, but he doesn't know when to quit." My social standing was surely moving up.

2

I found real pleasure in my association with the carpenters. As a rule I worked as assistant to Frank Hyde, a man of rough exterior but a really kind heart. He swore at me and made biting remarks if I was not on the job promptly at seven o'clock, but often when he thought I was tired he sent me on unimportant errands or in other ways eased my burdens.

Frank was a "character." He had no talent for fine cabinetmaking, hence was employed mostly on what he termed in self-derision "outside work." Often when he had by chance made a perfectly fitting joint—perhaps it was only a rough studding job—he would say to me, with a twinkle in his eye, "Pip, that's inside work." His quips and trenchant sayings, often acute generalizations, had a wide circulation among the workmen.

Frank was dramatic and declamatory. Often he would stop in the middle of a repair job and with a saw in one hand and the piece of lumber he had been sawing in the other, recite a bit of poetry. Frank was very much what horsemen would call "over on his knees." I can see him now, standing in front of me, with sprung legs wide apart and a soiled carpenter's apron hanging low between them. After an oratorical gesture with the hand holding the saw, he would ask, "Pip, have you ever heard—

> 'Three crows they sat upon a limb
> And they was black as crows could be.
> Said one old crow unto his mate
> Where shall we get some food to eat?
> There lies a horse on yonder plain
> That's by some cruel butcher slain.
> We'll perch upon his bare backbone
> And . . .' "

At this point he assumed a horrid expression, and turgidly hissed his words,

> " '. . . pick-his-eyes-out-one-by-one.' "

Then he would go back to work.

One day he surprised me by an invasion of Latin literature. He asked: "What does this mean, Pip?—*ingens hiterab-imus equod?*" Mr. Underwood had introduced me to some very elementary Latin with the aid of an interlined Latin reader full of *Dies ira! Dies illa!* but I really knew little more about the language than Frank did. Later I discovered a passage in Vergil which I think must have been the original of his quotation: *Cras ingens iterabimus aequor.* Where Frank Hyde came across that scrap of Latin I cannot imagine.

For some reason he took a fancy to me. Often I was invited to go home with him, and the evenings spent at his house are among the pleasant memories of those years. He lived in a neat little cottage at Oneida Castle. When the whistle blew at six o'clock we betook ourselves to a shed near the shop or, if we were on a distant job, to some barn where his shiftless-looking black horse had stood all day hitched to an equally shiftless buggy. On the way home Frank was full of the job we had been doing. This being outside of work hours, he felt free to give his ego a sort of field day and his comments were, I think, aimed to impress upon me that he knew more about carpentering than Uncle Abram.

"I told Abram the whole underpinning was rotten. But no, he was sure all that we needed to do was shore it up. You saw, Pip. You know, I never ask him; just go ahead and do what I know needs doing. When he sees that we put new sills all round today, he'll holler. I won't even argue with him. Do you know what I'll say to him, Pip? I'll tell him he can't make me do a poor job."

I remember Aunt Julia Hyde—she told me to call her Aunt Julia—out on the porch prepared to scold her husband for being late. He interrupted her opening remarks respectfully but with assurance, "I've brought Pip home to spend the night with us."

To do her justice, Aunt Julia was always the soul of hospitality. While we ate at a table covered with a red tablecloth, in a low room which served as both kitchen and dining room, she bustled back and forth from the stove to the table. We must have had apple pie for supper since I remember Frank saying to his wife, "Ma, you must be sure to put away plenty of pie timber for the winter." And "Ma's" answer, with her nose in the air, "Don't I take care of you all right?"

I enjoyed everything—the room, the red tablecloth, the food—although quite different from that to which I was accustomed—and even the peculiar odor which clings to a room that has been cooked in for years. It was the home life of a successful carpenter. I was being accepted.

After supper I followed Frank around while he did the chores and then we sat on his little stoop until a late hour, later, I think, than was the custom of a man who must arise before six in the morning. On the darkening porch Frank became mellow. He often turned the conversation to the stars or some other semiscientific subject, deferring to me as though, with my callow thirteen years, I had more education than he. Early in our acquaintance he conceived the idea that I was "too good for the work" I was doing. He told Uncle Abram that I ought to go to college. At the time this displeased me, so determined was I to establish myself as a competent workman and an earner of sufficient money to support myself and my mother and sister.

3

During those years I worked as assistant to other carpenters. Bill Padgham is fond of telling a story of my carpentering days in which he spanked me with a shingle. According to him, we were shingling one of the company's houses at Turkey Street. I had discovered that a shingle nail thrown from the flat palm of the hand sang through the air like a mosquito, and on that particular day I was amusing myself by throwing nails at boys who passed below. Padgham had told me positively to quit it. Later he saw me working my way slyly to the edge of the roof and as I raised my arm for the throw, he hit me a smart blow from behind with the butt end of a shingle.

I once fell from the roof of a tenant house; which reminds me of my towering ambition to be a strong man among strong men. We were shingling the house. I had been told by all of my bosses—had, in fact, been ordered—not to try to carry a bundle of shingles to the roof. Unfortunately, the desire to demonstrate my ability to do whatever they did proved stronger than my traditional attachment to obedience. I was sure I could accomplish the feat. Therefore, when I thought no one was looking I shouldered one of the heavy bundles, nearly as large as myself, and successfully mounted a ladder. There a more difficult task confronted me. The foothold was insecure, and while attempting to transfer the shingles from my shoulder to the roof I lost my balance. Seeing that a fall was inevitable, I heaved the bundle to one side and fell clear of it. I was not seriously hurt except in my feelings.

The best period of my day was the noon hour, when I ate with the men. They usually sat around on lumber piles in the shade of a row of maple trees which then bordered the path to the Mill. There was about those noon gatherings a pleasurable atmosphere of rest for tired bodies which was heightened by rambling conversation, uttered between mouthfuls, by men who were frankly giving their brains a rest along with those tired bodies. Not that anything they said seemed banal to me. During the noon hour I enjoyed an intimacy with my superiors more complete than ever while on the job.

Working men are friendly men. There exists among them a sort of fraternity of labor and, sitting before our open dinner pails, they took me into that fraternity with special consideration for my youthfulness. Oren Morrison often insisted on sharing his pie with me. Frank Hyde would take from his dinner pail a bottle and, holding it aloft, address me in a declamatory tone, "Pip, how would you like a drink of switchel?—good old switchel!" It was that spiced vinegar beverage we children used to call "medicated."

4

Another memory seems relevant to the story of my carpentering days, because it suggests that my mind was active in spite of long hours of labor. After each shingling job the ground round about was always strewn with little nails carelessly dropped by shinglers who, with a hatchet in one hand and a shingle in the other, carried nails in their mouths. It was my task to pick up the scattered nails. I knew the cost of shingle nails because Uncle Abram had allowed me to wait on farmers and others who came to the shop to buy things, and it occurred to me that picking up nails did not pay anyone. So I timed myself and weighed the nails recovered.

Sure enough, the nails I had gathered would not pay for my time. Triumphantly, I produced the statistics, but to my chagrin no one seemed interested in them. I was especially nonplused that Uncle Abram refused to take my demonstration seriously. I can only think that the thrift, or perhaps the consciences, of the nineteenth century made the wasting of a nail, produced by elaborate human labor, seem a crime regardless of profit and loss statistics.

Throughout one summer I worked sixty hours a week and the work was hard. By putting in an extra quarter hour at noon we got off at four-thirty on Saturday. I recall that Frank Hyde and I, with no other help, built wings on two of the company's tenant houses. We built even the chimneys. I mixed the mortar and carried both that and the bricks up a ladder to him. By this time I was earning eight cents an hour.

When I returned to Mr. Underwood's school in the fall I was threatened with the nickname "Stub." I was broad-shouldered and strong for my age, but the shortest boy of my class. It was generally agreed I had been stunted by over-work.

Chapter IX

I Become a Turkey Street Boy

I

DURING most of the year 1884 we lived at Turkey Street. Ormond worked in the trapshop, and in order that he might be nearer his work my mother had exchanged a portion of her Oneida Community, Limited, stock for a house. This removal emphasized my separation from the old Community life. It was in March that we moved to the house in Turkey Street. My mother had a sociable disposition and was very democratic and she soon had a coterie of Turkey Street friends who dropped in evenings for a "sing" or to have their fortunes told. I remember Ellery Williams, who came with two young ladies. He sang in a high falsetto, and praised my mother's piano playing so extravagantly and in such an unctuous tone that I disliked him. Dan Teal also came. He did not sing, but talked in falsetto. He was usually dickering with Ormond over some kind of "trade." He got the best of those trades so regularly that Mother and I were annoyed and when, in our absence, he persuaded Ormond to exchange a dozen useful articles for a bulky printing press that never performed she protested.

Active boys are seldom satisfied with home associations, and I was no exception. I knew that the neighborhood boys were a rough lot, for among them were the same hoodlums who had persecuted Humphrey and me and shocked us with their profanity in Community days. They were, however, the only available boys. Every evening after supper they foregathered at Johnny Moore's store on the corner opposite our factory, and I soon began making their acquaintance.

I find myself a little astonished that I braved the dangers of the gang at Johnny Moore's store. They were Irish and congenital fighters. There must have been a liberal element of timidity mixed with the desires which impelled me to approach that corner. I remember stormy scenes between my mother, Ormond and myself, in which they both inveighed against my associating with bad boys, and I also recall the stratagems I employed to get out of the house after supper and away to the corner. The lure of companionship was stronger than fear of my mother or the boys.

A favorite pastime of the older boys and men who congregated at the store consisted in starting fights between the younger ones. I happened to be at just the age preferred for such exhibitions and, though not a fighter by choice, found myself frequently engaged. It was the price I had to pay for Turkey Street companionship. One boy would elbow another violently, then stand in front of him in a truculent attitude, or someone would put a chip on a boy's shoulder, whereupon he was bound to dare another to knock it off.

I particularly remember my fight with a certain "Stub" Hovey. He was a year older than I, and heavier, but my reach of arm was longer and I must have been more muscular. In every round—if boys' battles can be divided into rounds— I was the victor. I knocked him down, and still retain a mental picture of Stub lying on the ground, his mouth opening and shutting like a fish; I "wrastled" him down; I threw him down and fell full length upon him; and again I knocked him down, but always he got up and attacked me. Never did he seriously hurt me, and yet he won the fight. In the end I ran away; there seemed no other possibility of finishing. I was undoubtedly humiliated by the outcome of my fight with Stub Hovey, but memory stresses only a generalization which afterward became for me a working formula. In colloquial language it ran thus: "He who won't be beaten can't be beaten."

2

My mother, having attached herself neither to the loyalist party nor to the seceders at the time of the breakup, had no "pull" with the local managers of the Oneida Community, Limited; and when Ormond was awarded only the standard rate of ten cents per hour, she showed her quality by starting out vigorously to earn money herself. She gave piano lessons to ambitious Turkey Streeters at twenty-five cents a lesson, and experimented with canvassing for books. I remember *Samantha at Saratoga.* I also remember evenings when she would proudly show sales of three or more books as a result of a long day's journey on foot along the turnpike.

During those years my mother must have longed for some substitute for John Humphrey Noyes's spiritual leadership. Frequently she hired one of the company's horse-and-buggies and took us all to Sunday service at the Oneida Castle church. My recollection of the sermons is meager. I do remember one in which eternity and hell-fire were raised to the nth power, by imagining a sparrow flying with a grain of sand to some planet and having deposited it there, returning for another grain. This was repeated until our entire globe had been transported to the planet; then the sparrow brought it all back again. I remember the preacher's solemn asseveration: "After this process had been completed a thousand times, Eternity would have only just begun."

I think I resented Reverend Corcoran's hell-fire partly because it was not offset by the positives always present in

Perfectionist theology, and partly because I looked on him as one of the detested "clergy." The principal figure in my memory of the Oneida Castle Sunday school is a tall brunette who seemed the last word in female charm.

During that summer I worked, as mentioned before, sixty hours a week, each morning before seven o'clock walking a mile and a half to the mill. Late in September I returned to the Community school. We did not find in our new teacher's pedagogy the same interest Mr. Warne had inspired and he failed to arouse any personal affection capable of restraining us from annoying him whenever it could be done safely. I remember a plot which ended in the sound ferruling of Elliot Hinds, the same Elliot Hinds who, during the World War, was killed in an airplane crash on the French front.

It occasionally happened that a scholar, entering the schoolroom a little late, asked if the bell had rung. On this particular day a dozen boys and girls purposely delayed until school was in session, then entered one at a time and each asked the apparently innocent question, "Has the bell rung?" By the time four or five had asked the same question, Mr. Underwood became suspicious. He scolded the next entrant. Then came Elliot, and his question proved the last straw. Those still outside repaired with Bert to his father's laboratory above the schoolroom where, through a ventilator, we listened to the indictment and castigation of Elliot.

I owe it to Mr. Underwood to add that, when in later life I became better acquainted with him, I found him not at all the dry pedant we thought him in schooldays. His enthusiasms were for subjects uninteresting to boys. He had studied oratory under Frobisher and phrenology with Foster, and he loved Latin. *Gallia est omnis divisa* and the rest, written in his fine Spencerian handwriting, stared at us from the blackboard until even the younger children could repeat by rote the first four lines of *Caesar*. In later life, I was attracted by Mr. Underwood's intelligence and active interest in all scientific subjects, but for a thirteen-year-old boy oratory, cranial bumps and Latin compared unfavorably with Mr. Warne's microscope and walking-school. Perhaps a portion of Mr. Underwood's unpopularity should be laid to boys' prejudice. At the start of his teaching we labeled him "peculiar," partly, I think, because he ate hardtack and would drink nothing but specially filtered water.

3

During the winter Mr. John Cragin visited us at Turkey Street. He had, soon after the breakup, rushed off to New York City expecting to make his fortune and had returned completely discouraged. Now he was filled with a new love of the old Community home. He urged my mother to sell her house and return to the Mansion. At the time she negatived his suggestion; although I was at the time pleased with her independence, I suspect that she was not, at heart, disinclined to the idea.

In the meantime Ormond had developed an obscure disease which would now, I think, be diagnosed as ulcers of the stomach. Mother hovered over him. I remember how sternly she reproved my unthinking ridicule of his voracious appetite which usually resulted later in a total loss of everything he had eaten.

It was sometime during January, 1885, that Grandfather Worden wrote of an opening for Ormond in Vineland, which involved lighter labor and promised more pay and more opportunity for advancement than the trapshop. A family council discussed this proposal. Ormond was eager for the change, and both Stella and I urged enthusiastically a return to the Mansion House. Mother surrendered. She succeeded in renting her house, and when Ormond departed for Vineland we three moved back to the old home.

With that return, and for some reason I have never been able to explain fully, a rightabout-face in my outlook and ambitions began. My spiritual depression was over. I recall an emotional expansion, and a stirring of ambition which demanded for the future something more satisfying than a carpenter's career.

Part V—Emergence

Chapter I

Repatriation

I

DURING that winter my satisfaction over escape from the comparative isolation of Turkey Street was measurably heightened by the frequency of entertainments in the Hall. Most of these were concerts or miscellaneous programs employing home talent, but occasionally there came to us outside entertainers. This social renaissance may have betokened a feeble reaction against joint-stock individualism; men and women who had lived together as a great family for so many years, having got their second wind, may have welcomed even secular gatherings as substitutes for the old evening meetings.

I particularly recall an entertainment given by a certain Captain Thomas and his Four Musical Daughters. I remember it because of the surprising access of ambition it stimulated in me, an effect hardly to be accounted for by the performance itself. The captain was a burly, good-natured faker who astonished us by producing white rabbits from a hat, eggs from his ears, and finally a bowl filled with water from the front of his shirt. His conjuring, however, was not emotionally important. It left no more lasting impression on me than did the antics of a trained bear which a wandering Italian, at rare intervals, exhibited in front of the Mansion. It was the daughters and their magical music that have made that concert seem a signpost on which I can still see fingers pointing toward the promised land of possible achievement.

One of the girls played a cornet, another a clarinet, a third the piano, while the youngest, seemingly about my own age, performed marvelous feats with her violin. She played the "Carnival of Venice" with variations, and with her instrument held in many awkward positions. At the last, having loosened the hairs of her bow and slipped the violin between them and the stick, she repeated the tune, this time adding beautiful chords.

It sounds ridiculous to say that an acrobatic rendition of the "Carnival of Venice" stimulated in me prodigious ambitions, but that is an understatement. My imagination was set on fire. I was dazzled by the colorful glimpse, the dramatic suggestion of pleasures and possibilities to be found in the world from which those bewitching maidens came. I made a mighty resolve to go out, explore, experience and attain.

Later, like many other country boys, my first experience in a real theater added tinsel and glitter to the prospect of worldly success, but that was a feeble flash compared with the flare of that evening in the old Hall. To be sure, my exaltation soon faded; it was provoked by the witchery of music and pretty girls; but for years thereafter whenever I heard the "Carnival of Venice," I stood up a little straighter and renewed my resolve to do something worthwhile in the world.

2

There were, of course, other influences working to alter the direction of my ambitions. Even before I left Turkey Street, Frank Hyde's suggestion that I go to college instead of working in the carpenter shop had taken root. College was out of the question for financial reasons, but something within me had already begun to reach out for a different companionship. Although I had grown fond of the men with whom I worked, their unwillingness to discuss seriously anything outside of their own immediate problems or neighborhood affairs gradually undermined the satisfaction I had felt over progress as a carpenter. Those months of hard work and small pay had raised in my mind questions that were perhaps unusual in a boy of fourteen, for I remember trying to discuss the relation of capital and labor.

I asked my working companion, "Why don't men who work get the things they make?"

His answer disappointed me. "They don't want them. They want to sell them."

I tried to put what was in my mind another way, "Why do those who don't work have more things than those who do?"

He laughed. "You'd better be glad to earn good wages."

It was not altogether this unresponsive attitude that dulled the edge of my eagerness to become a carpenter. I had seen workingmen's lives at close quarters and, while I still admired their independence, their opportunities in the year 1884 appeared too limited.

I recall that I brought back from Turkey Street an enlarged appetite for reading, but suspect that this was a sort of narcotic employed to deaden my new discontent, for in general the books I chose were not of a sort to suggest literary or intellectual precocity. I soaked in stories of adventure. My mother sought to raise my literary standards by reading to me such classics as Edward Eggleston's *Hoosier Schoolmaster* and *The Circuit Rider,* also tales of explorations in the arctic and in darkest Africa.

This passion for reading must have seemed to someone misdirected or a little excessive, for I remember adopting a certain corner of the gallery that was not under observation from the hall below, as a sort of hideaway for Sunday afternoons when I wanted to indulge in an orgy of E. P. Roe or one of the nineteenth-century "yellow-covers."

3

During this brief repatriation I must have been more observant than hitherto. In particular I began to notice among the ex-communists a changed attitude toward the new regime. They had settled down stoically, if not always contentedly, to earn their living wherever in the Oneida Community, Limited, industrial machine fortune or preferment had placed them. Those no longer able to work, mostly aged persons who had served long in the Community and had been allotted more stock than the average member, were living with reasonable comfort on their dividends. All seemed to have adjusted themselves in one way or another to the world's system of wages and salaries, board and rent, and pay-for-what-you-get—even more important, what you can afford.

For the terror of that first plunge into individualism had left most of our people with an economy complex which persisted as long as they lived. This passion for economy was the most characteristic quality of my elders in 1885. They guarded their personal finances jealously and kept the company expenses always under critical inspection. The $1,200 salary paid its president was an object of persistent criticism. Old Mr. Abbot, whose duties had never been more complex than inspection of the springs at Spring Grove and care of the family's water supply, offered to take the job of "presidenting" for ten cents an hour.

Uncle Abram once became greatly exercised over the

jets of steam escaping from retorts in which cans of corn
were being sterilized. He appeared before the board of directors and accused the canning department of waste. When
told that this circulation of steam was necessary in order to
raise the temperature above 212° Fahrenheit, he was still
not wholly appeased.

4

Most of the religion to be found outside people's hearts
was divided between the inconspicuous and strictly limited
gatherings of those loyalists who still remained at Oneida
and the enthusiastic meetings of a small group of men and
women belonging to the opposition party who had embraced
orthodox revivalism. Many of the loyalists had moved to
Niagara Falls to be near the man who was still their spiritual
leader. Those left at Oneida held themselves aloof, not alone
from the backsliders (that is how they thought of the re-
vivalists), but also from the generality who, they felt, were
rapidly drifting away from spiritual things and toward the
pagan god, Mammon. Not but that some of the loyalists
themselves revealed mammonistic tendencies; these strove to
maintain connection with Mr. Hamilton and other spiritual-
minded persons, but economic pressure involved them deeper
and deeper in occupational interests.

5

Politics—joint-stock politics—had become quiescent.
Stockownership among the loyalists gave John Humphrey
Noyes unquestioned leadership, and he must have used his
power with wisdom and moderation, since men of the opposing parties, like Mr. Hinds and Uncle Frank, held im-

portant executive positions in the business organization. On the other hand, Mr. Hamilton, president of the company and my father's recognized vice-regent, failed to reflect his spirit of conciliation or even practice wisdom in executive relations. His interferences irked superintendents and responsible officers and prepared the way for his downfall.

Mr. Hamilton's intrusions extended to personal affairs. This was, of course, a leftover from that paternalistic system which alone had made possible more than thirty years of communism. I remember a typical example. Uncle Abram decided to build himself a house and move out of the Mansion. He was then past fifty years of age. Mr. Hamilton, still living in a past when young men like Abram made no important moves without permission from Central Members, called him to his office and took him to task for going ahead with his plan without consultation. What especially sticks in my mind is a certain lack of complete conviction in Uncle Abram's explosive indignation over Mr. Hamilton's interference in his private affairs.

"By jolly!" he exclaimed. "I'm not obliged to get his permission."

The words were defiant, but in his tone there lurked a suspicion of guilt.

Early in January, 1885, my father, having evidently listened to complaints from others than his own partisans, wrote to Mr. Hamilton that he felt he had been president long enough and asked him to retire. Uncle Frank told me the story: It seems that along with the president's retirement went that of the other officers, and one of them, the secretary, proved unreconciled to demotion. A few days after word of the proposed changes had gone out, this officer accosted Uncle Frank exultantly, "Well, Frank Smith, Mr. Hamilton has decided to keep the presidency."

It turned out that Mr. Hamilton had written my father that he could not afford to lose the presidential salary because he was helping to support his brother Charles in Syracuse: the worst possible argument to give John Humphrey Noyes. He promptly wrote back, "The Oneida Community cannot be run to support your brother Charles. More than ever I think you should retire." It is a tribute to the sincerity and loyalty of Mr. Erastus Hamilton that later he moved to Niagara where he built a house and maintained a close fellowship as long as he lived with the man who had deposed him from office.

So Mr. George Campbell ascended to the presidency just as we were returning from Turkey Street. He was religious, but from a managerial standpoint hopelessly beyond his depth. His quality was that of a bookkeeper. He did his best, but during his term of office the company's businesses prospered in proportion as departmental managers brushed aside his futile attempts at supervision.

In the role of religious leader, Mr. Campbell was an even worse failure. He had no personal magnetism and no ability to make religion attractive, with the result that under his leadership the secularization of the Oneida group proceeded more rapidly. He was president four years. After my father died in 1886, the business element revolted, politics revived and, with a new alignment of parties, Mr. Campbell was dethroned.

But in the winter of 1885 the Campbell regime was new and I remember a general hopefulness that living and working conditions would be more comfortable under a less dominant president. His leadership, or lack of leadership, seemed likely to fit the attenuated social and spiritual aspirations of the group at Oneida.

6

There was one other phase of life at the Mansion House which impressed me at the time. The fear of social ostracism, so rampant at the breakup, had lost its poignancy, but in its place had come a sort of mass inferiority complex. At home our people forgot their social taint. It was only when they visited outside or went to live in other places that their old timidity was evidenced by petty concealments and evasions. Certain people who had insisted that the office send their dividends in envelopes without the Community letterhead and use blank stationery were very angry when by mistake the telltale "return" notice appeared in the mail.

Again, while our men, both managers and others, worked with confidence and enthusiasm in the company's businesses, I found myself surrounded by a new realism which more or less openly admitted that Community folks were ill equipped to compete as individuals in the world's economic struggle. I often heard the remark, "We are all better off to stay with the company."

Several memories suggest that, with no practical plan to support my hopefulness and nothing in my past experience to warrant it, I was loath to accept the prevailing defeatism. One day two of my fellow workmen twitted me about my dependence on the company. They were, I think, in a bad humor because compelled to spend an afternoon carrying lumber from the yard to the mill instead of at more congenial work in the shop. It started with an expression of sympathy. One of them said:

"You ought not to have to do such heavy work at your age."

The older man broke in, cynically, "He'll have a soft job enough in the end. He's a Community boy."

Carrying heavy scantling did not encourage much talk on my part, but when passing the men on my way back to the yard, I threw out, "I don't want a soft job. I'm going somewhere else."

I am sure that those carpenters laughed derisively at this explosion, because my memory of the episode is mostly one of resentment that my newly aroused ambitions had been ridiculed.

At another time, Uncle Abram told me that if I stuck to my job and learned all about the work, I could someday take his place as head of the carpentry department. He intended his words as encouragement, but this prospect, which would have thrilled me one year before, now left me cold. Somewhere in the world there was surely something more important that I could do.

7

In all this description of my life after the breakup, I have said little about my own spiritual state. (In the Community there was much discussion of members' "spiritual states.") Searching my memory, I am led to believe that while my early religious faith undoubtedly remained intact, it had small part in my emotional life. God and Christ and the angels and the Primitive Church were still there—somewhere, but death and the judgment day seemed, to a fourteen-year-old boy, far away, and my guardian angel, in the absence of Papa Kelly, did not intrude as it had in the old days.

Perhaps I felt about my soul much as I always have about the machinery of my physical body. I knew I had a heart whose regular beating was of the highest importance and lungs whose breathing kept me alive, but I trusted both and forgot them. A similar psychology may have prevented my devoting much thought to the condition of my soul. After all, the existence of a heavenly hierarchy was, like the existence of my internal organs, necessarily a matter of faith.

During the winter of 1885, however, something happened which temporarily jolted me out of that religious complacence. Mr. Pitt—he with the billowy white hair and whiskers—gave a lecture in the Hall on the subject of "Christian Evidences." Until that moment I had never suspected that doubt existed as to the truth of religion or that the story of Jesus Christ required any bolstering evidence. I was shocked and disconcerted.

My mother tried to lessen the effect of Mr. Pitt's lecture. She said:

"He likes to parade his learning. You and I know that the Bible is true without any of his miserable evidences."

Mr. Pitt did not destroy my belief, but he altered permanently my relation to the heavenly powers. He changed that which had seemed an unquestioned reality into a less stable object of faith.

Chapter II

A Year with My Father

I

OUR return from Turkey Street had seemed a favoring turn in my road, but that home-coming was a gentle curve compared with the short right turn which presently came in sight. On the 26th of March, 1885, I was invited to go to Niagara Falls for a visit or, if I so desired and my mother was willing, to make the Stone Cottage my permanent home. Two of my brothers, Humphrey and Holton, a sister Gertrude, and my cousin George had been living in my father's family for some time. While the stories of their doings, which came to us at Oneida, were not wildly exciting, they suggested to my restless imagination that Niagara was a door opening out into the real world.

Recalling an earlier visit, I pictured my father as a venerable figure, pacing back and forth on the long veranda of the Stone Cottage in full view of the falls, presumably thinking great thoughts, save only when at each turn he paused to beam abstractedly on Bert and me engaged below in some simple sport. I respected him, but, when looking forward to life at the Stone Cottage in 1885, this did not prevent me from hoping to adventure in ways that I must have known would not fit exactly with his ambition for Community boys and more especially for his sons. I planned no disobedience, much less rebellion. It was simply that my natural optimism saw in this new field, limited only by the

267

guardianship of a rather self-engrossed elderly man, opportunity for a new approach to the outside world.

I sometimes wonder whether my father felt any trepida-
tion when he invited me to join his group of young people.
Certainly there must have been times during my stay at
Niagara when he regretted having introduced a discordant
element among his hitherto obedient children; and yet, in
general, during that year he showed me kindness and affection.

Which anticipates my story. In March, 1885, I was
eager for the change and my mother consented because Ormond, working in Vineland, wrote of ill-health. She decided
to go there and care for him. Certain loyalists outfitted me
with new clothes and contributed money for my railway
fare to Niagara. On the 28th of March I left Oneida.

2

The train stopped at Niagara Falls, New York. That
was not my getting-off place, but there was a long wait at
the station, long enough to permit my going out on the platform. I remember a bedlam of yelling hackmen and hotel
runners soliciting patronage from the new arrivals.

"See the Falls, twenty-five cents!"

"Goat Island and the Falls, fifteen cents!"

"Rooms one dollar!"

"Fifty cents!"

And a confused jargon of other strenuous bids for
custom.

Someone had told me, on my previous visit, that people
who fell into the clutches of those hackmen and hotelmen
were always swindled. I thought of the spider's invitation in
our old school reader:

"Come into my parlor, said the spider to the fly," and all the people around me seemed either spiders or flies.

That five- or ten-minute train stop gave me a permanent distaste for the town of Niagara Falls, New York, and—strangely enough—struck another blow at my exaggerated respect for the "competent Outsider." It seemed an exhibition of militant sham and futility. I remember a sort of surprised contempt for the population of Niagara Falls, New York, and their victimized visitors, and with it an access of confidence in my own ability to compete with such a world.

In those days the train crossed the lower Suspension Bridge and ended its journey in the little village of Clifton, on the Canadian side of the river. I do not recall who met me; probably Mr. Herrick or the boys with old Fanny and the surrey. What I do remember is my father standing on the Stone Cottage veranda, bareheaded, with welcoming arms held out to me and a happy smile on his face.

I found myself in a large family where simple pleasures were the rule and spiritual implications discovered in everyday happenings. All worked for the comfort and prosperity of the family with just such a naïve enthusiasm as I remembered in the old Community. We boys were treated as responsible members and, outside of certain play hours, divided our time between work in the garden, helping about the house, and attending a homemade school whose lack of pedagogic system would have shocked any State Board of Regents.

The Stone Cottage was not a small cottage, nor was it a large building, although the long stone shed connecting with a barn as large as the house lent to the whole an appearance of amplitude. Its Gothic lines, steep roofs, sharp gables and leaded windowpanes added an architectural charm.

Located a little back from the brow of a steeply terraced hill and partially concealed by fine old trees, it seemed withdrawn from the hurly-burly of life below.

Inside, two large pleasant rooms, the parlor and dining room, occupied most of the first floor. The dining room was the most attractive room in the house. Two wide, French windows opened onto the veranda and faced Niagara River. The parlor, too, was large and well proportioned. These rooms, together with a large hall and stairway, left space for only two small bedrooms. Upstairs there were two front bedrooms, long and narrow, and others of lesser size. The ample low-ceilinged kitchen occupied a first section of the one-story wing or shed, and behind this came the inevitable Turkish bath, a necessary feature of every Community ménage.

3

In 1885 the Stone Cottage family consisted of eight adult members plus, at all times, two or three visitors from Oneida. My father lived in one of the upstairs front bedrooms. His windows looked out on the gorge and the great falls and the ever-mounting, swirling cloud of mist which rose from its vortex. He spent much time in his room, alone or talking with Mr. Herrick or Aunt Harriet. He seemed much older than when I had last seen him; and yet his mind was as vigorous as ever and his will as dominant. After supper he usually sat for a time in the parlor while the assembled family conversed with each other, or fell silent when he had an inspiration to talk.

It was the same at mealtimes. Sitting at the end of a long table, he watched silently, often smilingly, the sociability of the grown folks and the animation of the children. At times Mr. Herrick explained, close to his ear, on account of

JOHN HUMPHREY NOYES
Taken at Niagara

THE STONE COTTAGE AT NIAGARA

his increasing deafness, interesting topics of the current conversation or the cause of some boisterous explosion of mirth.
Occasionally, however—and we came to know by the character of his silence that he was going to speak—he would
start with a simple text and develop into an old-fashioned
"home talk" some thought on which his mind had been
working.

As I remember it, after such talks he would go at once
to his room, and something about those departures suggested
to me that he retired in order to ponder more deeply the
subject discussed. Always a respectful silence ensued, broken
after a time by Aunt Harriet's or Mr. Herrick's sympathetic
comments on what he had said. Still later, the discussion
would become general and I remember gaining new respect
for Humphrey and George because they often joined in the
conversation.

That my father's dissertations were not always general
is shown by a note in one of our visitors' diaries.

When Mr. Noyes got up from the supper table last night, he
came round where Pip was sitting and put his hand on his shoulder
and said something like this to him:

"Conversion is not a painful thing—it is a happy thing. You
will be converted when you begin to notice God's providences.
That is the way I was converted and began to be religious. If you
see a providence, believe in it and confess it, and that will be conversion. From that you will go on till you see God in all the Universe."

The regular evening meetings had been abandoned,
probably on account of my father's health. In their place he
encouraged evenings of sociability and games. I particularly
remember mind-reading experiments, and a little play, *John
Gilpin*, given somewhat extemporaneously by a combination
of young people and old. On one occasion my father himself

recited a funny piece. After he went upstairs, we usually
played backgammon or authors or Mother Noyes read aloud
to us.

Each Sunday afternoon there was a general gathering of
the clans at the Stone Cottage; old Community members
who lived over the river or nearby on the Canadian side,
came with their children. For adults the afternoon was mainly
devoted to visiting with my father and each other. For the
younger set there were games. In the end we were all rounded
up to sit in a crowded parlor and listen to a talk by Father
Noyes. Afterward refreshments were served, usually cookies
and lemonade; but once we had wine and cake. My father
called it "a spree for the gods." I can remember how the
faces of stanch old loyalists like Mr. Barron, Mr. Kinsley
and Mr. Miller beamed as they sat talking with my father.
They beamed on me too, but I felt that their approval was
founded on an assumption that, since I was privileged to live
near him, I must be growing up to be a worthy young man.
Altogether there lingers about the memories of those Sunday afternoons a pleasant aroma of spirituality so humanized
as to be inoffensive to a boy.

'4

Next to my father the most important member of
the family was Mother Noyes, the wife of his youth. She was
three years older than he, and physically more decrepit although she survived him by nearly ten years. Being unable
to climb stairs, she occupied a ground-floor room. My memory pictures her sitting by one of the French windows in the
dining room sewing, knitting, making flowers out of fish
scales and silver thread, or playing solitaire. Three times a
day, however, she washed the dishes, perched on a special

high chair in front of the kitchen sink, always humming to herself. Mother Noyes insisted on washing the family dishes until unable to leave her bed. In spite of rheumatism, which at times caused her to suffer cruelly, she was always a cheerful member of the household.

It was only on the few occasions when something I did or said registered in her mind as disloyalty to my father's principles that I remember any cross words from Mother Noyes, and even those had more the quality of apostolic severity than crossness. She had been more a disciple than a lover when she married my father in 1838 and she remained his unfaltering disciple to the end.

5

Aunt Harriet Skinner was equally unfaltering in her discipleship. Through all the vicissitude of his stormy career, she had stood stanchly beside him and now she watched over his physical and spiritual comfort and interpreted him to us of the younger generation. She seemed especially anxious that we be well grounded in his theology.

Toward me her attitude was peculiar. I shall always think that her affection for me, if not greater, was more acutely personal than for her other nephews. There was in it some of the quality the Biblical father felt for his prodigal son. It was not alone my evil associations in Vineland and Turkey Street or the reports of my ambitious toughness that distressed her, but linked with regret over that prodigal career was, I believe, a haunting fear that the worldliness of my Cook ancestry might permanently submerge the spirituality of a Noyes boy. On the whole, however, I think that her faith exceeded her fears.

6

At the Stone Cottage our activities were varied enough
to make each day interesting. We had great freedom as to
what we would do and when we would do it. We boys lived
under an inspirational government and, as long as we seemed
en rapport with the central inspiration, this worked out in
a rather unusual immunity from oversight.

Both my father and the adult portion of his family
had, by 1885, reached ages where their satisfactions were
mostly of the mind, and they evidently found vicarious
pleasure in the enthusiasms and physical activities of the
younger members. My brothers must have been very satisfactory proxies. I found that at mealtimes or in the evening
they were in the habit of relating to an interested family
many details of their work, their play or their adventuring
in the world roundabout. Furthermore, they had lived with
my father so long that their descriptions were couched in
the ingenuous language of Perfectionist neophytes, and their
imaginations, quickened by belief in the nearness of heavenly
agencies, found many coincidences which approving elders
agreed were "special providences."

That was not all: my father's religion, with all its
austerities and severities, encouraged happiness—pleasure, if
you please. What he criticized as "pleasure seeking" was
pleasure sought "beyond the freedoms licensed by one's degree of perfection." In reality, I think that he had a sympathetic nature which, quite outside theological sanctions,
loved to see people enjoying themselves. The undeviating
loyalty of his followers, through so many years, suggests
that his social sagacity often approved concessions to his
sympathy with human happiness.

Whatever the motive or motives, he certainly granted

us a surprising freedom of action. I note from Humphrey's diary that the very next day after I arrived we crossed the ice bridge, and I climbed almost to the top of the ice mountain. It illustrates the family passion for discovering "special providences," that Humphrey should write a few days later, "I think it was quite providential that we went over the ice-bridge Sunday as it has begun to break up."

We boys wandered widely and almost at will. On the far side of the whirlpool, we explored a ravine which my father believed to be the original bed of the river. Mr. Herrick went with us on most of those expeditions. After much climbing about and examination of strata, he would let us go swimming at a point where the waters of the gigantic eddy moved slowly. I recall wandering four or five miles to St. David's for bank swallows' eggs; often we saddled old Fanny and took turns riding out into the country; we played lacrosse with the Clifton boys; once Humphrey captured a runaway horse. Sometimes—and here we were experimenting just a little outside bounds—we strolled up the Clifton road at four o'clock in the hope of meeting the high school girls and felt greatly set up when they stopped and talked with us. Once they pinned flowers in our buttonholes.

7

This freedom to go was, of course, limited by work to be done, and definite hours of school. But even work was not all boredom. Mr. Herrick added an element of sport by injecting into the performance of each task an enthusiasm similar to that of the old Community bees. It was, "All hands at one o'clock to set out strawberry plants" or "to cultivate potatoes" or "to clean up the shed" or "to repair the bridges on the path below the hill"; and he would add,

"Let's see how quickly we can do the job." He usually set the pace and made us feel the accomplishment well worth-while.

Mr. Herrick also had a knack, which I think he learned from my father, of lifting things out of the ordinary by applying to them whimsical names, sometimes taken from the Bible. I remember "Tophet," a depression in the ground at the far side of our orchard, where we burned rubbish. Somehow wheeling loads to Tophet had a slightly different flavor from taking them to a dump or a garbage heap. The Stone Cottage family embroidered life—as did the Community family in its best days, with a thread of sentiment, but it was a naïve and withal a sturdy sentiment.

8

Neither work nor play was allowed to interfere with school, from nine o'clock until noon. When I first arrived, we did most of our studying at home and recited at the North Cottage, a small house on the other side of the Michigan Central Railway tracks, which had been rented for the purpose. We boys slept in the second story of the North Cottage.

Our study courses were not courses at all in the modern sense. The main consideration with our elders seemed to be that we study; and if there were side glances at what was being done in schools elsewhere, formal courses found little sympathy at Niagara Falls. We leaped from arithmetic to geometry. We worked assiduously at phonography, now called shorthand, so that we might report my father's talks; and we studied Greek, largely, I think, to enable us to trans-late the Greek New Testament. We read aloud from the book *Home Talks* or the *Berean* or Mr. Alfred Barron's *Foot Notes*.

Our curriculum was evidently aimed at what the Community called improvement rather than any plan of academic advancement. Like all other activities of the Stone Cottage family, education was influenced by spiritual considerations, and in general the initiation of new studies awaited my father's inspiration. I quote again from Humphrey's diary, "Father wants Pip to study more, so the latter commenced studying Greek with our class."

9

I found among the boys at Niagara an unmistakable pride in the number of outside people they knew. They called by name, with an unconvincing nonchalance, most of the carpenters who worked on the Kelly House; also the ticket taker at the Suspension Bridge, and the man on the River Road who ran a "burning spring." This spring, by the way, was a typical Niagara Falls "wonder" and consisted of a pool of water into which was introduced city gas from a concealed pipe.

I remember one embarrassing episode brought about by my attempt to ape their familiarities. We happened upon a stonemason rebuilding a roadside wall. The boys said he was a friend of theirs and that his name was Buckshot. For some reason I thought it necessary to accost him first. I saluted: "Hullo, Buckshot!" He was a big, burly Irishman, and the expression on his face when he looked up at me should have been a warning, but I still thought him a friend of the boys'. I was, therefore, greatly surprised when he swore loudly, grabbed his stone hammer, climbed over the wall and started after me with blood in his eye.

At the moment I had no clue to the cause of his anger, but that he was really angry I could not doubt. Fortunately, I was on a little rise of ground which gave me a head-start, and I ran and ran fast. Afterward Humphrey admitted that while he knew the man as "Buckshot" he had never called him that. I can only conclude that the nickname was, for some reason, offensive to that honest mason.

10

My father seemed to have changed his attitude toward Outsiders. He talked freely and on even terms with neighbors and tradesmen and often passed the time of day with Mr. Bardow who used our path as a short cut to his post of duty at Suspension Bridge. Then there was old man Zibach who ran one of those "museums" near the Horseshoe Falls where tourists were lured into buying Indian relics and "spar" jewelry said to be "made out of spray from the Falls."

What I remember is my father's neighborly conversation with this excessively "outsider-looking" museum keeper. He had taken us boys, as he often did, for a stroll along the river bank as far as Table Rock, an overhanging ledge from which could be seen the cataract's monstrous plunge into the mist-concealed cauldron from which a white cloud rose high and, carried by the wind, sometimes drifted as far as the Stone Cottage. (In later years Table Rock fell with a mighty crash into that same abyss.)

Zibach was standing in front of his store where, like the spider, he urged victims to walk into his parlor. What has stuck in my memory is the fact that I was disconcerted by father's talking on such equal terms with this man. It revealed him as willing to come down from the clouds of Mt. Sinai

and interest himself in the affairs of worldly men. I think that
I just a little resented his descent.

This new attitude was adopted by the entire family and
even we boys felt free to talk with carpenters working on the
Kelly house. When we were children at Oneida we were
punished for even speaking to outsiders. Now Humphrey
was permitted to go once a week to the house of one of those
carpenters, Wes McCready, to give him lessons in shorthand.

Which reminds me that, when I arrived at Niagara,
shorthand was a family enthusiasm. The other boys were already proficient enough to "take" Father's evening talks and
Humphrey made fairly good work with speeches at the Camp
Meeting. He was really talented and had a genius for anything
connected with language or literature.

I naturally joined the shorthand class. Our exercises consisted of shorthand attempts at passages from the New Testament read slowly to us by Mr. Kelly or Aunt Harriet. The
fact that these readings were mostly from the Bible is confirmed by the only relic of shorthand lessons left me; a "word-
sign" whose rhythm has, I think, preserved the memory—
"chess-en-ven," interpreted "which is in Heaven."

In spite of this breakdown of the old Community exclusiveness, the charm of life at Niagara was greatly enhanced
by a revival of the spiritual background of my childhood.
Again, as in the old days, my father's apostleship stood out as
the most important fact in all our lives.

The atmosphere of holiness was pervasive. It grew denser
as we approached the upstairs front bedroom, but thinned
in the out-of-doors until it was hardly more oppressive
than the blue sky or those cirrus clouds which add beauty
to a scene but in no way interfere with a boy's activities.
I felt no more temptation to rationalize the illusion of heavenly presence than I had as a child to destroy the bene-

diction of the clouds by resolving their substance into mist.

I was happy at Niagara. Even the assumption that we were living in full view of and close alliance with the heavenly powers, an assumption which pervaded all activities of the Stone Cottage family, was pleasing to me after the ill-fitting materialism of Oneida. If a greed for "pleasure seeking" (to quote my father's words) and my new self-confidence did later lead me to unauthorized experimentation with "the world, the flesh and the devil," I can truly say that those worldly wanderings were neither caused nor excused by any loss of respect for his religious principles. Perhaps the "Cook spirit," for which my mother was criticized in the Community, prevented that complete surrender to spiritual leadings which he hoped to see develop in his children.

I entered the Stone Cottage family as something of an Outsider. My allegiance was on trial. I felt admitted, but never quite a full-fledged member, and yet the ability of my father to add a spiritual quality to daily living by finding in the simplest and meanest activities evidence of the angelic presence touched some obscure capacity for idealism in me.

Chapter III

The Kelly House

I

IN an earlier chapter I referred to the building of the Kelly House. That ugly, three-story, wooden building was a monument to the persistence of communistic ideals among our older generation; perhaps even more to their desire to be near him who had—to quote Bernard Shaw—so "mightily shepherded" them. I have no doubt that the origin of the project could be traced to one of "Father Noyes's inspirations," but so far as I knew at the time Mr. William Kelly was the promoter and the largest investor.

This Mr. Kelly, the Papa Kelly of Children's House days, had, in 1883, moved to Niagara Falls and rented a small house not far from the Stone Cottage, asking only that he might be of service to Father Noyes. He was appointed head schoolmaster, and his little stuccoed cottage on McGrail Street became the schoolhouse for all those children whose parents had moved to the Falls.

When I arrived in 1885, plans for the new building were far advanced. It was designed for communal living, and paid for largely with money supplied by elderly Oneida members who hoped to live there. My father contributed as much as he could afford. I think that he selected the site, less than a hundred yards from the Stone Cottage, it being an important part of the scheme to provide space for a more ambitious school. My father referred to it as an academy. In addition, there was to be a room that he could occupy whenever he desired a change.

Communism at the Kelly House was never expanded beyond the dining room. Those elderly couples who moved on from Oneida in 1885 and 1886, lived in separate apartments and in general maintained separate finances. The school, however, was a communistic enterprise.

Soon the foundation of the Kelly House was completed, and the superstructure begun. My father proposed, with an amiable presumption regarding my accomplishments, that I be freed from other duties so that I might work with the carpenters on the House. It was an example of his genius for making life interesting and meaningful for his associates. The same instinct led him to encourage George's giving phonography lessons to Mr. Burgess, the station agent, and later, Humphrey's tutoring Wes McCready, one of the carpenters. I worked hard and with a pleasurable feeling that I was proving a profitable addition to the Stone Cottage family. The other boys helped at odd times. They were not carpenters, as I was, so they carried materials to the workmen or "cleaned up around."

2

The first to move to the Kelly House from Oneida were the Leonards, Stephen Leonard of favorable boyhood memory, who, as keeper of the bees, doled out spoonfuls of honey to small boys, when honey was not included in the Children's House dietary; and his wife, Fanny Leonard, whose goiter distracted my attention from that first criticism at Wallingford.

The Kellys and the Leonards were soon joined in the new house by the Ellises. Mrs. Ellis was none other than the Harriet Hall whom, in the faith-healing stage of his religious experience, John Humphrey Noyes cured of a fatal malady and thereby brought on himself and his Putney flock a storm of clerical condemnation. That was in 1838. Now, in 1885, she was well past seventy and spry for her years.

That adjective "spry" comes inevitably to mind when I think of Mr. and Mrs. Charles Ellis, both of them. Mrs. Harriet Hall Ellis was both spry and sprightly; as for Mr. Ellis, his body was thin, his voice was thin, his straw-colored beard was thin, and he was physically weak, but his motions were spry. Mr. Ellis, by the way, has appeared before in this chronicle. It was he who tried to freeze himself to death in 1883, and after being thawed out in the Turkish bath was saved from serious physical consequences by a Community criticism.

When I was a child my simple mentality sorted the grown folks of the Community into three classes. There were, first, the few about whom clung an atmosphere of extra holiness, created partly by their grave demeanor (or impressive whiskers), but more from observation of their intimate relation with my father. Surrounding these came a considerable group of old or middle-aged persons who, by no stretch of a child's imagination, could be invested with the halo of apostleship, but who seemed to have a special standing indicated by the magic word "Putney." I was foggy regarding Putney. I knew that the word had a historical significance, but it registered in my mind as "Bunker Hill" or "The Boys of '76" did in the history of our country. I remember being surprised when in 1879 and 1880 certain members of the Putney class were reported as "seceders." Beyond these Putneyites came the majority of Community members whom I thought of as simply "our folks."

My early impressions of Community folks placed the Leonards in the second class, particularly Mrs. Leonard. At

Wallingford "Miss" Fanny Leonard and Putney were in some vague way linked together in my mind. The Ellises belonged in the third class in spite of Mrs. Ellis's Putney experience.

3

Over at the Stone Cottage our interest in the tenants of the Kelly House was overshadowed by a general enthusiasm for the new school facilities. The school rooms were well lighted and large, occupying most of the space on the third floor. In addition, a larger teaching staff and an ambitious program of studies were planned, one more in line with standard academic courses. We boys made desks for ourselves and for the girls out of fence pickets. This school was one of my father's last enthusiasms. He often came to visit us during recitation periods, and although he could not hear questions and answers, he smiled on us.

The school or the possibilities of the Kelly House must have revived his youthful passion for the printed word. He was always an ardent propagandist. From the day of his theological apostasy, he devoted much time and often more money than he could well afford to publishing weekly or monthly journals—the *Perfectionist* (New Haven) in 1834; the *Witness* in 1837; the *Spiritual Magazine* in 1846, and during the life of the Oneida Community the *Oneida Circular* and *American Socialist*. He often declared that the "paper" was the chief concern of the Community.

And now, with his race almost run, he saw in the Kelly House the facilities for again printing a paper. It was in his mind during his last illness. To Mr. Herrick, as he sat by his bedside, he frequently talked about it; and Mr. Herrick, always ardent in support of any of Father Noyes's enthusiasms, discussed the project hopefully in family meetings.

Chapter IV

Camp Meeting

I

No chronicle of my year at Niagara Falls would be complete without an account of the "camp meeting affair," more specifically our adventures with the camp meeting girls. Near the village of Clifton, in a thick wood, Reverend Osborne and the Methodist brethren conducted an annual camp meeting which, during the preceding year, my more amenable brothers and Cousin George had attended in the utmost good faith. So far as I know, they went solely for spiritual benefits. They certainly listened attentively to the services, for each morning they edified the family at breakfast with detailed reports of proceedings the night before.

At the start, I think I attended the meetings in equal good faith. I could not take phonographic notes of the sermons as the others did, but I remember listening interestedly for something to tell at the breakfast table. It was not long, however, before I discovered that the woods were full of attractive girls. Probably the other boys had not overlooked their existence, but my father was particularly definite and emphatic in his disapproval of fraternization with outside girls.

If I was the first to cross the Rubicon of disobedience, I do not recall any reluctance on the part of the others to follow my lead. There may have been an interim of timid experimentation; if so, it was short. Very soon we were all frankly turning the freedom of camp meeting into opportunity for getting better acquainted with the opposite sex.

That we were conscious of guilt is shown by the systematic deceit we practiced. Each evening one boy was sacrificed to the exigencies. He attended the services while the other three betook themselves to somebody's porch or a more private rendezvous and there enjoyed their first thrills of courtship. Meanwhile the unfortunate delegate to the meeting took careful notes. We four slept out in the shed over the Turkish bath, and each night before we went to sleep all were posted on leading points of the sermon. Thus the morning report to the family was insured, with all its accustomed minutiae.

2

Those camp meetings were of the old-fashioned kind. The main service was held in a great barnlike auditorium surrounded by dense woods. Within, tiers of benches furnished seating capacity for at least a thousand people, and faced a roughly planked rostrum on which a large number of elders, exhorters and devout believers sat or walked, punctuating the speaker's address with loud hallelujahs. Between the audience and the rostrum there intervened a sort of sawdust ring.

The presiding cleric preached hell and damnation in no half-hearted way. When he had worked up the emotions of the congregation to a point where he thought a sufficient number were ripe for religious ecstasies, he called on all who wished to be saved to come down in front. One after another rose and went to the sawdust arena. There they were stimulated further until they "got the power." Men, women and even children danced and sang and shouted. It was a distressing exhibition, but on the whole entertaining to thoughtless youngsters. The "penitents" would grovel in the sawdust for a time, then suddenly spring to their feet and emit terrifying yells. This might happen several times, the paroxysms growing more violent with each demonstration. Finally, the frenzied contortionists passed out entirely and the success of the meeting seemed measured by the number of human beings who, at the end, lay unconscious in the sawdust.

I remember braving detection one night by taking my young lady to what our youthful associates called the "holy show." We sat far back where the lighting was dim and chances of ministerial attention seemed small. I never repeated that experiment, not with a girl. One of the exhorters came up the aisle laboring with individuals as he went and presently directed his attack at us. It was not alone that I feared his attentions might reveal our presence to some acquaintance in the audience, but before he was through there seemed a real danger that the man's religious zeal would persuade either the girl or myself to go down in front. We had underrated the emotional compulsion of a Methodist exhorter's arguments. After that, my free evenings were spent on friendly benches in the woods or with others far away at the home of one of our sweethearts.

3

While I was the discoverer of what turned out to be a fool's paradise, the other boys grasped the opportunities with no less avidity than I. Our folks were surprisingly unsuspicious. We took to prinking in a way which should have suggested to them that something out of the ordinary was going on. Every day we spent much time brushing our best suits and shining our shoes and always left for camp meeting early, with flowers in our buttonholes.

I am reminded of one amusing—at the time, embarrassing—incident which resulted from our efforts to compete with neighborhood boys. Those rivals wore chokers and carried dandy-canes. The chokers we accomplished. When the folks saw the result of our attempt to turn up turn-down collars, they permitted us to buy the real articles.

The canes were different. We had not the temerity to ask for them, and it was Humphrey who solved our problem by carving from one of the ever-useful fence pickets a cane as slender as the Biggar boys were swinging so jauntily. He also solved the color problem by coating his cane thickly with shoe polish from the box in the shed. Soon we all had fashionable black canes and went off to camp meeting feeling the equals of any Drummondville lads.

Our triumph was of short duration. I was sitting in a hammock on a young lady's porch with her beside me when she exclaimed suddenly, "Look at your hands!" I looked. The awful truth flashed through my brain—that cane!—the shoe blacking! My hands were covered with it. Then another more dreadful thought! "What about her nice white dress?" Holton's hands were blacker than mine. I have forgotten how I got word to him or what excuses we made for our sudden departure. All I remember is the mass humiliation when we all foregathered that night in our attic and the loathing we felt for those canes. Next day we broke them into small pieces and burned them.

4

Our hedonistic exploitation of camp meeting lasted for several weeks. Then came the crash. One morning Father

Noyes (he always seemed Father Noyes with capital letters when he rose to admonish) called the four of us to the woodshed. There he informed us in a tone of ominous import that he knew all about our deceitful doings. He launched into a vitriolic criticism. The tragedy of that criticism cannot be appreciated by anyone not acquainted with John Humphrey Noyes's ability to make a victim think very poorly of himself. When he was through with his verbal castigation, I felt as small and mean as I have ever felt in my life.

In one respect he astonished me; I think he surprised us all. After scathingly characterizing what he referred to as my leadership in the affair and humiliating me still further by a brevity which said plainly, "I might have expected that of you," he turned his attention to the others. It was George; the fact that George W., his true disciple, had fallen, that outraged him most. He bore down on George until tears stood in the boy's eyes.

The outcome was interdiction of camp meeting. I think we were all relieved that our punishment was not more severe. I also think that the others accepted the deprivation with more contentment than I did. My father represented himself as a rescuer of sinners but, as time went on, I thought of him as Adam must have thought of the angel with the flaming sword who barred his return to the Garden. Afterward we pledged ourselves to good behavior so that we might attend the last three days of camp meeting. We kept those pledges faithfully, and I am rather proud of this because by that time the flaming sword was, for me, becoming less fiery and the memories of my ladylove were growing more alluring.

5

I hardly know whether to be ashamed of my part in those adventures or attempt justification. Surely my father, on his side, forgot that I was then fifteen years old—forgot what it meant to be fifteen. If he did not forget, he must have thought he could dominate the life of boys as he had dominated the lives of those devout followers whose chief concern in 1848 was the salvation of their souls.

On the other hand, I cannot free myself from the charge of deceit and ingratitude. I suspect, however, as I review the events of that year, that my intransigeance was a symptom of something more fundamental, a sort of duel between my father and me. Not that I had any such thought at the time; far from it. I went to Niagara Falls with an ambition to be a good member of his household and the previous narrative has, I hope, evidenced my genuine respect for his character and a lively satisfaction with living in the area of his inspiration. It was a case of youth struggling against the religious sanctions of a fading era. My father was determined to convert me; I refused to be converted.

This refusal was not grounded on disloyalty to him or any of the less threatening features of his creed. I think I was pleased with his assurance that God or His appointed angels took an interest in my welfare, and, even more, was glad to believe that in the end they would see to it that I was saved. I also accepted his theory of "special providences." I remember his once telling us that through those providences God was teaching us to read. He went on to say in his piquant metaphorical style:

"A great many people grow up without knowing how to read. They don't even know their letters. You think them dreadfully ignorant, but people who can't read God's providences in everything around them have grown up in a worse kind of ignorance. They have not learned their letters. Do you want to grow up in such a state that the angels can point at you and say, 'See those poor creatures; they don't know how to read'?''

It was, I believe, his insistence on a perfect spiritual totality, a complete surrender of self-determination that alarmed my love of adventure. Another quotation from one of his talks will suggest the subtle threat I saw in his theology. He likened sin to a tree:

"A tree," he said, "has many branches, but it is all one tree. Just so there is one sin. If you try to stop sin by cutting off one branch here and another there, you will fail. Your work will come to nothing. You will only strengthen the root. In the cultivation of vineyards the vines are pruned to strengthen the roots."

From this and others of my father's talks I inferred that conversion entailed the cutting out of all sin. I held no brief for sin, but I did have definitely in mind a sampling of the world's stock of pleasure, and if his conversion meant no expeditions outside the "New Yard fence" of perfection, I was not going to be entrapped.

There is a quaint passage in Humphrey's diary of the time:

"I read a portion of Pip's diary today. It was quite edifying though not strictly instructive with regard to moral culture."

I am intrigued by this ambiguous comment. I can find no trace of my diary to which he refers and Humphrey cannot recall what he meant by moral culture. He says, however, that all felt that I was unconverted if not secretly rebellious.

Chapter V

Farewell to My Father

I

DURING the last four months of my stay at Niagara our lives went on much as they had in the earlier months, before camp meeting—a happy combination of work and play and school. I think I felt closer to my father, possibly as a result of the struggle we had been through. He was not one to prolong criticism or persist in condemnation, and I certainly had no just cause for resentment. My punishment had been mild considering the offense. I came to value my father's good opinion more than freedom to seek pleasure out of bounds.

On September 5th he contracted a cold that laid him up for several days. This was the beginning of a series of alternating ups and downs which by the middle of November brought him to bed with his final sickness. I remember his telling the family that his first attack followed a struggle with Satan. He had spent the entire day writing a letter to an agnostic nephew, Joseph Skinner. The letter was a triumphant answer to Joseph's skepticism and a challenging defense of his own theology. He was again the crusading apostle. When he finished the letter he was shaking with a chill.

2

During my father's successive illnesses, Mr. Herrick and other members of the family devoted themselves almost exclusively to his care. This threw much of the responsibility for family affairs on the boys, which enlarged our sphere of operations and thereby brought us new satisfactions and a new dignity.

Then, in November, when Father's condition began to look more serious, a great solemnity settled down on the little colony of believers. At the Stone Cottage especially, it was solemnity rather than gloom. Downstairs, Mr. Herrick and Aunt Harriet discouraged talk of his sickness. In frequent family meetings they spoke with ringing words of faith and submission to God's will. They urged that Father Noyes had been a true disciple of Jesus Christ and that God had His own plan for his future, which made weeping and wishing on our part impertinent.

Upstairs, Father ate little and talked with Mr. Herrick about future plans, especially his scheme for a printing establishment at Kelly House. Whenever we were allowed to visit him, his smile belied his haggard looks. Once he referred to himself humorously as "generally dilapidated." I remember that on an abnormally warm day in September when he felt better, he came downstairs in his summer coat and insisted on Mother Noyes's putting on a muslin dress.

3

My father's illness led me to serious thinking about his past and speculation as to the real story of the Oneida Community. My viewpoint was, I believe, less partisan than my brothers'. I knew him to be a man of God; living with him had convinced me of that. What I tried to decide was whether religious fanaticism had led him astray or he had been, as Aunt Harriet said, "ahead of his time." I think I concluded, if I actually reached any conclusion, that it was a little of both.

I was, however, much impressed by the virility of his mind at the age of seventy-four. I noted the fact that he had retained his youthful passion for championing unpopular causes and for converting others to his beliefs. More grand crusades against religious and social error which gave birth to the Oneida Community having lost their objectives with the passing of the Community, he turned for satisfaction to attacking lesser heresies.

As an instance, having decided that geologists were wrong regarding the original course of Niagara River, he spent much time in research aimed at proving that in an earlier age the outlet of the great whirlpool was westward to the St. David Gorge instead of through the present northern gateway. During 1884 he frequently visited the section where the lie of the land suggested this conclusion. Through all the summer when I was at Niagara, Mr. Herrick did most of the exploring and we boys accompanied him on expeditions to the V-shaped, wooded ravine which rises from the western shore of the river.

We struggled through miles of dense woods and clambered up cliffs to examine the strata. I remember that we became as partisan as Father in defending the St. David thesis. He made, from a block of wood, a relief map of the entire terrain, on which the water in the present gorge was shown in blue and the various ravines and depressions, where he believed the old river had run, were green. This map hung in his room and was shown to all visitors.

Another of the windmills he fought was the popular

hostility toward the Jews. I am under the impression that this defense of the Jews was a revival of a theme he had mixed with his early theological preachments. He called attention to the fact that Christ was a Jew, Paul was a Jew, and all members of the Primitive Church whom the Community reverenced were Jews. He took exception to Christians condemning the Jews because they killed Christ. I especially remember his dramatic statement that if Christ had appeared in the United States he would have been mobbed and probably killed. My father clinched his case for the Jews by saying, "God chose the Jewish people for the great mission of his son—why? because they were the most godly people."

4

On October 1st my half brother Ormond died. He had been sick in a New York City hospital and, feeling a little better, had started for Oneida. While crossing the city he collapsed in the street. By a strange coincidence, Mr. Edwin Burnham, a former Community member, noticed the crowd surrounding an ambulance, and, approaching to learn what caused the excitement, recognized Ormond. Before he could get through the crowd, the ambulance drove away. Mr. Burnham, however, learned the name of the hospital and telegraphed my mother where Ormond had been taken.

It was by the merest chance that Ormond's whereabouts were known and that my mother reached the hospital before he died. It all seemed one of my father's "special providences." At Niagara we had no word of the tragedy until Ormond had passed away and his remains were on the train to Oneida. Then I had a letter from my mother.

I am puzzled to determine why I did not go to her at once. I remember that my father, on his sickbed, suggested that I go and I am sure I was ready to leave Niagara if she asked me to come. I remember long, affectionate letters from her; once she sent five dollars to have my picture taken. I have searched for those letters which would undoubtedly solve the riddle of my seeming neglect, but my care for correspondence, as for all relics of the past, has always been casual and I am left to surmise that she thought I was a comfort to my father whom the folks at Oneida believed to be on his deathbed.

Whatever the explanation, I stayed on at Niagara for another two months. Then, on the 13th of December, Uncle Frank wrote from Oneida that my mother's persistent efforts to communicate with Ormond through spiritualist mediums were affecting both her body and her mind. With a reversion to the characteristic vernacular of the Community, he asserted that she had "come under the influence of Hadean spirits," and added, "in trying to reach Ormond, she receives messages from devilish spirits which she mistakes for good spirits." My father called me to his bedside and insisted that I go to my mother at once. Early next morning I took the train to Oneida.

5

I wish that I could remember details of that last interview with him. He was greatly emaciated, but so hopeful that I came away with no feeling of discouragement. Earlier, when his illness threatened the end, Dr. Theodore Noyes had come on from New York City and remained at Niagara for several days. My father seemed very happy in his company. After all, the doctor was the child of his youth. He rallied from that sinking spell, but died five months later, April

13, 1886, with his son Theodore, Mr. Herrick and his immediate family at his bedside.

As I leave the Stone Cottage, I find myself a little disappointed that I have not been able to reproduce the peculiar psychic tint of my life there. Perhaps the true reason for this failure lies in my own vagueness. It is only in rare moments that I am able to recapture that subtle quality of happiness which differentiates the year at Niagara from all other experiences of my life, and those fleeting glimpses vanish before I can find words to fix them, as photographers say, for effective analysis.

If I cannot describe the exact coloring which made life at Niagara unique, I can with some assurance account for its source. The presence of Father Noyes was the outstanding reality in all our lives. Just how that presence impinged on boys—bringing in coal, cleaning the cistern, working in the garden or adventuring in the world outside—is beyond me; but memory asserts that it did add an imponderable something which gave to both work and play a peculiar zest.

Old members of the Community have said to me that those who got within the effective area of Father Noyes's personality were reluctant to lose him; that life seemed brighter and more worthwhile when he was about. Another of his long-time associates tried to analyze for me his unquestioned power to attract and hold the loyalty of both men and women. He accounted for it thus:

"Most people subconsciously fear life just a little or have become disillusioned by its futility. Mr. Noyes had no doubts regarding life or himself. He plowed through difficulties, disappointments and dangers with an inextinguishable faith in an Edenic world plan and the ultimate triumph of righteousness. He was a source of light and power for all about him.

His was a golden dream and always we were bent on sharing it with him."

It must have been something of this confidence and optimism that percolated through the devotion of a believing family at Niagara to the less subtle sensibilities of a boy and caused the sun to shine for me a little brighter at the Stone Cottage.

Chapter VI

An Interim

I

HUMPHREY and Holton took me over the river to catch an early morning train. Their last words were: "You're coming back!" And my answer: "I surely am!" I meant it too; but when at the Oneida depot I took my mother in my arms (I had grown taller than she while I was at Niagara Falls) I knew I would never return to the Stone Cottage for anything more than a visit. The joy in her face told better than words what my absence had meant to her. She was thinner than I had ever seen her and there were dark circles under her eyes. I was filled with remorse.

My uncles and aunts were much relieved that I had come. Aunt Cornelia took me to task for not coming before, but my mother rebuked her: "Don't say that, Cornelia. It is good for him to be with his father. I want him to go back— after a while." I never knew before how much I loved my mother.

Life at the Stone Cottage had done for my mental growth as much as the healthful regime had done for me physically, so that my mother and I found in each other a kind of companionship we had never known before. I did not strive with her about her sorrowful search for Ormond in the spiritland, as my maternal aunts insisted that I do. It was not necessary. With returning health and the dawning of a new happiness, she soon came out of the shadow, and again sought in religion the solace spiritualism had promised but failed to bring her.

Stella was now a child of eight. My mother's sorrows and anxieties had developed her beyond her years, and Mother told me that Stella had been a great support and comfort to her during the long months of my absence.

My memories of that winter at Oneida are, in general, pleasing memories. We had three comfortable rooms in the Mansion House, and ate in the co-operative dining room. We were able to find more interest than worriment in the problem of our finances. The board for three of us cost less than six dollars a week; our rent, $9.50 per month. The $371 per year was still forthcoming from dividends and guarantees, and with this, plus what my mother and I earned, we did very well.

I have always counted that winter a sort of interim. I plunged into life at the old home among my old companions with all the avidity of healthy youth and the plan of returning to Niagara Falls disappeared in an amazingly short time. It was a year of physical activity and social expansion. Our school was mostly a social affair. The teacher was a young woman only a few years older than I. During study hours we boys planned our after-school sports, arranging appointments by passing notes from desk to desk. I assume we studied—some.

Girls of my own age had been too long our companions, almost our sisters, to possess any considerable glamour. We aspired to older girls. They seemed a little strange, and we got thrills out of their complacent if on the whole niggardly acceptance of our attentions. On rainy afternoons or Sunday evenings Bert and I used to dress in our best, put on tall chokers and wonderful neckties, and carefully brush

our hair in preparation for a euchre party with Virgie and
Maud, girls some years our seniors.

2

I have called the winter of 1885-1886 an interim. It
seems just that, if I look backward at the spiritual chasten-
ing of my year at Niagara and then forward at my later
ambitions. And yet during that interim changes were taking place within me more radical than ever before in my
life. Those changes were undoubtedly connected with adolescence. I did not so connect them at the time, but looking
back on my sixteenth year I find myself converted to the
overpowering influence of inheritance rather than the implications of behaviorism.

The mental habits of a spiritually nurtured childhood,
as also the inhibitions of a cramped boyhood, were being
sloughed off. I hardly knew myself from month to month.
That otherworldly outlook, the reverences, the obediences,
the timidities so carefully cultivated by Papa Kelly faded
until they were little more than memories. Similarly, the
tissue of social misgivings and lowly ambitions, which developed after the breakup, was replaced by eager interest in all
that was happening or had happened in the world and an
even more eager desire to take part in what was going to
happen. A truly ridiculous self-confidence was bursting
through the humility taught me in childhood and the sup-
pressions of my economically lean years.

One influence alone, my mother's, drew me toward the
verities. Often at suppertime, ignoring my evident restless-
ness to finish the meal and join my comrades outdoors, she
would suggest in a tone I could not always resist: "Let's have
a nice family evening; we three together." Upstairs, she

would encourage me to play games with Stella or do something to amuse my sister until she went to bed. Then she
would read to me—she was an excellent reader. Before the
evening was over, we always had a good talk. She would
inquire about school, and even interest herself in my games.
But in the end she always discussed the Bible and God and
Christ and told me of her religious experience.

I would not exaggerate the elevating effects of my
mother's influence. Honesty forces me to admit that on the
whole I romped through that winter with both religion and
improvement very much in the background. I grew serious
only when I thought of the future.

Chapter VII

On My Own at Last

I

THE "slings and arrows of outrageous fortune" had really made of me a serious-minded boy and the interim ended with a new ambition, new in both aims and direction. On that day in 1875 when, as a five-year-old, I graduated into the South Room and found myself free to explore a larger world, I took counsel with Dick as to how we could make the most of our new freedom. Similarly, at the age of sixteen it dawned on me that I was on the threshold of real life in a very real world, and again I took counsel, this time with my cousin George, as to the necessary equipment for success. And George furnished the spark that lit the fire of a new ambition.

He had moved from Niagara Falls to Oneida in the early summer. Deprived of my father's religious instruction, which had been for him the breath of life, he found a substitute in the pursuit of education. My own zeal for education, then emerging, was of mixed origin. I was ready to stop trifling with life and decided that ignorance of what had been thought and done in the past would be a handicap in a struggle with educated men. But that was not all. I am certain that in the summer of 1886 education meant more to me than practical efficiency. I had glimpsed the enchanted world of ideas and the glimpse left me with a strong desire to explore that world. Some obscure reaction from the defeatism and pressure of the previous five years or a long-suppressed hereditary necessity must have burst through the superficialities of boyhood; for, suddenly, the thing most worthwhile in all the world was the development of my own mind.

One day George and I walked in from the straw-thatched summerhouse where we had been kindling each other's ambition, to inform our families that we had decided to go to college. Mr. Herrick, George's stepfather, was far better able than my mother to finance a college course. In fact, looked at realistically, my chance of going away to school did not appear good. But I have a peculiar quality of optimism. Obstacles grow dim when seen in the glare of extreme desirability. In this case, however, I suspect that my optimism was reinforced by confidence in my mother's resourcefulness and her habit of trying to get for me anything I wanted.

George and I sent to Cornell for a catalogue. From that we made the surprising and disappointing discovery that we were in no way prepared for college, and a detailed study of the entrance requirements showed that two or three years of preparatory work would be necessary before we could pass college examinations. Not until then did we realize how sketchy and informal our schooling had been.

Mr. Herrick encouraged George to correspond with Cascadilla, the preparatory school for Cornell, and half promised that he could enter there in the fall. Cascadilla was patently out of my reach; it was too expensive to be considered. So I investigated the possibilities of local schools and finally, in despair, resolved to prepare myself with the aid of textbooks alone.

It was then that my mother's persistence and resourcefulness triumphed. As I have said, she was a very sociable person. She had a friendly acquaintance with all kinds of

tradespeople in the village of Oneida. How she happened to
discuss my schooling with the young man who worked at
Bemis's five-and-ten-cent store, I shall never know, but she
came home one day with his statement that a year in Colgate Academy cost him little more than two hundred dollars. He was not going back to school in the fall, but this
good-natured young man offered to give her a letter of introduction to one of his fraternity mates who would help
me get started.

My mother saw light. On my sixteenth birthday I
would get from the Oneida Community, Limited, under the
"Agreement to Divide and Reorganize" $200 in cash. Not all
of that money would be available for schooling since on the
same day my annual "Guarantee" of $100 ceased, and our
total family income, always a close fit, would be inadequate
without this and the earnings I had contributed as a result
of two hours' work on weekdays and half of my Saturdays.

2

In this dilemma she told Uncle Abram of our plan.
He was interested and promised to contribute a sum which
would ensure one year of schooling at the academy. He also
agreed to go with me to Hamilton before termtime to arrange details of my entrance in September.

I shall never forget our interview with Dr. Ford, the
principal of Colgate Academy. As I intimated before, Uncle
Abram was a simple, unsophisticated man. Not that he
viewed himself in that light. Had he not for years nego-
tiated the purchase of lumber with old man Carter at Con-
stantia-on-the-Lake and with even bigger dealers in Buffalo?
Was he not accustomed to deal with customers of his department, also with carpenters, masons and men who sold build-

ing supplies? He felt fully competent. He went with me to Hamilton as a man of the world, bound to assure himself that the institution was a suitable place for his ward. He intended to question the principal of the academy narrowly.

When we were ushered into the presence of the dignified Ford Ph.D., it was all different. Uncle Abram lost his assurance and after the bare statement that I wanted to enter the academy, he fidgeted in his chair and seemed at a loss just how to begin. Dr. Ford was the soul of politeness, but extremely academic and inclined to question Uncle Abram in considerable detail regarding my qualifications. We both felt that we, rather than the academy, were under investigation.

However, the worthy principal, being a diplomat and, I dare say, desiring more students, brought the interview to a satisfactory conclusion. At the end he patted Uncle Abram on the back for his interest in education and Uncle Abram went home convinced that he was a forward-looking guardian determined that I should have the right start in life.

This interview with Dr. Ford proved a piece of good fortune for me. Uncle Abram not only helped me in the academy, but afterward contributed $100 a year to my college expenses. Perhaps he would have helped anyway, but that peep into the academic world gave him a more personal interest in my educational career.

3

On the 14th of September, 1886, I entered the dignified halls of Colgate Academy and with a hundred other boys registered as a student. At last I was out on my own and set to make a place for myself unaided in that world

PIERREPONT NOYES
Taken while he was attending Colgate Academy

into which I had been reborn at the age of ten. I knew when I planned to go away to school that, with the breakup of the Community only six years past and Hamilton less than twenty miles from Oneida, I would face a certain amount of obloquy. I did not relish the prospect—no boy would—but I felt able to meet the issue.

When, back in 1881, I opened my eyes on that new world of joint-stock, I found myself possessed of few qualifications for survival except physical health, but either the challenge of the next six years or some inner quality emerging with adolescence had now dispelled most of the negatives. Partly, no doubt, this resulted from living a year with my father. On the other hand, I had seen enough of Outsiders to lose my earlier fear of them and, with the optimism or insolence of youth, had decided to ignore their opinions. I suppose there were still times when I suffered embarrassment about my birth, but never again humiliation. In general, my relations with my fellow students must have been good, for my memories of life in Hamilton are happy memories. I recall that on one of my first visits home my mother asked rather anxiously, "How do you get along with the boys? Do they treat you well?" To which, brushing aside the implications of her question, I replied, "They treat me all right. They are fine fellows."

4

Later my mother visited Hamilton. I knew she longed to see the school and feel nearer to my new enthusiasm, but a fear that her presence would embarrass me held her back. Finally, on the occasion of one of my week-end visits at home, I persuaded her to return with me. We hired a horse and buggy from the company and drove up the valley and

over the hills to Hamilton. My mother was nervous. She
still feared that her visit might in some way injure my relation with the school or the boys.

I understood her feeling and may have shared it to a
certain extent. If so, my embarrassment registered in reverse, so to speak. I introduced her to all my companions
and when the boys at the club invited her to dine with us,
I accepted on her behalf. As a matter of fact, when actually
on the ground, she threw apprehensiveness to the winds and
enjoyed herself wholeheartedly. I remember a warm feeling
of gratitude and happiness when one of the older boys told
me afterward that he liked my mother.

Then there was our interview with Dr. Ford. As always,
he was courteous; with her he was even more, he was cordial.
My mother's cup ran over when he told her that they were
very glad to have me there and that I was doing well in my
studies. As we left, he urged her to visit the school whenever she felt like it. That visit of my mother's was a final
triumph. She and I had, together, shaken off the last shackles
of worldly fear and could now be partners in this new enterprise—getting an education.

5

Colgate Academy and then the college! I doubt if any
of my classmates found such romance as came to me during those years. Often the academy courses seemed to stretch
away endlessly, into a distance I had not fully contemplated,
and when I looked toward College Hill the path to learning
appeared infinitely long and steep; but beyond—life was
going to be a great adventure just as I had pictured it when
a child.

Afterword

*T*HE boy whom the author leaves at Colgate Academy is now sixty-seven with the energy and vitality of a man twenty years younger. In the fifty years after the close of this book, Pierrepont Noyes has lived a busy, useful, and highly intelligent life. He has made a success of almost everything to which he has turned his hand, but he is little impressed with his own achievements. Undoubtedly the accomplishment that has mattered most to him is the preservation of the Community at Oneida, not alone as a successful business enterprise, but as a way of life, an ideal of social relationship. The briefest of visits to the Mansion House is sufficient to attest to the extraordinary degree in which the Community of John Humphrey Noyes still underlies the life of his descendants and those of the other Perfectionists. This Afterword contains the briefest possible outline of Pierrepont Noyes's life and career, but even so it suggests how truly the child was father to the man.

From Colgate Academy Pierrepont Noyes went on to Colgate University, where he remained till the end of his sophomore year. His appetite for education grew steadily as he went along, and he decided to transfer to Harvard University so that he might study history and political science. In order to do this he was compelled to make up much ground which he had not yet covered; in the midst of a strenuous course of study at home, his mother's ill health made it necessary to drop scholastic work and care for her.

She died in the fall of 1891, and in the following Janu-

ary Mr. Noyes went to work in the Niagara Falls factory of
the Community. Later he established, with his brother, a
silverware business of his own in New York City, and in
1894 married Corinna Kinsley, to whom he refers in his account of the Children's House.

Reports from Oneida were, at this time, discouraging,
and in 1895 he joined the minority directors in a campaign
to secure control of the company. In a very close election,
Mr. Noyes's faction succeeded in electing Dr. Theodore
Noyes as president of the company, and in the following
January Pierrepont Noyes sold his New York business and
moved to Oneida. Unquestionably, he was largely motivated
by a desire to preserve the Community, and he brought to
its problems a clear vision and a driving energy. Within two
or three years the older generation had placed on his shoulders and those of the young men around him the entire management of Oneida Community, Ltd.

Within fifteen years the profits from the Community's
silverware business had grown to the point where they were
annually as large as the total capital of the enterprise when
Mr. Noyes and his associates first took hold of it. Throughout this period, the Community enterprises were developing
along social and industrial lines as well. Profit sharing, and
intelligent planning for the housing and social needs of the
increasing numbers of Community employees have continued to be a feature of the Community's labor policy to
the present day.

Mr. Noyes believed that the management of a business
should not remain in the hands of one man too long; it ought
to pass, like "shingles on a roof," from one generation to the
next. Accordingly, in 1917, he relinquished the control of
the business and went to California, intending to stay a year.
However, when the United States entered the war in April

he returned home and attempted to enlist in the air force.

Realizing that at the age of forty-seven he was little likely to see active service, he applied for work in Washington, and for a time had a position on the War Trade Board, and shortly after found himself transferred to the Fuel Administration, ultimately being appointed as Fuel Member on the Priority Committee which limited and apportioned industrial production throughout the nation.

Shortly after the conclusion of the war, Mr. Noyes went abroad, intending to visit Italy on business. The Peace Commission was organizing in Paris at the time, and Mr. Noyes's work during the war was fresh in the minds of many of the Americans at the Peace Conference. He found himself drafted to serve as the American member of the Rhineland Commission, which was in charge of the occupation of Germany.

Here he at once found himself in conflict with the plans for the military occupation of the Rhineland, which he felt to be brutal. In co-operation with Sir Harold Stuart, the British member of the Commission, he drafted a tentative revision, but ultimately decided to write direct to President Wilson in Paris. Unprecedented as this step was, it got results. A special committee was appointed which drafted an agreement with Germany along the lines laid down in Mr. Noyes's letter to the President.

For more than a year he was President of the Coal Commission for occupied Germany. In the course of his service on this commission he went into the coal mines themselves and settled German strikes; telling Herr Thyssen, now the famous German industrial magnate, in no uncertain terms that the demands of the miners were just.

Upon his return to America after a year and a half in Germany, he spent a year in making addresses in the different cities in the United States on the war danger inherent in the existing European alignments and in the French policy of chauvinism in particular.

Out of these experiences abroad both of Mr. Noyes's previous books arose. *While Europe Waits for Peace*, analyzing the situation in Europe, predicted that the League of Nations would never succeed without the participation of the United States. *The Pallid Giant*, a novel, dealt with the danger of war and the fear which man feels of man, a fear that leads inevitably to military struggles. He hoped to impress on the American public the knowledge of what another war would mean for civilization.

After this period, Mr. Noyes returned to active participation in the affairs of the Community. In 1930 Franklin D. Roosevelt, then Governor of New York State, appointed him Chairman of the Saratoga Springs Commission, which had been given an initial one million dollars toward the development of a spa. "Commissions" for this purpose had been appointed successively for nearly thirty years. As Mr. Noyes says: "Either fortunately or unfortunately for the state, I took the appointment literally and went ahead and built the new spa. Physically it is now completed, and I hope to retire from the Commission as soon as the institution can be put on its feet financially."

THE PUBLISHERS